Iran

Iran

From Theocracy to the Green Movement

Edited by

Negin Nabavi

First published in 2012 by
PALGRAVE MACMILLAN®
in the United States—a division of St. Martin's Press LLC,
175 Fifth Avenue, New York, NY 10010.

Where this book is distributed in the UK, Europe and the rest of the world,
this is by Palgrave Macmillan, a division of Macmillan Publishers Limited,
registered in England, company number 785998, of Houndmills,
Basingstoke, Hampshire RG21 6XS.

Palgrave Macmillan is the global academic imprint of the above companies
and has companies and representatives throughout the world.

Palgrave® and Macmillan® are registered trademarks in the United States,
the United Kingdom, Europe and other countries.

ISBN: 978–0–230–11461–6 (HC)
ISBN: 978–0–230–11469–2 (PB)

Library of Congress Cataloging-in-Publication Data

Iran: from theocracy to the Green Movement / edited by Negin Nabavi.
    p. cm.
    Includes bibliographical references.
    ISBN 978–0–230–11461 6 (hardcover :alk. paper)—
    ISBN 978–0–230–11469–2 (pbk. : alk. paper)
    1. Iran—Politics and government—1979–1997. 2. Iran—Politics and
government—1997– 3. Iran—Social conditions—1979–1997. 4. Iran—Social
conditions—1997– 5. Social change—Iran—History—20th century. 6. Social
change—Iran—History—21st century. 7. Social movements—Iran—History—
20th century. 8. Social movements—Iran—History—21st century. 9. Islam and
politics—Iran—History—20th century. 10. Islam and politics—Iran—History—
21st century. I. Nabavi, Negin, 1965–

DS318.825.I644 2012
955.05′4—dc23   2011052925

A catalogue record of the book is available from the British Library.

Design by Newgen Imaging Systems (P) Ltd., Chennai, India.

First edition: September 2012

10 9 8 7 6 5 4 3 2 1

Printed in the United States of America.

Contents

Figures and Tables

Figures

Tables

Note on Transliteration

Persian words have been transliterated so as to follow Persian pronunciation, and with a few exceptions for *ayn* (') and *hamzeh* ('), diacritical marks have been omitted for the most part. In cases where Persian names and words are already established in English, the spelling used in the mainstream media has been adopted. For Arabic terms like *Muharram*, *ijtihad*, *fiqh,* and *umma,* the transliteration system developed by the *International Journal of Middle East Studies* has been used.

Preface

Recent Iranian history has been full of unexpected turns. Whether it was the 1979 revolution, which resulted in the establishment of the first ever Islamic Republic in the history of the Muslim world, the rise to power of the reformist movement in 1997, or most recently, the emergence of the Green Movement, an opposition movement that took shape spontaneously in the days immediately following the presidential elections in June 2009, the world was taken unawares at every juncture. While on the one hand, this unpredictability points to the complexity of events in Iran, on the other hand, it highlights the need for a greater understanding of the everchanging internal dynamics of postrevolutionary Iran, with its many transformations, contradictions, and unintended consequences.

This book has been in the making for some two years. It had its beginnings at a conference entitled "The Iranian Revolution: Thirty Years," organized by the Center for Middle Eastern Studies at Rutgers University in February 2009, to mark the thirtieth anniversary of the 1979 revolution. However, 2009 transpired to be much more than a passing anniversary; it was the year of the controversial tenth presidential elections, the year when huge crowds filled the streets of different cities in Iran in protest at the results of the elections, and when a spontaneous opposition Green Movement came into being, giving a name and expression to a mood of defiance, pre-dating the so-called Arab Spring that would only begin to engulf the Arab Middle East and North Africa in spring 2011.

The book, therefore, had to undergo a makeover of sorts because it could not afford to ignore what had turned out to be perhaps one of the most important challenges in the history of the Islamic Republic, namely the Green Movement. To this end, new chapters reflecting on the significance of this new development, were solicited and written specifically for the volume, while a little less than half of the essays that form the nucleus of the book had grown out of the original conference. This book, therefore, brings together essays that both shed light on the many transformations that Iran has experienced in the different political, economic, intellectual, and societal domains in the 30 years under the Islamic Republic, and also speculate on the import of the developments of 2009.

Part I, entitled "Religion, Politics, and Discourse" consists of four chapters that concentrate for the most part on the aftermath of the tenth presidential elections and the Green Movement. Farideh Farhi gives an assessment of the significance of the tenth presidential elections by putting them in the context of the previous 29 elections (that include the three founding elections in the early years of the revolution, the election of the Constitutional Assembly and the approval of the Islamic Constitution) that have taken place in the Islamic Republic since 1979. She argues that, regardless of the turn of events in the future, the tenth presidential elections will remain consequential for the Islamic Republic because they have challenged the credibility of the two institutions that have been fundamental to the Islamic Republic since its founding, namely the office of the leader and the exercise of elections.

The aftermath of the tenth presidential elections is also the subject of Fariba Adelkhah's chapter, although she focuses more specifically on the Green Movement and the significance of its emergence. She argues that contrary to conventional wisdom, the Green Movement is not so much the manifestation of the confrontation between state and society or a clash between conservatives and reformists, as it is the culmination of the tensions and contradictions, both political and economic, inherent in the Islamic Republic. Adelkhah describes the Green Movement as primarily a social movement, not unlike that of *Solidarność* in Poland. In doing so, she puts the Green Movement in the context of other social movements that began to make their presence felt in Iran in the 1990s, thus making the point that its appearance was not as sudden as some may have thought at first. Furthermore, she explains the predicament of the Green Movement in terms of the political and economic rivalries and factional politics that make the Islamic Republic such an opaque and convoluted system. Ultimately, Adelkhah concludes that even if the Green Movement fails, it has already achieved success "in transforming the relationship between state and society." In her words, "Big failures can hide huge successes. Mir-Hossein Mousavi, who would never have met the expectation of his supporters had he been elected President, has since become a hero of one of the most impressive and original social movements of the last decades."

One of the most interesting developments resulting from the revolution, has been the emergence of new concepts and discourses, some of which were unintended. Whereas in the ideology-stricken first decade of the revolution, terms such as *"shahadat"* (martyrdom) and *"mostaz`af"* (the dispossessed) were current,[1] the reformist era (1997–2005) gave rise to a totally new discourse with a range of new concepts. Terms such as *"jame`eh-ye madani"* (civil society), *"qanun-gara'i"* (lawfulness), *"mardom-salari"* (democracy), *"hoquq-e shahrvand"* (citizens' rights), and *"hoquq-e bashar"* (human rights), among others, gained prevalence, leading some historians and social scientists to regard this development in discourse to be tantamount to "a cultural turn"[2] or an "intellectual revolution."[3] Even though reform as politics failed in view of the fact that Mohammad Khatami, and the reform movement that he endorsed, were easily suppressed by the more hard-line elements of the establishment, the reformist discourse did seem to have gained a life of its own. Negin Nabavi discusses this reformist discourse, outlining some of the shifts in emphasis that it underwent between the years 1997 and 2009. More specifically, she argues that by 2009, on the eve of the tenth presidential elections, a "discourse of rights" had supplanted that of reform, and gained prominence among several sectors in society. In her chapter, therefore, Nabavi considers how this "discourse of rights" took shape, how it was influenced by earlier discussions regarding what constituted "reform" and "reformism," and the extent to which it was informed by and further promoted by the women's movement. She contends that inasmuch as the women's movement had succeeded in gaining recognition for their cause, adopting a pragmatic and nonideological approach, and rising above politics, the women's movement provided a new paradigm and played a significant part in enabling a general discourse of rights to supplant that of reform.

Babak Rahimi, too, explores the notion of discourse although from a different perspective. In his essay, he considers the many transformations that Shi'ism has undergone since the 1979 revolution and the establishment of a theocratic system of rule in Iran. He discusses the development of competing visions of Shi'ism among the clerical as well as the lay religious circles at different stages of the 30 year history of the Islamic Republic, and argues that in terms of discourses and practices, these changes have not only taken place in the domain of the state but also that of society. Thus, while these changes have resulted in a rethinking of what he calls the "theocratic underpinnings of the Islamic Republic," they have also contributed and enabled new conceptualizations of the sacred and the profane on a societal level. In this way, Rahimi brings attention to the ultimate paradox of the Islamic Republic, namely the "fragmentation" and "contestation" of Shi'i religious authority despite and, perhaps, in response to the persistent efforts at the centralization and consolidation of Shi'ism as represented by the office of the *Velayat-e faqih*.

Contestations do not limit themselves to the domain of Shi'i discourse and practice. As the chapters in Part II illustrate, contestations extend themselves to other areas such as debates regarding national identity and the economy as well. Rasmus Elling examines the complicated identity politics of the Islamic Republic. He questions the conventional wisdom that characterizes the Islamic Republic as a system that necessarily prioritizes the Islamic *Umma* over the Iranian nation. He contends instead that the reality is far more nuanced as represented by the emergence of various degrees of what he calls "overt nationalism" at different times in the three decades that have passed since the revolution. The symbolism of state-sponsored ceremonies such as the return of the "Cyrus Cylinder," or references to "*maktab-e Iran*" in 2010, by Esfandiyar Rahim-Mashaei, Ahmadinejad's controversial adviser and confidant, are but the latest and most blunt expressions of nationalism. While mindful of the fact that this may have been an instance of factional politics, and a ruse on the part of Ahmadinejad and his supporters to win over the disenchanted middle classes, Elling sees this development also as a continuation of attempts at a bringing together of nationalism and Islamism throughout the history of the Islamic Republic. He, therefore, argues that the contraposition of Islamic versus national identity is at best simplistic, if not misleading. Through a detailed analysis of two works that he regards as representative of the "official ideological literature" sanctioned by the state, he assesses the ways in which Islamism has been reconciled with Iranian nationalism, and the extent to which this nationalism has been inclusive of different ethnicities. However, he adds that ultimately in the absence of genuine political pluralism, regardless of the claims made by the politicians in the Islamic Republic, there can be no true cultural diversity.

Kjetil Selvik tackles the very different topic of the private entrepreneurial business sector in the Islamic Republic. He challenges the oft-repeated assumption that the Islamic Republic has been hostile to capitalism, and shows that despite the ideological facade and posturing, for the most part, a new entrepreneurial class has managed to emerge and gain recognition in Iran. Based on personal interviews with a number of industrial entrepreneurs, as well as written surveys, Selvik outlines the social backgrounds of this new emerging class and discusses both the advantages that they have secured as well as the trials and tribulations that they have undergone throughout the different phases of the Islamic Republic. He adds, however, that unless the fundamental contradiction between ideology and a "laissez-faire" philosophy is resolved, the business community will continue to remain in a "state of limbo," and, like many other sectors of the Islamic Republic, thwarted in its growth.

There is of course much more to Iran than the politics and the ruling ideology of the Islamic Republic. One of the intriguing features of Iran is its dynamic society, in particular, the growing assertiveness of women and the youth not only in the political domain but also in society at large. The two chapters in Part III address aspects of this phenomenon. Fatemeh Sadeghi considers the significance of the Green Movement in terms of the women's movement. While mindful of the fact that women have been an active presence in major events in the course of modern Iranian history, whether it was the national movement headed by Mosaddeq, the 1979 revolution, or the 1997 reform movement, Sadeghi argues that what distinguishes the Green Movement from previous turning points, is that women both participated in the Green Movement and used it to subvert many of the long-established "social norms" with regard to gender. She gives many examples of instances when women and men took advantage of the unanticipated development that was the Green Movement to challenge the "public/private binary, and the male/female divide" that have laid the basis for the gendered power relations in postrevolutionary Iranian society. In this sense, she argues that the Green Movement represents much more than the "shaking up of the political order." As she says, the Green Movement "was not only advanced by women, but also provided an opportunity for them, alongside men, to defy social attitudes towards gender, and patriarchal arbitrary rule over the country in unprecedented ways."

Finally, Marie Ladier-Fouladi addresses the question of the youth and their changing aspirations in Iranian society by taking a sociodemographic approach to this issue. Basing her chapter largely on the data provided by Iranian censuses in 1976, 1986, 1996, and 2006, as well as two sociodemographic surveys carried out in rural areas in 2002 and 2004, she compares the prerevolutionary youth—what she calls the youth of "yesterday"—with the postrevolutionary youth of "today." She argues that the assertive and rebellious behavior of the youth "today" may in part be explained by substantive changes that have occurred in the family structure as a result of a continuous decline in fertility as well as of the greater availability of education to larger numbers of young people, both men and women. In a situation when children often surpass their fathers in the levels of education they have attained, not only are children no longer submissive to their fathers, but they also contribute to the destabilization of the patriarchal order. Ladier-Fouladi contends that such social changes are bound to play a part in future political transformations as well. She concludes that "the Islamic Republic may temporarily be able to curb the spread of this new movement for freedom but it won't be able to eradicate it given that the aspiration for democracy and modernization of the social arena has its origin in the profound changes that have occurred within the Iranian family and the relationships among its members."

I would like to thank all of the contributors whose work has made this volume possible. I would especially like to thank Ali Banuazizi for his generosity and invaluable advice at different stages of completion of this book. Thanks are also due to Ali Gheissari, Mohiaddin Mesbahi, Azar and Ahmad Ashraf, Shaun Marmon, Farideh Koohi-Kamali, and Sarah Nathan. Last but not least, many thanks go to Simin Nabavi and Jawid Mojaddedi for their constant support.

NEGIN NABAVI

Notes

1. See Ervand Abrahamian, *A History of Modern Iran*. Cambridge, UK: Cambridge University Press, 2008, 188.
2. Ibid.
3. Mehran Kamrava, *Iran's Intellectual Revolution*. Cambridge, UK: Cambridge University Press, 2008.

Part I

Religion, Politics, and Discourse

I

The Tenth Presidential Elections and Their Aftermath

Farideh Farhi

Introduction

The crisis that has engulfed Iran since its June 12, 2009 presidential elections is the most significant event in the life of the Islamic Republic.[1] With the exception of the revolution itself that deeply restructured the political map of the country, no other event—including the Iran-Iraq War, the March 1989 purging of leadership designate, Ayatollah Hossein-Ali Montazeri, the 1989 revamping of the constitution, which turned the office of the leadership into absolute leadership, or the rise of reformist politics—has been as politically significant.

The significance of the recent events lies in the fact that the two institutions fundamental to the Islamic Republic, namely elections and the office of the Leader (*rahbar*)—designed to manage or moderate political competition, conflicts, and systemic contradictions have been challenged and failed to perform their tasks. The office of the Leader failed, first, by the inability of Ayatollah Khamenei to stand above the fray that is the constitutional mandate of his office, and, then, by the ineffectiveness of his order for harsh response to demonstrations that continued on and off for another eight months after the elections.

Elections—amazingly the twenty-ninth of which was witnessed in June 2009 in the short history of the Islamic Republic, if one includes the three founding elections held in the immediate postrevolution years regarding the change of regime, election of the Constitutional Assembly, and approval of the Islamic Constitution—have been the method of choice for managing popular participation, socializing the newer generations into the Islamic Republic, and regulating and ultimately, negotiating intraelite competition.

In this crisis, irrespective of whether there was fraud or mere perception of it—or what former president Akbar Hashemi Rafsanjani called the "doubt" surrounding it[2]—electoral politics not only failed to temper conflicts, but also resulted in heightening or inciting them further. Electoral politics also failed to act as an agent of socialization, preserving or deepening allegiances to the political system. This electoral failure was the direct cause of street confrontations and violence—or electoral politics by other means—that ensued. In the process, the damage that has been done to the legitimacy of elections will either have to be repaired in profound ways or have serious consequences for Iran's future power structure.

So, while the events engulfing Iran must be seen as entailing an uncertain and ultimately improvised outcome, no matter which direction events take the country—whether heightened authoritarianism or increased political dysfunction, persistent political stalemate, state breakdown, or eventual addressing of some of the democratic demands—the only thing for certain is that the 2009 presidential elections were seriously mishandled or mismanaged, and that both sides in this very intense competition miscalculated and underestimated their opponent's power and capacities. In understanding these miscalculations, a closer look at the history of electoral competition in Iran is necessary.

Electoral Competition in an Authoritarian Context

The Islamic Republic of Iran was the first political creature in the Middle East— the second was the post-2003 Iraq—that came into being through an election; a referendum to be exact. To be sure, the referendum that was held in March 1979 was an "engineered" one limited by an up and down choice regarding the creation of an Islamic Republic. Still, people did come out to vote and while the 98 percent participation cannot be trusted, the reality of revolutionary fervor turning a majority of the Iranian population toward an affirmative vote for an Islamic Republic cannot be denied either. Since then the country has had ten presidential, eight parliamentary, and four Assembly of Experts elections regularly, adding three provincial elections to its inventory since 1998.[3] This is a significant achievement and testimony to the importance of elections for the identity of the Islamic Republic that has weathered the systemic purge of its first elected president, the assassination of its many key leaders, including a president and a prime minister, a brutal eight-year war, and an almost continuous state of being under external pressure via sanctions or threats of war.

Although all Iranian citizens of a certain age[4] have been endowed with the right to vote—or not to vote—these elections have not fulfilled the democratic criteria of being fair; of being underwritten by free expression of political and civil rights, including freedom of the press, freedom of association, and freedom to campaign without fear of reprisal. Perhaps, most importantly, they have not assured that elected officials possess real authority to govern and are not subject to the tutelary control of other unelected leaders. Still, Iran's electoral regime, at least up to now, cannot be considered a "facade"—one in which electoral institutions exist but yield no meaningful contestation for power (such as Egypt under Hosni Mubarak, Singapore, and Uzbekistan in the 1990s). Several recent elections—municipal, parliamentary, and presidential—have been truly contested with results not known in advance. Newspapers, some with identified linkages to organized political parties, have editorialized in favor of their preferred candidates and in two key presidential elections—1997 and 2009—television debates among candidates played a significant role in introducing challengers to the public and increasing voter turnout.[5]

Elections in Iran have also been meaningful in so far as their results have led to partial turnover of the political elites with significant impact in the policy direction of the country, particularly in the economic and cultural arenas. Even foreign policy has been impacted in, for instance, the change away from the "policy of détente" advocated during the presidency of Mohammad Khatami (1997–2005) toward an "offensive foreign policy" espoused by his successor Mahmoud Ahmadinejad.

More significantly, the rules governing Iranian elections have themselves been contested, particularly after the death of the founder of the Islamic Republic, Ayatollah Ruhollah Khomeini. Khomeini himself was of course never beyond meddling in the election process. For instance, in Iran's first presidential election, he effectively forbade Mohammad Beheshti from running for election on the account of him being a cleric. This criterion for rejection was clearly not articulated in Article 115 of the Constitution, which merely states that the president must be elected from among religious and political personalities possessing the following qualifications: Iranian birth; Iranian nationality; administrative capacity and resourcefulness; a good past record; trustworthiness and piety; and convincing belief in the fundamental principles of the Islamic Republic of Iran and the official religion of the country.[6]

However, it is after Khomeini's death that the manipulation of state institutions by conservative forces as a means to shape election results began in earnest, leading to vociferous objections by factions who clearly understood that without the presence of a protective overlord like Khomeini, their electoral fortunes would be on the decline unless they found ways to counter the institutional bias against them through increased voter turnout. It is in this sense that electoral politics in Iran distinguishes itself from what Ellen Lust has called "Competitive Clientelism in the Middle East."[7] Drawing a picture of the relation between authoritarian elections and democratization processes in the Middle East, Lust argues that elections in authoritarian regimes of the Middle East not only fail to push the democratic transition process forward, but they also tend to strengthen the incumbent regime by serving as mechanisms to create competition for access to the limited state resources, hence, reducing demands for change, and creating a competitive clientelism. Elections in Iran, on the other hand, while manipulated by nonelective institutions in a myriad of ways, have instead served to destabilize Iran's version of competitive clientelism by threatening to bring into the political process a section of the electorate that has lived and survived outside clientelist relationships.

This is the mostly secular urban middle classes that have always had a tenuous relationship with the Islamic Republic. Unlike many of their peers, who emigrated mostly to the West, they have stayed either by choice or by fortune. They have been allowed to go about their way economically, running or working for private businesses or even maintaining nonmanagerial state jobs as teachers, university professors, and government employees. There are no restrictions on their movement inside the country (i.e., no reporting to police stations when traveling or moving from one city to another such as in China or the former Soviet Union). The only catch is their identification as "outsiders" (*ghair-e khodi*) versus those who are "inside" the system (*khodi*) and the checking of their political aspirations; something they occasionally forget to do by engaging in the only overt political opportunity afforded to them, which is voting. I can think of no other country in the world in which there are such huge swings in voter turnout in successive elections with about 20 percent of the electorate making a decision about whether to vote or not essentially in the last few weeks prior to the election. In Iran, the voting participation rate for both presidential and parliamentary elections generally waivers between 50 to 60 percent with some significant variations among Iran's 31 provinces. In the 1996 parliamentary elections, however, it went as high as 71 percent and in 1997 presidential election, it inched close to 80 percent. In the 2009 presidential election, it reportedly was close to 85 percent.

Mobilization of this electorate has given energy to the demand for change that in turn has led conservative forces occupying nonelective institutions to become increasingly more overt in their manipulation of electoral rules. Ironically, however, this increasingly overt manipulation began not with an election for republican institutions such as the presidency or the Parliament (*Majles*) but with the 1991 election for the clerical Assembly of Experts. It was in the events leading up to this election that the Guardian Council—the body in charge of ascertaining the constitutional and Islamic nature of all laws—reinterpreted the law for eligibility of candidates for the Assembly of Experts in significant ways. This change was eventually backed by the new leadership (*rahbari*) of Ayatollah Ali Khamenei. The reinterpretation not only tied eligibility to higher religious expertise—changing the language to one of "candidates must have *ijtihad* to the degree of being able to deliberate on issues of *fiqh*"(Islamic jurisprudence) rather than being "fully acquainted with the basis of *ijtihad*"—but also transferred "the source of assertion" for the eligibility of candidates from well-known teachers in religious seminaries to the clerics sitting on the Guardian Council.

The Guardian Council went farther in another ruling in December 1991 in which it clarified Article 99 of the Constitution, which gives the body "the responsibility of supervising the elections of the Assembly of Experts for Leadership, the President of the Republic, the Islamic Consultative Assembly, and the direct recourse to popular opinion and referenda." The Council did more than clarify its power when it announced that its supervisory role entailed "approval supervision" (*nezarat-e estesvabi*). This meant that all candidates for the above-mentioned offices had to be approved by the Guardian Council irrespective of approval by the Interior Ministry. In one swift move, the Council's role changed from supervision to approval of elections with serious implications for the election process. Now rival political forces would be restrained through political machinations by government bodies rather than through the electoral process.

Since then, the forces that later came to be known as "Reformist" have tried a variety of tactics to show their displeasure about the political process that as early as the 1992 parliamentary elections entailed disqualification of close to 50 percent of registered candidates, including incumbents.[8] Their tactics have included complaining about the process, threatening electoral boycotts, contesting individual disqualifications, and bargaining behind closed doors. While in some instances, such as the 2005 presidential elections, these tactics proved successful in the requalification of certain previously disqualified candidates, nothing substantive was done to increase confidence in the impartiality of state institutions in charge of running and ultimately, approving election results. The end result has been a peculiarly Iranian form of "competitive authoritarianism"[9] in which the coexistence of democratic rules and autocratic methods aimed at keeping certain groups in power creates an inherent—and increasing—source of challenge and tension during election times. At least since the 1991 election for the Assembly of Experts, challenges by forces participating in elections but dissatisfied with the way election rules have been implemented have repeatedly posed serious dilemmas for the Islamic "system" (nezam). On the one hand, outright and overt manipulation of rules is costly, largely because the challenges tend to be both formally legal and widely perceived as legitimate. On the other hand, without such manipulation, groups powerful enough to control nonelective institutions could lose elective ones such as the office of the president and the Parliament if they let democratic challenges run their course. Since the early 1990s, elections in Iran have thus been occasions through which contradictions inherent in a system that allows for competition for elected offices in the midst of an authoritarian setup have been made public, forcing nonelective offices and individuals to choose between overt manipulation or violation of democratic rules at the cost of domestic conflict, or allowing the challenge to proceed, at the cost of possible defeat of their favored groups and individuals.

Until the 2009 presidential elections, what had made the Iranian competitive authoritarianism peculiar was the persistence or recurrence of elections whose rule implementation was challenged by the participants. This persistence had in turn led to differing responses to the challenges posed by participants, ranging from public assertion of fraud despite the eventual acceptance of the results in some cases, to immediate preparation for the next elections despite flawed results. In other words, unlike in other countries where the result of contested elections brought about a situation of crisis for the regime—as it happened in Mexico in 1998; Nicaragua in 1990; or, Peru, Serbia, and Ukraine in 2000—until the 2009 presidential election and subsequent crisis, the response to the candidacy of those seeking to reform the system had been variegated, ultimately averting a crisis while at the same time maintaining the ideological commitment of the Islamic Republic to electoral competition, albeit a limited one.

An inventory of the electoral competition since the 1991 Assembly of Experts elections gives a sense of the variety of responses by conservative or nonelective institutions. In the 1992 parliamentary elections, the Guardian Council used its newly appropriated vetting prerogative to disqualify 1,060 candidates—including 30 sitting parliamentarians from what at the time was considered to be the left of the political spectrum—out of a total of 3,150 candidates. This tactical maneuver combined with the negative campaigning against the Left by the conservatives paid off with the result of the Fourth *Majles* (1992–1996) having a conservative makeup in contrast to the Leftist-controlled Third *Majles* (1988–1992). There were complaints about the vetting process but few doubted that the small number of candidates from the left of the political spectrum who were eventually allowed to run, lost the election due to their inability to garner votes in an election in which close to 58 percent of the electorate participated.

Political dynamics changed in the 1996 parliamentary elections with a split among the conservative forces and the entry of one wing of the conservative movement as a centrist force calling itself the "Servants of Construction." It was in these elections that for the first time the possibility of marginal manipulation of results—as distinct from electoral engineering through the disqualification of candidates prior to Election Day—was entertained. In these elections, which registered the highest parliamentary participation rate in the history of the Islamic Republic (71 percent), the daughter of the then president Akbar Hashemi Rafsanjani, running as a candidate for the "Servants of Construction," was declared to have received the second highest number of votes in the city of Tehran. Her ranking was behind that of the former Interior Minister Ali Akbar Nateq Nouri in the face of widespread rumors that votes were manipulated to assure Nateq Nouri's higher standing as a means to guarantee his position as the new Speaker of Parliament. Despite this alleged manipulation, there was very little questioning of the makeup of the Fifth *Majles*.

The increased competition for the Fifth *Majles* set the stage for the 1997 presidential elections, which featured no incumbents because of term limits. The candidate of the "system" was Speaker Nateq Nouri and the main challenger was Mohammad Khatami running on a platform of the "rule of law." Initially, societal expectation was that Nateq Nouri would win but a series of television appearances by all candidates introduced Khatami to a wider public, and a savvy campaign particularly in the urban areas mobilized both the youth voting for the first time as well as a large part of the electorate that had not voted in previous elections.[10] As Election Day neared and the reality of higher participation rate began to sink in, various officials occupying both elective and nonelective institutions were faced with a choice: allow voters to decide election results or attempt to manipulate the results and court the possibility of a political crisis. They chose the former and in the process gave birth to the reform movement.

This approach, more or less, continued in the 1999 municipal elections and 2000 parliamentary elections, which brought reformists into power in droves. In both these elections participation rates were quite high—64 and 67 percent, respectively—confirming a correlation between the improved fortunes of reformers or challengers and higher participation rates. However, the importance of higher participation rates for the success of reformers was really driven home in the 2003 municipal elections. These were the freest elections held in the life of the Islamic Republic with almost no political vetting of candidates (candidates were vetted based on preestablished criteria for qualification) since at the time the Guardian Council was not tasked with supervising municipal elections and the body in charge of vetting was the Sixth *Majles,* which was controlled by the reformists. However, dissatisfaction with the inability of the reformists to prevent the obstructionism of nonelective institutions in allowing the pursuit of the reform agenda kept many voters home. A 49 percent turnout throughout the country, and even lower turnouts in larger cities such as Tehran and Tabriz, resulted in the defeat of reformists across the board. And a lesson was learned by both sides: Voter turnout matters.

This lesson was put to good use in the 2004 and 2008 parliamentary elections. In both these elections a combination of highly publicized and politicized vetting process, low voter turnout (51 and 57 percent, respectively), and marginal manipulation of results particularly in large cities assured conservative victory.[11] The reformists complained about manipulation of results particularly in the city of Tehran but essentially accepted that it was low voter turnout that made marginal manipulation of election results both possible and effective.

In the 2005 presidential elections, vote rigging again became an issue in the first round of an election that fielded seven approved candidates. Mehdi Karroubi, who was running second to the front runner Hashemi Rafsanjani throughout Election Day, woke up in the morning to see his name dropped to third place, below the name of the eventual winner of the election Mahmoud Ahmadinejad. He publicly charged fraud but was unable to find takers for his call for a recount. At the end, his complaints were overshadowed with Ahmadinejad's clear victory in the second round, which was deemed credible over Hashemi Rafsanjani. Again lower voter turnout (less than 60 percent) and the reformist inability to mobilize behind one candidate until it was too late was considered as more of the reason for the loss than disqualifications and vote rigging.[12]

It was with this background that various political factions entered the political fray in the 2009 elections. A history of increasingly aggressive vetting by the Guardian Council, marginal manipulation of election results, and conservative backing down in the face of high voter turnout convinced the reformists that winning would be hard but not impossible if the right candidate could mobilize voters in numbers comparable to the 1997 elections. Everyone understood that the usual 60 percent or so turnout would favor Ahmadinejad. It was this theory that pushed most reformists to put pressure on former president Khatami to run again given the belief that he would be the only one that could generate enough enthusiasm to do a repeat of 1997. Khatami withdrew his candidacy once Mir-Hossein Mousavi declared his. As it turned out, a Khatami presidency was not necessary to generate 1997-like enthusiasm. Where the reformists miscalculated, was their assumption that similar dynamics that generated the 1997 high turnout would yield comparable results.

The 2009 Presidential Elections

The foremost miscalculation on the part of the expanded ranks of the Mir-Hossein Mousavi's political supporters was their belief that although a degree of electoral manipulation was a given, massive manipulation would be unlikely as it would be dangerous and destabilizing for the system; hence, they did not think it would be tried.[13] As mentioned above, they understood from the beginning that their path to winning the presidency was a difficult one, dependent on their ability to mobilize a large sector of Iran's silent voting bloc.

They entered the race highly skeptical of Mousavi's ability to expand the participation rate. He was deemed as lacking Khatami's charisma but, more importantly, there were abundant worries regarding an electorate that had become rather jaded about the possibility of any executive bringing about change after what was deemed as the failure of the reformist era. Still they did, however, assume—wrongly it turned out—that if Mousavi managed to mobilize that block of silent voters, he could overcome the presumed 5 million vote deficit he had to contend with because of the conservative ability to tinker with votes by marshalling organized votes of supporters, stuffing ballots, and voiding the opponents' ballots by the Ahmadinejad-controlled Interior Ministry.[14] Once former reformist president Mohammad Khatami withdrew his candidacy, the reformists simply neither took into account the possibility of massive fraud particularly since Mousavi had made his commitment to the Islamic Republic quite clear.[15] Nor did they take into account the likelihood that a mobilized population would take offense to the election results and would come into the streets in droves to express its anger and shock. Finally, they did not foresee the likelihood of the security forces loyal to the office of the Leader reacting the way they did to the popular response to the election results.

As mentioned above, the model they still operated under was that of 1997 when a 79 percent participation rate pressured the highest authorities of the country to assure a fair election out of concern for the popular reaction. In fact, prior to that election, the two most prominent leaders of Iran—then president Hashemi Rafsanjani and Leader Khamenei—had been informed of the political mood in the country by the security and intelligence apparatus and came out to assure the public that its preference on election day would be respected. Undoubtedly, concern about possible riots was what brought the two leaders together. In 2009, the reformists wrongly assumed that once they had mobilized the population, the same pressure would be at play. The genuine shock expressed by Mousavi along with his supporters was the direct result of this miscalculation.

However, Mousavi's supporters were not the only ones who miscalculated. On the conservative side, miscalculations occurred in the opposite direction. First, what the conservatives underestimated was the ability of reformist candidates to energize what to them was happily considered to be a cynical electorate. Hence, they assumed that, like the 2005 presidential elections, an over 60 percent Ahmadinejad victory in an election that entailed only a 60 percent participation rate would be a disliked but accepted outcome by the electorate.

The 2009 elections turned out differently because of a combination of factors that included competition between the two reformist candidates, increased outrage at Ahmadinejad's blatant (and much discussed) misrepresentations of the state of the Iranian economy as well as his own record, and past declarations during extensively watched television debates. All these elements energized the electorate in the last few weeks of the campaign in ways not foreseen by either candidates or political pundits. The animus against Ahmadinejad and savvy campaigns run by his two main candidates—Mousavi and Mehdi Karroubi—did the unthinkable and, if the total number of votes announced by the Interior Ministry is to be accepted, it brought into the electoral process at least an additional 11 million voters out of the announced total eligible electorate of 46.2 million and raised voter turnout from close to 60 percent in the first round of 2005 to about 85 percent, the highest in the history of presidential elections in the Islamic Republic.

As such, the second miscalculation was the underestimation of the impact the debates would have in energizing the population, and in encouraging them to see the elections as a contest between real alternatives. Having confidence in their man's aggressiveness and debating capabilities, the conservatives simply did not grasp the impact of either Ahmadinejad's comfort with making up data about the positive state of the Iranian economy on national television or that of other candidates standing their ground and engaging in fierce push back.

The one-to-one debates between the sitting president and Mousavi, and former Islamic Revolution Guard Corps (IRGC), Commander Mohsen Rezaei, were particularly consequential as they showed to the Iranian electorate that not only were there real differences among the candidates, but also that these candidates took their differences seriously and were willing to expose what they considered to be the president's mendacity as well as wrong-headed policies. Ahmadinejad's public charges of corruption against key figures of the Islamic Republic whom he identified as real forces behind Mousavi's candidacy also further buttressed the belief that the competition was real and consequential.[16]

Third, those who conducted the elections at the Interior Ministry did not feel the need to adjust their model of Ahmadinejad receiving two-thirds of the vote once the participation rate threatened to go above 80 percent. While they must have known that the additional voters beyond 60 percent have historically voted for change and never entered the fray in order to vote for the status quo, they simply chose to ignore this reality probably because they underestimated the role the preelection rallies had had in creating networks and links among people from different backgrounds and that would lead them to come into the streets after the elections without much effort and leadership. This was their fourth miscalculation.

In the end, like their reformist counterparts, conservatives, too, assumed certain similarities to the events of the late 1990s; although what they had in mind were student demonstrations in the summer 1999. This was when student demonstrations were prevented from spreading across the population through the use of sporadic—and what can really be described as goon—violence: the indiscriminate use of plainclothed club-wielders attacking a small group of the population—usually students in dormitories—in order to cause fear and send everybody else home.

It was the failure of this system of crowd control to put a quick end to the demonstrations in summer 2009 that ultimately forced the hand of the Leader Khamenei to enter the fray with full force and use the card that he had not been forced to use and probably should not have used until later. This resulted in Khamenei being projected as the person responsible for the fraud that had taken place on the side of one candidate, and thus becoming identified as the leader of a part of the government of Iran that has always operated in the shadows and is willing to impose violence on the Iranian population on a periodic basis.

He not only threatened violence but also made explicit that in the ideological fight about the future direction of the country, he stood with Ahmadinejad and not his life-long friend, former president Hashemi Rafsanjani, who in an open letter a few days prior to the elections had warned him of turmoil in the event of an electoral manipulation. Khamenei made clear that in the months and years to come it was really his office that would be the bastion standing against compromise with popular sentiments for a less austere and securitized political system as well as compromise with the outside world. In effect, in one quick step, he made the electoral contest over the office of the president less significant in comparison to the unelected bastions of the Islamic Republic who were going to be fighting for the future and survival of the Islamic Republic.

We will probably not know for some time what led Khamenei to incur such a heavy cost to his office in order to give support to postrevolutionary Iran's most polarizing political figure. However, it is significant that in his Friday prayer speech on June 19, 2009, he really did go further than he needed to at that moment and revealed something that he had kept ambiguous for a long time. He revealed that in the deep, ideological fights that have mired the Islamic Republic, he and his office have not been the consensus builders but the partisans, fueling and inciting the schisms rather than alleviating them.

This is something many had suspected and whispered about in Iran. However, to publicly align his office with the hard-line security apparatus of the country that in the minds of many in Iran are responsible for an Ahmadinejad presidency was a line that the Leader had previously tried not to cross and, in fact, had avoided by giving the impression that a Mousavi presidency would also be fine with him.

So why the change? In retrospect, it was probably fear of losing control— or fear of reformers not being able to control their supporters—that must have frightened the hard-line sectors of the Iranian elite in general and the office of Leader Khamenei in particular. The extent of fear was revealed in a speech given by the commander of IRGC, Mohammad Ja'fari in September 2009.[17] In this speech, he openly acknowledged that at least since February 2009, well before the June elections, the IRGC was closely monitoring the reformists of all hues in order to keep in check their presumed efforts to weaken or undermine the office of the Leader Khamenei. This acknowledgment came in reference to an attribution of a statement to the former president Mohammad Khatami, which according to Ja'fari was uttered in February 2009 in a private meeting presumably secretly taped by IRGC. According to Ja'fari, Khatami had said, "If in these elections Ahmadinejad falls, then the Leadership (*rahbari*) will be effectively eliminated; if at any cost reforms return to the executive branch, *rahbari* will have no authority in society...through the defeat of principlists (*usulgarayan*), we must contain the power of *rahbari*."

Indeed, in Ja'fari's telling, the IRGC had to enter the fray well before the elections took place in order to prevent the weakening or even the elimination of *rahbari*. It did this by taking note of what the reformists were doing and identifying them as enemies of the Islamic state as embodied and represented in *rahbari*. Such an attitude, formulated prior to Election Day, can also explain the widespread arrest of reformist leaders immediately after the elections and the aggressive postelection campaign to identify the elections and their aftermath as constituting a "velvet" or "soft" revolution—and eventually referred to as a "sedition"—inspired by external forces intent on overthrowing Iran's Islamic system.

It has become common wisdom to suggest that what has happened in Iran is an effective take over of the Iranian political system by the IRGC. And, indeed, it is possible that these elections were an attempted capstone of a process that had been going on for a while; an attempted take over of the Islamic state by the security establishment whose public face for now is Ahmadinejad and perhaps, even Khamenei himself.

However, if, indeed, this was an attempted coup, it was at least a partially botched one. While the coup leaders can probably cow some people for a period of time to accept the new arrangement, the mismanagement of the elections and their aftermath has exposed deeper domestic rifts about Iran's place in the world and the contours of state-society relations that cuts across all institutions and strata of the society. It is really about different visions and the ability of these contending visions to fight it out in a peaceful way, win or lose, via a game that is not rigged and takes everyone's citizenship seriously. Given Iran's highly polarized elite structure, it is hard to imagine any institution—including the IRGC—free of elite schisms.

The 2009 presidential elections once again confirmed that a large sector of the Iranian population and elite yearns, and has been yearning for decades, to have a say in the policy direction of the country. More than 30 years ago, a significant sector came into the streets and took part in a revolution in order to make the same point. On June 12, 2009, and after several days of millions of men and women marching, a significant sector again came out to make the same point through an election.

On June 11, 2009, one could marvel at the fact that Iran had come a long way since 1979. The population was no longer wishing to reshape the structure of the state or *nezam* in order to have an impact on the political process but was nevertheless insisting on having a say in the direction of the country. It was making a choice among candidates who during their campaign had convinced the electorate, rightly or wrongly, that they would lead the country in different domestic and foreign policy directions.

By June 13, 2009, and continuing until today, however, it is clear that Iran's century-old yearning for an end to arbitrary rule, and the creation of a set of agreed upon rules that could manage and moderate conflicts and competition without violence has yet again not been fulfilled. However, the reaction to the perceived brazen rigging of the rules also suggests that the dream of hard-line or security-state consolidation by its advocates and beneficiaries is not easy to realize. In the past three decades, the Islamic system has operated on the basis of a moving line or balance between social and political repression. It has relied on partial political repression while in fits and trials allowing for a gradual expansion of personal and social freedoms. Now trying to balance the two will be hard since allowing more social freedom so that the population can vent will immediately turn into political agitation. It will be hard for the government to draw the line. And, of course, this means constant contestation in the streets, on the rooftops, factories, and even government offices.

So the Islamic Republic remains in limbo, still searching to find a compromise to the fundamental contradiction of a populist and anti-imperialist revolution that cannot find the proper balance or accommodation among the contending societal and political forces that all want to have a say in the direction of the country and all have the means to prevent themselves from being purged.

As such, if it keeps its commitment to the holding of regular elections because as its founder Ayatollah Khomeini said "the people's vote is the standard," then it will continue to keep itself vulnerable to and hobbled by periodic and unpredictable outbursts unless it manages to put in place rules that are accepted by all sides and can resolve conflicts in a peaceful fashion. Even if it manages to control the crowds dissatisfied with electoral outcomes through a securitized political environment, the systemic inability to quiet dissatisfactions about the rules of the game among the Iranian political elite assures the continued dysfunction of a political system often paralyzed by intense policy disagreements. Electoral contenders unhappy with electoral results will end up behaving as spoilers and contribute to the political gridlock that has been exacerbated, rather than lessened, by each electoral cycle.

Notes

1. The significance of this event is accentuated by the fact that massive protests continued for eight months after the elections and resurfaced again in February 2011, in the wake of protests throughout the Middle East and in spite of the government's claims of "victory" against "the enemies" of the Islamic Republic.
2. Akbar Hashemi Rafsanjani, Friday Sermon, July 17, 2009.
3. The date and official participation numbers and percentages for Iran's elections until the 2005 presidential elections can be found at Ministry of Interior website. See, http://www .moi.ir/Portal/File/ShowFile.aspx?ID=f3e81a22-f3c0-4e89-8b24-7dc1684f26f4.
4. The original voting age in the Islamic Republic of Iran used to be 15 years. It was raised to 18 years for all elections starting with the 2009 presidential election.
5. The 1997 television debates were significantly different from the 2009 debates. As discussed later, in 2009, candidates directly confronted each other on a one-to-one basis in a series of debates. In 1997, all four candidates appeared at the same time on television and were simply asked questions by the moderator. Still the joint television appearance was instrumental in introducing a candidate who was not initially favored—Mohammad Khatami—to the audience, particularly outside the capital city of Tehran.
6. Constitution of the Islamic Republic of Iran. http://www.iranonline.com/iran/iran -info/government/constitution.html.
7. Ellen Lust, "Competitive Clientelism in the Middle East," *Journal of Democracy* 20, no. 3 (July 2009): 122–135.
8. In 1992, the Guardian Council disqualified 1,060 from a total of 3,150 registered candidates, including 30 incumbents. *Ettela'at*, April 1, 1992, cited in Mehdi Moslem,

Factional Politics in Post-Revolutionary Iran (Syracuse, NY: Syracuse University Press, 2002).

9. Steven Levitsky and Lucan Way, "The Rise of Competitive Authoritarianism," *Journal of Democracy* 13, no. 2 (April 2002): 51–65.

10. In the 1988 elections, when Hashemi Rafsanjani was elected President, close to 55 percent of the electorate (16.45 million people) voted. In his reelection campaign, the percentage had dropped to near 52 percent (16.78 million). According to official data, an increase in voting age population as well as an increase in voter participation brought the numbers participating in the 1997 election to more than 29 million (nearly 80 percent of the electorate).

11. For an analysis of the 2008 parliamentary elections, see, Farideh Farhi, "Iran's 2008 Majlis Elections: The Game of Elite Competition," *Middle East Brief* (May 29, 2008), Crown Center for Middle East Studies, Brandeis University, http://www.brandeis.edu/crown/publications/meb/MEB29.pdf.

12. The additional factor of Ahmadinejad being able to portray himself as the "challenger" or "force for economic change" against the perceived establishment candidate Hashemi Rafsanjani also played a part in his unexpected election.

13. The reformist political elites were divided in the 2009 elections in their support for either Mousavi or Karroubi. As Election Day neared, it became clear that Mousavi would have a better chance than Karroubi, but the reformist miscalculation regarding massive manipulation was across the board.

14. The issue of how many more votes the reformists needed to counter conservative vote tinkering was discussed publicly in Iran. For instance, in an interview with *E'temad* on October 8, 2008, Alireza Alavi-Tabar, a leading reformist commentator, said that 5 million votes out of an approximate total vote of 46 million was the maximum that could be manipulated, but overcoming such a hurdle was unlikely in the event of a voter turnout of between 50 to 60 percent. Higher turnout, however, would neutralize the hurdle, he said.

15. Given the fact that no empirical studies have been done regarding what caused the higher voter turnout and what networks or resources were used, it is difficult to speculate with confidence about the reasons. However, again like the 1997 election, widely-watched television debates—this time much more confrontational and accusatory in terms of assertions of corruption and incompetence—no doubt had an effect in convincing people that the election did indeed offer a choice and hence, was worth participating in. Indeed, by the eve of the elections, the carnival-like atmosphere throughout the country had made clear that turnout would be significantly higher than the previous presidential elections, giving the challengers as well as the additional participants a clear hope for victory.

16. The reasons for allowing such heated and acrimonious debates on national television are still debated. In an interview published on December 11, 2010, in *Qalam-e Sabz,* an online newspaper published by Mousavi's supporters, Mousavi said, "After the election it took me two months to realize that the famous debate was not intended to push me or Mr. Karroubi out of the field. Rather it was for a complete settling of scores with all competing forces, and a purification of the country. I was just one of the objectives and an obstacle on the way."

17. Fars News, September 2, 2009.

2

The Political Economy of the Green Movement: Contestation and Political Mobilization in Iran

Fariba Adelkhah

The Iranian presidential elections on June 12, 2009, led to social and political mobilizations on a scale not witnessed since the 1979 revolution. The campaign itself was heated and included hard-hitting televised debates between the incumbent president, Mahmoud Ahmadinejad, and the other candidates, notably Mir-Hossein Mousavi and Mehdi Karroubi. Voters and spectators filled the main streets of the capital following those TV programs, lending a festive atmosphere to the campaign, not unlike that which reigned during the big football rallies of 1997–1998. On the day after the first round of voting, hopes faded as Mahmoud Ahmadinejad was declared the victor, despite all evidence to the contrary. This, however, did not put an end to the rallies; in fact, it had the opposite effect. Immediately following the official announcement of the results, opposition supporters gathered in the streets to ask what had happened to their votes. The intensity and momentum of the ensuing protests can be explained by the stark contrast between people's expectations and the reality surrounding the elections; that is, the relative freedom with which people had been allowed to express their views about the sitting president throughout the campaign, and a combination of the speed with which his victory in the first round was declared and the severity with which all expression of doubt regarding the legitimacy of the results was repressed. Still, by the fall, protests resumed, generally during official national celebrations or religious ceremonies. The protests peaked during the Ashoura[1] commemoration in December 2009, following the death of Ayatollah Montazeri.

Interpreting events as they occur is a tricky affair, in part, because it is difficult to obtain both reliable sources of information and the means to independently and immediately verify those sources. In the case of the 2009 elections, the main press was largely controlled by those in power. There were also reports and comments from weblogs and pictures taken with mobile phones by the protesters, which could not be confirmed. As a result, it has been impossible to determine the exact number of votes won by each candidate. In retrospect, it is tempting to view the crisis that developed as a resurgence of the antagonism between state and society, as described in the writings of Homa Katouzian (2003).[2] Alternatively, one can, as the reformists tend to do, brush aside the events' antecedents and characterize the Green Movement as simply a protest against fraud and dictatorship. Nevertheless, it is clear that the Green Movement was (and is) a "social movement" (Touraine, 1984) and by organizing considerable political demonstrations it has challenged some basic political assumptions about the Islamic Republic and its authoritarianism. Not surprisingly, the advent of the movement triggered a wave of repression and arrests throughout the country that were, in turn, followed by televised trials, complete with false confessions, and the delivery of a number of death sentences.[3] While most analyses, thus far, have focused on the electoral and political aspects of the Green Movement, I propose a different approach in this chapter, namely to underscore two important and yet neglected aspects of the protest movement, which might explain why, on the one hand, the movement has not been completely suppressed, despite numerous episodes of coercion; and why, on the other hand, it has neither been able to progress nor achieve major concrete political concessions, despite its popularity.

First, the Green Movement should be understood in its context as one of a series of social movements, some of which promote regional and ethnic identity, and others, the specific grievances of teachers, bus drivers, and low-salaried workers. While the Green Movement grew out of the June 2009 elections, it benefited from the experience of these earlier social movements, which in turn provided activists with an opportunity to renew their grievances. Moreover, the Green Movement has enabled disparate special-interest groups to unite in a national movement, thereby creating a whole which is greater than the sum of its parts. In doing so, the Green Movement has evolved into something more than a monopoly of Tehran-based elites; and its focus now extends beyond mere opposition to Ahmadinejad or support for Mousavi. Therefore, the very lack of a specific political ideology can be considered a strength since this is what has, to a large extent, allowed the Green Movement to garner the support of people with wide-ranging professional and local grievances.

Second, and more controversially, the Green Movement has affected state institutions and the economy. It operates in a situation where multiple power centers are at work, which can then be interpreted both as evidence of the state's muscular authoritarianism as well as of its fragmented nature. The Green Movement, by polarizing the main political actors, illustrates once again the contradictions at the heart of the Iranian economy where political factions, in part because of their heavy business affiliations, are engaged in a constant tug-of-war. Therefore, it seems that the Green Movement demonstrates how the alleged tension between state and society (*mellat / dawlat*) is an inappropriate, if not misleading, model for understanding the current social dynamics in Iran. Under Ahmadinejad and during the tenure of previous presidents, the Iranian economy continued to lend great weight to state organizations, while simultaneously and furtively pushing for greater integration of those institutions into the market economy through liberalization.

This analysis helps us to better understand the current authoritarianism of the regime and to make sense of the support it continues to receive from both a significant segment of the population and the political elites. It is instructive to compare the Green Movement with other social movements born under authoritarian conditions. A case in point is Poland's *Solidarność* movement, which is particularly analogous to the Green Movement in that both movements merged workers' demands with calls for national independence and allegiance to their religious faith by creating an alliance between the unions, intellectuals, and the clergy. Likewise, both have enjoyed popularity; addressed grievances, in addition to those that were originally dealt with at the formation of the movement; and each movement was able to limit its ambitions for the sake of its own survival.

To sum up, if one accepts that the electoral crisis was linked to the existence of a civil society that was trying to negotiate with the regime, then one can focus more on the actual functioning of state institutions and less on scenarios about attempts at regime change, or the people who are leading them at any fixed point in time. Moreover, following Habermas, a public sphere is defined by its relationship with, rather than its opposition to, the state. I would like to point out that the regime and the Green Movement, thus, share a common vision that is defined by three criteria: Islam, Iran, and the revolution. These shared references, at least under the existing political and ideological thinking, render it difficult to make any clear-cut distinction between the regime and its opposition. While rooted in the pluralism of the institutions of the Islamic Republic and supported by its strong figures, the Green Movement also exists because of their fierce rivalries. This institutional pluralism, however, also poses an obstacle; it precludes the Green Movement from developing a distinct political identity. Furthermore, I would further argue that authoritarianism in Iranian society seems as much rooted in a specific religious or political project as it is the inevitable consequence of an institutional pluralism that emerged with the evolution of the revolution, and that gained in strength because of the Iran-Iraq War and the economic liberalization that followed the 1988 armistice. Of course, this does not imply that we should deny the authoritarian nature of the current political leadership but implies that those in power are dependent on the institutional logic and balances of power that permit the survival of the regime and that of its opposition, the Green Movement.

The Beginnings of the Green Movement: Making Use of the New "Repertories" of Contention

For the purposes of this chapter, I employ Charles Tilly's (1986) work on protest and social movements in France,[4] because of the assumption made earlier that the Green Movement has been able to mobilize elements of previous social protest movements. One such important factor has been the memory of Iran's war with Iraq, which is still vivid. What emerged from that period was not only a consolidating nationalism but also a reassertion of ethnic identities among those who were involved in and affected by the war. There remain multiple accounts (in novels and songs) that describe the ways troops were organized (according to region, town, and ethnic group) and how this organization helped young soldiers cope with hardships in the trenches, enabling them to return to civilian life; and numerous regionally oriented media productions (songs, radio programs). These cultural productions, paradoxically, have become legitimate channels for acknowledging and sometimes cultivating local identities. A good illustration of this point is a book by Zahra Hosseini, a woman veteran and member of the female *basij*. Titled *Da* (*mum* in vernacular Arabic), and based on personal diaries, it describes her three-pronged battle as a woman, an Arab, and an Iranian,[5] I suggest that although the war strengthened nationalistic feelings and a desire for a more coherent society, it also provided legitimacy to claims regarding regional and provincial diversity. Subsequently, (particularly in the 1990s and beyond), three kinds of events created the foundation for significant mobilization on a national scale: elections, social grievances, and court cases. Each, in turn, lent momentum for mobilization and contestation, and offered the opportunity for larger interaction between the regime and the society.

Elections

At the electoral level, the 1996 legislative elections appear to have been a watershed moment, occurring a year before Mohammad Khatami's surprise ascension to power offered a political face to the endogenous reforms of the Islamic Republic's institutions. These elections took place in the wake of a lively campaign—particularly in the provinces—that came to be dominated by colorful personalities (including the following three—two of whom represented Tehran, and the third, Mashhad):

> Faezeh Hashemi (daughter of the then President of the Republic, Akbar Hashemi Rafsanjani), the champion of women's rights in sports, who later became the founder of the Federation of Islamic Countries' Women's Sports Solidarity;
> Farhad Ja`fari, the youthful "free thinker,"[6] who became the overnight favorite candidate of high school students in Mashhad—in part because of his good looks; and
> Hojatoleslam Seyyed Ali-Akbar Hosseini, a cleric also very well known for his sarcastic and humorous televised comments.

Each of these candidates, in addition to others with lower national profiles, managed to highlight social and cultural concerns that clashed with the revolutionary spirit of the first decade of the republic without overtly challenging it. Three segments of the future Green Movement—women, youth, and the clergy—received recognition at that time, eventually becoming an integral part of the electoral scene. Furthermore, everyday concerns such as women's access to sports, male and female dress, and marital relations raised questions about the status of the family, women, and youth; as well as the autonomy of the private sphere and society vis-à-vis the state.[7]

Court Cases

Two legal cases also had a profound impact on the general public: the lawsuit (in 1997) against Gholam Hossein Karbaschi, the mayor of Tehran, and the court action brought against Abdollah Nouri (in 1999), a former Interior minister, parliamentarian, and editor in chief of the daily *Khordad*.[8] The two trials were televised—each highlighted the fact that there were different interpretations of the Islamic Republic within the regime. Public support for the two defendants, whether reformist or otherwise, was significant but not surprising, given the open proceedings. These lawsuits were understood to constitute a dispute between close collaborators of Ayatollah Khomeini, since both had been in positions of authority and were seen as dedicated in their service to the republic. The proceedings revealed that what was at stake were different interpretations of Ayatollah Khomeini's message and legacy. Furthermore, the ensuing battle did not appear to be peaceful between the two dominant political trends—reformist and conservative—which, needless to say, were at odds. The aggressive response of Hezbollah, with attacks on women cyclists, assassinations of intellectuals, and legal cases brought against the press, demonstrated that the conflict was an unusual one; this was to be confirmed by the bloody July 1999 repression of the student movement.

Social Grievances

Various social movements—mostly involving unions—arose during the 1990s. They were mostly apolitical and dealt, more often than not, with group interests. Although the movements were repressed, they did lead to negotiations with the authorities. The groups were careful not to question the legitimacy of the republic, either out of caution or because the political chessboard was not promising. In that context, the protesters' primary focus was on social rather than political demands. Their demonstrations targeted issues such as urban planning (Mashhad, 1992), the increase in public transportation fares (Islamabad, 1992), low income and high inflation (Tehran and Qazvin, 1994), low salaries for the Ministry of Education teaching staff (2001, 2002, 2004, 2006), the student grievances (2004), and freedom of the press and of ideas (1999). For instance, there were spontaneous uprisings in Mashhad, Zahedan, Qazvin, and some of Tehran's suburbs; ethnocultural demonstrations in Azerbaijan; politico-religious demonstrations by the Sunnis of Khorasan (1993, 2006) and Baluchistan (2006); opposition to the division of certain provinces such as Khorasan (Sabzevar in 2001; Quchan in 2002), Fars (Oqlid in 2007), and Isfahan (Semiram in 2003). Each of these grievances was linked to a specific segment of the population, either by profession or ethnicity, and lacked an explicit political agenda. Most of the protests simply faded away as promises were made and settlements partly reached. An exception, however, was the more recent and tremendously successful "One Million Signatures Campaign" that opposed gender discrimination. It emerged three years before the Green Movement, in 2006, and one could argue that it provided a new paradigm for social movements. It was interested neither in questioning the legitimacy of the regime nor in contesting the principles of religion; rather its aim was to challenge laws within the legal framework of the Iranian Constitution.

These instances of public engagement were, in turn, influenced by a changing political environment. For example, Hashemi Rafsanjani's election as president of the republic, and the ascension of Ali Khamenei to the position of "Leader" in 1989, serve as two cases in point, for they led to a period of reconstruction and economic liberalization. Economic liberalization was largely linked, not to the Leader who symbolized the legitimacy of the Islamic Republic, but rather to the president of the republic and his "government of action" (*dawlat-e kar*), whose ministers were technocrats of various political persuasions charged with running the state. It was at that time that a movement called "Reconstruction" (*kargozaran*) became a third political force, ideologically situated between the Society of Clergy (*jame'eh rohaniyat-e mobarez*) on the right, and the Association of Clerics (*majma'-e rohaniyun-e mobarez*) on the left. The latter had had a parliamentary majority until 1992 but was then held in check by the Council of Guardians, which vetted candidates for the election. Thus, the triumphant election of Mohammad Khatami to the presidency of the republic, while unexpected, grew out of these earlier events. It was, nevertheless, transformative. His election exacerbated tensions within the political class, causing not only alarm among those on the right—whose champion, the Speaker of Parliament, Ali Akbar Nateq Nouri, was defeated—but also by provoking a rapid divorce between the pro-Rafsanjani "reconstructionists" who helped Mohammad Khatami get elected and the "reformists," largely from the left, who claimed to be his heirs.

In addition, this new political landscape seemed to provide an opening for civil society: football fans took to the streets to celebrate their national team, newspapers proliferated, and youth and women felt less restrained in their public comportment. The Khatami era (1997–2005), while disappointing in terms of its failure to promote democracy and better governance, did radically alter the relationship between state and society in ways that made the Green Movement possible and its repression largely a failure. The election of Mahmoud Ahmadinejad in 2005 did not, in reality, jeopardize the results of Khatami-style liberalism. Certainly, the new president was the spokesperson for a movement referred to as "fundamentalist," adhering to a form of neoconservatism, and arising out of recognition of the inability of the traditional right, which had lost elections in 1997, 1999, 2000, and 2001, to stop the reformist wave. However, ideologically, the new president united a revolutionary spirit of social justice with economic liberalism, despite the fact that the two were sometimes incompatible, as in the case of labor rights.[9]

This conundrum was resolved through the use of public funds and petroleum price increases in a seemingly populist manner. Although painful to the Central Bank and economists, including those on the right, the distribution of public funds contributed to a renewed social dynamism, most notably in the border regions of the poorer provinces. The resulting inflation also had its benefits, at least in the short term. It provided speculative opportunities to many Iranians and a concomitant increase in the value of their homes.[10] Moreover, Ahmadinejad and his advisers could be iconoclasts on such issues as the presence of women in sport stadiums, the permissibility of satellite television, and the wearing of the veil. Perhaps, finally, his devastating criticism of the enrichment and corruption of "the sons of the elites" (aqa-zadeh), which formed the basis of his campaigns in both 2005 and 2009, contributed to minimizing the role of Islamic ideology in the republic and to making it, seemingly, more mundane.

Paradoxically, during Khatami's tenure, demonstrations were limited out of concern that they would provide the conservatives with an easy target. In any case, the reformist press was not inclined to cover popular protests against the government's objectives, on the grounds that they would threaten national security—as reformist members of parliament (MPs) alleged during the 2001 teachers' strike. Ahmadinejad's assumption of power removed such inhibitions. This was particularly true of social movements whose discontented members had held back for several years and who now accepted the word of a president whose slogan was social justice. Strikes by teachers, bus drivers, and factory workers took place, as did demonstrations by women. In 2006, the "One Million Signatures Campaign" was founded on the initiative of Noushin Ahmadi Khorasani along with 50 or so other women, and aimed at fighting gender discrimination. Thanks to its novel methods of collective action and organization, its message, and its refusal to challenge the legitimacy of the Islamic Republic, the campaign laid the grounds for the Green Movement, although it did not take sides in the 2009 presidential elections.

Signs of general discontent further increased in reaction to Ahmadinejad's imposition of economic sanctions against South Korea, China, and Britain following their 2005 International Atomic Energy Agency (IAEA) vote that attempted to bring the Iranian nuclear issue before the United Nations Security Council. In addition, in 2008 strikes erupted in Tehran's bazaar in opposition to the increase in the value added tax (VAT), the first since the revolution. In short, the Green Movement was not just a clap of thunder in a clear blue sky.

Institutional Pluralism: Islamic Corporatism

One complication the Green Movement faces is that, while its leaders consist of individuals who have played a central role in the shaping of the Islamic Republic in the early years, they have not only been marginalized, in the aftermath of the 2009 presidential elections, but have also been accused of constituting a "fifth column" and of organizing sedition against the system. However, the Green Movement has been unwilling to raise the question of regime change, because its aim has been to work from within the confines of the regime. In other words, I would like to argue that the Green Movement is rooted in and supported by the pluralism of the Islamic Republic's institutions. A first point to consider is that the constitution of the Islamic Republic, with its series of revisions, created multiple centers of decision making with conflicting mandates and overlapping memberships since many in positions of power have multiple mandates.

For example, the Expediency Council and the National Security Council include among their members individuals from different factions of the regime's major political institutions. Second, the constitutional requirement that elections be held at regular intervals means that officials have had to compete for voters' support—a fact which has contributed to the creation of four more or less stable factions—the traditional right, the pro-Rafsanjani reconstructionists, the reformists of the Islamic left, and the pro-Ahmadinejad neoconservatives. Finally the religious arena, to which the Islamic Republic is linked, albeit with a separate identity, is, by definition, distinct and competitive. Several *marja*' (high religious authorities)[11] coexist, each offering a unique interpretation in the areas of law and politics. Furthermore, numerous religious sanctuaries such as Astan-e Qods[12] in Mashhad, Hazrat-e Ma'sumeh in Qom,[13] Haram-e Motahhar, Ayatollah Khomeini's sanctuary in south Tehran, Shahzadeh 'Abdol'azim in Rey,[14] and Shah-e Cheragh in Shiraz[15] compete for the allegiance of the faithful while supporting different electoral candidates. Hasan Khomeini, the grandson of Ayatollah Khomeini and the manager (*tawliyat*) of the Imam's sanctuary, famously supports reform and, thus, the Green Movement; whereas the managers administering Hazrat-e Ma'sumeh and Astan-e Qods, while being conservative, and those administering Shahzaheh 'Abdol'azim, leaning toward the fundamentalists, have not joined forces with Mahmoud Ahmadinejad, contrary to what might have been expected.

This pluralism, inherent in both the institutional architecture and religious orientation of the Islamic Republic,[16] was further broadened during the country's post–Iran-Iraq War reconstruction and economic liberalization. Hashemi Rafsanjani's government not only required institutions to self-finance, but also provided them with the means to do so by liberalizing the economy, most notably in the area of international trade with the creation of border markets, free trade, and special-economic zones. At the same time, the maintenance of multiple exchange rates, customs procedures for imports, requirements that exporters repatriate their profits, and controls on bank credits provided those able to straddle the public and private sectors with a means to quick and easy wealth. In short, the increasing economic stakes of the factional struggle, because of liberalization, and the diversification of available resources, has led to an escalation of the political debate.

Thus, the political game is no longer a mere discussion of economics, but has become more convoluted. Similarly, it is overly simplistic to view the Revolutionary Guards as the unique beneficiaries of this evolution or even as its instigators, although their influence has been increasing. The divisions within the conservative right, and between them and the neoconservatives, are numerous; affecting the political game every bit as much as do their fights with the reformist left, which is itself divided. For example, Astan-e Qods, a *vaqf* foundation, has neither an affinity with, nor does it identify itself with the *Mo'talefeh*,[17] which dominates the bazaar traders of Tehran and the Chamber of Commerce. In other words, the two movements follow parallel tracks, if only because of their different geographical bases. Astan-e Qods is thriving because of the *vaqf* of Imam Reza and the privileged role that the province of Khorasan plays in import/export activities with Afghanistan. For their part, the *Mo'talefeh* are mostly based in Tehran where they are linked to the powerful "Imam's Rescue Committee" (*Komiteh-ye Emdad-e Emam*) whose key constituency is also based in the capital city.[18] Therefore, the financial underpinnings of Astan-e Qods and the *Mo'talefeh* are different. The "Imam's Rescue Committee" possesses its own property, can count on the generosity of a metropolis with 12 million inhabitants, the wealthiest bazaar in the country—if not the entire Middle East—and a few hundred thousand annual pilgrims to Mecca.[19] The Astan-e Qods relies on its own wealth, notably, but not exclusively, because Imam Reza has *vaqf* throughout the world. Moreover, Khamenei, in his capacity as the Leader, does not appear to have the ability to bring these groups together. Politically, he is close to the various right-wing–political factions, although one should not underestimate his mystical and progressive leanings (as compared to those of the Hawzeh conservatives). For financing, he implicitly relies on the contributions of those political spectrums: he never misses, for example, his biannual visits to the sanctuary of Imam Reza, which serve both, as a sign of devotion and a means to collect donations from the faithful. Indeed, since the constitution does not allocate a budget for the *Beyt-e rahbari* (Headquarters of the Leader), the means to cover its operating expenses must be found elsewhere.

If one accepts the hypothesis that Ahmadinejad is the herald of the neoconservative movement, born in reaction to the right's inability to stem the reformist tide of the 1990s,[20] then it seems logical that Astan-e Qods be closer to the conservative establishment. All the more since during the first round of the 2005 presidential elections, Khorasan Razavi supported Mohsen Qalibaf while southern Khorasan supported Ahmadinejad. And although the results of the 2009 elections are not known, various declarations from Vaez Tabasi, the administrator of Astan-e Qods, suggest that he favored Mir-Hossein Mousavi in 2009, less because of his own personal political leanings than because of loyalty to his old ally, Hashemi Rafsanjani.

The Revolutionary Guards and Astan-e Qods do not share a level playing field. Despite its influence and affiliates outside of Khorasan, Astan-e Qods remains a regional institution, whereas the Revolutionary Guards constitute a national institution. Moreover, Astan-e Qods, one must keep in mind, is a religious institution; whereas the Revolutionary Guards are a political and military entity. Consequently, their agendas do not necessarily coincide when it comes to elections or administrative nominations given that the candidates in legislative and local elections must win the backing of Astan-e Qods.

It is true that in order to fight the drug trade, the Revolutionary Guards have been very much present along the border with Afghanistan and Turkmenistan. However, Astan-e Qods has its own security force, the *Khoddam*, which protects the sanctuary and other assets of Imam Reza Shrine. It also maintains direct relations with at least one part of the local *basij*[21] that is devoted to the service of the Eighth Imam, and for whom it can provide important advantages. Thus, the cliché that the *basij* are affiliates of the Revolutionary Guards must be questioned.[22] Finally, Astan-e Qods and the Revolutionary Guards do not act within the same economic domain. The *vaqf* of the Imam Reza shrine specializes in agriculture, animal husbandry, mining, agro-business, and various other activities. For their part, the Guards focus on construction companies, land-based- and port-infrastructure development, Islamic finance, in addition to the oil and gas sectors. There is nothing to suggest that the recent oil- and gas-trading activities of Astan-e Qods (since 2007), diminish the considerable comparative advantage of the Revolutionary Guards in these fields. It remains true, however, that the *vaqf* and the Revolutionary Guards have fought with blunt swords, apparently since the early days of the Islamic Republic. The revolutionary volunteerism of the Guards conflicts with a "petit bourgeois" concern for respectability that characterizes Khorasan's religious traditions. Astan-e Qods is the incarnation of this latter tradition, which is also found in religious circles such as *Maktab-e Narjes* (which directs a religious school for girls), *Kanun Ehya-e Tafakkorat-e Shi'eh* (a unit for the revitalization of Shia thought), and the *Hojjatiyeh*[23] (which refers to the Twelfth Imam)—the latter two being intellectual groups.

These differences in style and interest seem to have been accentuated particularly during elections, as in the case of Hossein Qazizadeh, an MP from the Fariman-Sarakhs district, backed by the Revolutionary Guards, who in the mid-1980s dealt a blow to Astan-e Qods' interests by digging wells without the permission of the *vaqf* and by legitimizing an illegal occupation of land. This conflict was further intensified with the denunciation of the "sons of the elites" (*aqa-zadehs*). The attacks on the *aqa-zadehs* were launched in the early stages of the "economic liberalization" –a policy the Revolutionary Guards disapproved of— since they considered it a direct rejection of Khomeini's message of social justice. In the early 1990s, for example, the sons of Vaez Tabasi, Nasser and Mostafa, and the sons of the "new Amir Kabir" or Hashemi Rafsanjani, namely Mohsen, Mehdi, and Yasser, were targeted for criticism. The Revolutionary Guards particularly resented Rafsanjani, primarily because of the military setbacks they had suffered at his hands at the end of the war.[24] Nasser Tabasi, whose father had entrusted him with the management of the Sarakhs special-economic zone, was denounced publicly. He was suspected of corruption, notably in his activities in Dubai, and was brought before the court only to be acquitted, as we will see later. He was also denounced by Khomeini's heirs for a lifestyle deemed as inconsistent with the ideals of the revolution: his haircut, dress, opulent office, and the fact that his wife went to the United States to give birth. The object of this polemic and these rumors was economic liberalization and the wealth accumulation it engendered. Criticism mounted, beginning with elections held in the mid-1990s, and exacerbated by reformists' speeches, as well as revelations by Revolutionary Guards such as Masoud Dehnamaki, Heshmatollah Tabarzadi, Abbas Palizdar, and Hasan Abbasi who opposed the regime, notably over its policy of economic liberalization.

Hashemi Rafsanjani, Mohammad Khatami, and Mahmoud Ahmadinejad all benefited from the denunciations of their predecessors' records. Ahmadinejad portrayed himself as the man best suited to lead a return to the true values of the revolution. Nevertheless, the various factions in the current political-economic conflict have not divided neatly between supporters of the president of the republic, the Revolutionary Guards, and the Leader on the one hand, and on the other hand, the adherents of liberalization such as Vaez Tabasi or Hashemi Rafsanjani. This point is illustrated in the case of Mohsen Rezaei, a founder and former leader of the Revolutionary Guards who ran as a candidate in the presidential elections of 2009 against Mahmoud Ahmadinejad, and who joined forces with Mir-Hossein Mousavi and Mehdi Karroubi, in denouncing the electoral fraud, in the aftermath of the elections; ultimately, however, Rezaei did not offer his support to the Green Movement. Moreover, as we have seen, the Leader is closely aligned with Astan-e Qods. In addition, Mohsen Rafiqdoust, a minister of the Revolutionary Guards from 1982–1988, later appointed president of the Foundation of the Oppressed (*Bonyad-e mostaz'afan*) under the authority of the Leader, was stripped of his role in 1999. Thus, factional- and related-economic alliances have proven to be volatile and change with circumstances.

Economic liberalization gave birth to institutional pluralism that in turn led to generalized corporatism and the simultaneous fragmentation of civil society. In retaining the management rules that had existed under the monarchy, the regime's principal institutions guaranteed for their personnel and constituents a comprehensive series of social advantages such as housing, basic needs, consumer goods, holidays, and pilgrimages. Nevertheless, the regime's corporatism and use of public funds to support favored special interests consolidated the support base for Ahmadiniejad, although the June 2009 electoral fraud had made it impossible to determine with accuracy the extent of this support. It is also true that the conservatives do not have a monopoly on corporatism. The reformists have their special niches as well: in the automotive industry, banking, steel, and oil- and petrochemical sectors, to cite a few examples, although they have lost their dominant position in the latter two sectors.

Thus, the political crisis reveals less a two-way split between conservatives and reformists or between civilian political forces and Revolutionary Guards than a complex game with a growing number of players. Ali Khamenei's ascension led to increased power for the new clerical elites, known as Tehran clerical elites, distinct from the clergy of Qom and Mashhad who are for the most part conservative and very critical of the clergy's involvement in state politics. This new clerical generation is less interested in endorsing Ahmadinejad than in administering the republic—of which they are the offspring and for which they serve as apparatchiks. Politically, they are split between the reformists, conservatives, and neoconservatives. Similarly, the Revolutionary Guards are hardly unified in their political stance; as is illustrated by the defection of several of their former leaders; and by the personal trajectories of Mohsen Rezaei, mentioned above, and Mohsen Qalibaf, the hero of the recapture of Khorramshahr from the Iraqi army in 1982. They both ran against Mahmoud Ahmadinejad in the presidential elections; Rezaei in 2009 and Qalibaf in 2005. In addition to their traditional rivalry with the army, the Revolutionary Guards must now contend with the antiriot forces that were created in response to the repression of the 1999 student movement when the regime recognized that they were unable to control Tehran's police force (given the latter's reluctance to use coercion against peaceful civilian demonstrators). At the time of writing, the use of police brutality against members of the Green Movement, too, seems to have been largely the work of this new antiriot force rather than that of the Revolutionary Guards or the *basij*, as has been often, and incorrectly, alleged.

In this political landscape, the powerful oil and gas sectors enjoy a privileged position. They represent the principal revenue stream of the government, constituting 80 percent of the budget. Iran has a prototype oil economy. Because of its economic importance, this sector acts as a state within the state, particularly so because it is protected from direct foreign investment (partnerships with foreign companies generally are legally accorded "buy back" status.) In some aspects, the Islamic Republic has never managed to take complete control of the National Iranian Oil Company (NIOC), which it inherited from the previous regime and whose independence it has been forced to acknowledge (a scenario repeated with Astan-e Qods and the Organization of Planning and Budget—before it was dismantled by Ahmadinejad in 2007). NIOC, which has consistently retained its legal status—determined by laws (in 1974 and 1977) during the Shah's rule—has dictated its wishes to a succession of ministers of petroleum.

Ministers come and go, but NIOC remains. Moreover, using the Petropars and Petro-Iran companies—created in the late 1990s under the administration of Mohammad Khatami—as intermediaries, NIOC conducts its foreign operations independently of, and without concern for either the Islamic Republic's foreign affairs, or financial and economic dictates. Neither has it been subject to the republic's economic and financial regulations. NIOC has also been able to adopt its own policies on employees' salaries and social benefits against any managing control. In 2008, under Ahmadinejad, (and calling upon the fatwas issued by Ayatollah Khomeini and other ayatollahs), NIOC was able to avoid integrating the common-salary regime and the pooling of pension funds mandated by the High Council of Administration.[25] Moreover, NIOC employees' pension fund has gained significant investment potential and operates on an international scale, notably, in India, Malaysia, Central Asia, and Azerbaijan.[26] Nevertheless, the oil sector has not completely escaped economic liberalization and is not entirely disconnected from the political class. It is revealing to note that Mahmoud Amadinejad's fiercest battles with the Parliament, during his first term as president, concerned the appointment of the minister of petroleum and that he has been forced to change ministers four times. Similarly, Behzad Nabavi, the leader of the Organization of Mojahedin of the Islamic Revolution, and Mehdi Hashemi, a son of Hashemi Rafsanjani, were forced out of the oil sector in the mid-1990s and the early 2000s, respectively. In addition, in what has become a crucial competition between companies, the oil exploration and exploitation sectors have become less important than the oil- and gas-transportation and transformation sector, which includes oil and gas pipelines, tankers, and various engineering and petrochemical derivatives. All these companies have emerged as a result of the privatization or partial break up of state-owned firms and are closely linked with other economic sectors: Khatam al-anbiya and Sadra, for instance, are presumably connected to the Revolutionary Guards and have been in the headlines of the financial and diplomatic pages for a while, and are operating in between the oil and engineering sectors. The control of the oil- and gas-transportation sector (pipelines, gas lines, and tankers) has been the subject of intense rivalry among these privatized companies. Moreover, the commercialization of oil triggered a speculative frenzy. The administration, foundations, banks, enterprises, Islamic banking, guilds, cooperatives, retirement accounts, and even the *vaqf* acted as traders, undertaking considerable risk.[27] They suffered serious losses when prices fell, some of which were covered by the state and the national banks.

These privatizations, along with speculation in oil, finance, and real estate affected levels of wealth and socioeconomic positions, ruined careers, destroyed alliances, and created a climate of uncertainty. This set the stage for the political and factional battles of recent years, thus, feeding both the electoral campaign slogans of Mahmoud Ahmadinejad and the growth of the Green Movement, although the public's understanding of the ins and outs of this economic battle was based solely on rumor and opinion.

The Political Economy of the Public Sphere

The political economy of the public sphere and social movements cannot be reduced in political science terms to principles of sociology alone.[28] A very important issue facing the Islamic Republic of Iran today is the legal and economic status of ownership—an issue not unrelated to political mobilization. Even though few Iranians still dream of socialism—and although some recent statements by Mir-Hossein Mousavi betray his support for a government-directed economy—this issue remains unresolved more than 30 years after the revolution.[29] Moreover, the wounds created by the confiscation of properties belonging to the supporters of monarchy, the so-called *taghuti*, and taken by the *vaqf* and the foundations, have not healed. Bitter conflicts still confront Astan-e Qods, with pious people being reluctant to use the prayer rooms adjoining the Imam Reza mausoleum that had been constructed on requisitioned land. In a similar vein, the farmers of Sarakhs were expecting the revolutionary regime to restore ownerships of all lands that had been confiscated by the Shah; instead, ownership was given to Astan-e Qods. Likewise, a group called Vaheb, was set up by the person dubbed the "Sultan of Sugar" (whose real name is unknown) to purchase the property rights of exiled Iranians in an attempt to profit from any resolution to the property-confiscation conflict.

The overlapping of the public, private, and *vaqf* sectors and the game of musical chairs that it provoked, raised growing criticism. Concerns centered on the intermingling of these different economic sectors, the opacity of the transactions, and the opportunity for profit it offered the political authorities. In a historical perspective, the *vaqf* institutions (or Islamic "evergesia") constitute a central feature of the religious public sphere, because they help delineate the differences between private- and state-owned properties and their management.[30] In such a context, Hojatoleslam Mesbahi-Moghaddam, the former chair of the Parliament's Economic Commission, insisted upon recognition of a "fourth sector" of the economy. In his view, this would help to alleviate the confusion between the management modes and the different status of staff not only within the *vaqf* but also within quasi-public organizations such as Social Security

Investment Company (SHASTA)—the retirement fund for public employees.[31] The relationship between a *vaqf*—be it a factory, a tract of land, a hospital, or a mosque—and the public sector is necessarily ambiguous given that the former has a public mission, even if it is run privately. Conflicts of interest are thus inevitable.[32] Today, this power struggle sets Astan-e Qods against the mayor of Mashhad who is obligated to support the millions of pilgrims whose donations go to the Imam Reza Shrine but whose costs linked to their stay must be met by the city. In other words, the *vaqf*, strengthened by its political relationships and the religious legitimacy granted to it by the Imam Reza Shrine, is able to impose on the public administration a financial burden under the pretext of the precedence accorded to religious practice.

However, one should mention that the real issue is almost dramatically trivial. In fact, Astan-e Qods, respecting its mission to provide assistance to pilgrims and the faithful, supplies them with thousands of meals every day, especially during numerous religious events, a generosity that is of course financed by gifts to the shrine. It is not a mere coincidence that the Coca-Cola served on such occasions is produced in Mashhad by Khoshgovar, a company run by Nasser Tabasi. It should be noted that this kind of practice is not limited to Astan-e Qods. Free-trade- and special-economic zones create the same sorts of conflict of interest and mismatches between resources and costs. Thus Chabahar's governor has complained that the free-trade zones attract floods of migrants but do nothing to address or pay for the problems posed by their arrival.[33] Provincial authorities also complain regularly about the need for their respective obligations to be legally determined.

During the 1980s and 1990s, the *vaqf* foundations benefited significantly from a multiple straddling of positions of power and of funding guaranteed by what Jean-François Bayart (1993) ironically called the *"République des initiés"* (the Republic of Insiders).[34] The various foundations have traditionally been largely exempted from paying taxes, and have enjoyed preferential bank loans, the repayment of which was not always required. They have been advantaged by easy access to the lowest interest rates, and import licenses necessary for modernizing their farms and businesses—even in times of war, and despite restrictions imposed by the scarcity of cash, and the socialist leanings of the government of the time.[35] In this type of political economy, exploitation and personal enrichment are easy.[36]

The privatizations brought on by the market liberalization of the late 1990s have exacerbated the mingling of public and private interests. For example, one means by which the state pays its debt to Astan-e Qods is by giving it shares in privatized banks and companies. As with all those who somehow benefit from these property transfers, the *vaqf* tends to sell its shares quickly and realize significant gains based on a marked undervaluation of the initial shares.[37] How these profits are used remains unclear, but one can imagine several possible scenarios. It is possible that the state undervalues any shares it sells for a variety of reasons: first, to make privatization acceptable to the political class that holds the levers of power in the public sector, and who may feel threatened by structural changes to the economy; second, to bolster the private sector in which it places its full confidence; third, to enrich itself by splitting the benefits of such operations; or fourth, as a means of financing political operations, notably electoral campaigns. Whatever the case may be, it is clear that the proliferation of these transfers creates capital gains while permitting their dissimulation behind a facade comprised of numerous groups who delineate the path of the privatizations.

In any case, the political landscape has been damaged by a speculative climate that has been reinforced, although not created, by privatization. Since the revolution, the real estate market, as well as international trade, has contributed to this speculative climate, as have the war in Iraq and international sanctions. Astan-e Qods, a major economic and financial power, is among the players; it, thus, often intervenes in the wake of other major institutional operators—key among them being SHASTA, the civil servant retirement fund—to resell shares of enterprises or banks given to it by the state. It is also probable that Astan-e Qods, following the example of the banks, insurance companies, and other financially able organizations, takes part in oil market speculation, and in any case, it is fully engaged in the financial sector. Thanks to its large agricultural holdings, it has joined the circle of so-called *zamin kharan* (land speculators). It is also involved, along with many other institutions, in the race to accumulate properties. The state's litigation will not be resolved any time soon. Thus, the state was forced to engage in a conciliation process, in 2001, between the *vaqf* (Astan-e Qods) and the agricultural workers in order to settle their dispute.

For purposes of clarity, I would like to expand upon one paradigmatic case that concerns the failed privatization of a commercial society, Almakaseb, founded in 1984 at the initiative of the National Bank of Iran (Bank-e Melli), itself nationalized in 1979. At the suggestion of the intelligence services, Almakaseb was based in Dubai, no doubt in order to escape the embargo on Iran and perhaps, also to get around the regulatory barriers instituted by the left-leaning government of Mir-Hossein Mousavi. Almakaseb has gradually become one of the principal players in the trade between the United Arab Emirates and the Islamic Republic. Astan-e Qods, and of course Nasser Tabasi, have worked extensively with Almakaseb from its inception, purchasing 51 percent of its shares in 1996 through one of its companies, Hamyari Kosar. The director is none other than Nasser Tabasi, who works behind the scenes. During Tabasi's trial in 2000–2003, it was revealed that in purchasing Hamyari Kosar, he benefited from a much undervalued selling price, and a five-year loan (which seems not to have been paid back). In the late 1990s, Hamyari Kosar resold its stake in Almakaseb to the "Green Line Company" which represented Khorasan's private group, Bazargani-ye Qods, which, as its name indicates, was owned by Astan-e Qods. Scandal erupted in 2000, seemingly at the initiative of factions within the Revolutionary Guards, involving not only the transfer of a publicly financed enterprise to the private sector on questionable terms, that is, below market prices, with easy credit, unpaid loans, and in nonobservance of regulatory requirements; but also consisting of multiple benefits that accrued to Almakaseb and its directors from the systematic mingling of the public and the private, and, of course, the sacred and the profane—because of the sanctity of the Foundation of Imam Reza. Almakaseb profited immensely from the growth in trade with Dubai, engendered by the creation of the free-trade- and Sarakhs special-economic zone, run by none other than Nasser Tabasi (until his guilty verdict for illegal enrichment). Almakaseb also gained fiscal and financial advantages, having had access to very competitive exchanges rates—at least until the unification of the currency rates, in 2002[38]—because of its commercial status and its offshore location. Its directors also enjoyed these kinds of benefits, many of which resulted from the misuse of public goods and commercial transactions based on fraud and abuse of confidence. The result of the trial, which brought all this to light, was the cancellation of the sale of Almakaseb to Bazargani-ye Qods. Almakaseb was returned to the National Bank (Bank-e Melli). However, the defendants, who against all evidence pleaded their ignorance of the fact that Almakaseb was a public entity, were acquitted. They were merely obligated to repay their loans to the National Bank and to avoid the spotlight. The scandal required Nasser Tabasi to relinquish his role in running the Sarakhs special-economic zone.

This affair illustrates the problematic, albeit legal character that privatization can assume when undertaken in a juridical and practical setting as ambiguous as that prevailing under Iran's economic liberalization. It brings to mind the "bat principle": "I am a bird, see my wings! I am a mammal, see my body!" The boundaries between the state, the public, and private sectors are, in some instances, deliberately blurred. In cases where there is disagreement, each of the parties can, in good faith, adopt its own interpretation of the law, as was the case with all those involved in the Almakaseb affair.

Property rights conflicts are equally revealing on this point. Astan-e Qods owns a number of properties in Tehran, whose inhabitants suddenly discovered themselves to be tenants of the Foundation of Imam Reza, and who had to undertake innumerable legal proceedings if they hoped to retain their property titles. The *vaqf* also owns the site of the Tehran International Fair, which is today the subject of a heated dispute. Intended as the premier commercial trade fair of the Middle East, that international fair has rapidly been eclipsed by that of Dubai. Its management is, as of this writing, in the hands of the Ministry of Commerce that hopes to turn over operating control to a private entity. Many worry about the lack of transparency in such a transaction. They are particularly concerned that privatization will result in a change in the use to which land is put and that the fair will be moved to a site on the outskirts of Tehran, near the new international airport on the road to Qom. It is unclear whether Astan-e Qods, which will in any case maintain ownership of the land, shares these concerns, given that it would be able to obtain higher rent than it now does from the Ministry of Commerce.

Lack of transparency in the political economy, caused primarily by the absence of "aggiornamento" of institutions and laws,[39] and the absence of independent and reliable media seems contrary to the very idea of a public sphere. Reasoned public debate requires a certain degree of transparency and reliable information if it is to overcome rumors, interfactional accusations, unsuccessful court cases, and conspiracy theories. These are not the least of the challenges confronting the Green Movement.

Conclusion

The difficulty with any analysis of the Green Movement is that it requires one to acknowledge the importance of the economic stakes involved in its dynamics, while simultaneously admitting that this movement cannot be reduced simply to a question of economic grievances. Explanations based solely on economic and social arguments are inadequate. Other factors such as the distinctions between the city and the countryside, or between disadvantaged regions and those benefiting from oil wealth—as well as demographic factors—like the differences between generations and/or the sexes, are important in determining the unpredictable character of the movement. Moreover, this uncertainty stems from a specific political genealogy: that of the modern mobilization brought on by the Constitutional Revolution of 1906–1911, the Mosaddeq episode in the early 1950s, the resistance movement of Ayatollah Khomeini in 1963, Mohammad Reza Shah's authoritarian modernization, and the nationalist and anti-imperialist fights of the Islamic Revolution. And it is that same logic that stems from the Islamic Republic itself, with its ideology, its institutions, its methods of socialization and of co-optation, and its takeover of social protections.

The Green Movement remains within the confines set by Khomeini's ideology when he proposed a path to modernity that was both uniquely Islamic and derived from Western intellectual and political traditions, most notably in its bureaucratic organization and its concepts of nation and republic. The Green Movement and the regime share close views on three strategic concerns: the revolution, the nation, and Islam. The novel participation of diaspora Iranians in domestic political mobilization tends to complicate things. On the one hand, the exiles bring their memories, frustrations, resentments, and interests to the table; on the other, their alliance with the Green Movement is linked to their endorsement of a critique of a republic that many of them have long feared or rejected. Certainly, the fact that they joined in the 2009 demonstrations is a further indication of the underground reconfiguration of the political landscape. Already, in the wake of the "One Million Signatures Campaign," Islamists along with secularists, and even monarchists, engaged in a dialogue and cooperated with each other; this trend has been consecrated by the Green Movement.

The Green Movement may eventually be considered as a driving force of the public sphere in the sense that it challenges political authority and the balance of powers, advocates for dialogue between the regime and the society, and allows everyone's participation in political debate and protest. In doing so, it embodies the tensions within the Islamic Republic, between Islamic ideas and values on one side, and material interests on the other. Without a doubt, it seems doomed to failure because of its internal divisions and the inability of its leadership to reframe its grievances, not to mention the ferocity of the repression directed at it. No doubt, it seemed to have reached its nadir when it was unable to participate in the demonstrations on the thirty-first anniversary of the revolution in February 2010. It has, nevertheless, already succeeded in profoundly transforming the relationship between state and society. Big failures can hide huge successes. Mir-Hossein Mousavi, who would never have met the expectations of his supporters had he been elected president, has since become a hero of one of the most impressive and original social movements of the last decades. The Green Movement has united various demands, mobilizing crowds from bottom-up according to their grievances, within the constraints of the Islamic Republic's legality, while profoundly destabilizing it.

However, how are we to understand Ahmadinejad's political success despite his authoritarianism and his debatable personal style? To what extent should we refer to his policies as mere coercion and to what extent do they offer a series of concrete social, economic, and political answers that could be supported and endorsed by, at least, a segment of Iranian society? At first glance, it is not simply a matter of personal rule; indeed, Ahmadinejad is constrained not only by a set of checks and balances—but above all by a 30-year-old political system in which he is only one link in a long chain of leaders.

Ahmadinejad is a shrewd political operative and some of his policies clearly benefit particular segments of Iranian society. He shapes and implements policies that do not always correspond to anything his political supporters would automatically endorse and he does not play only by their rules. Ideologically, he merges a claim for social justice with economic liberalism, though the two are often deemed incompatible—as in the case of the labor rights law that passed during his mandate. As we have seen, his answer to this conundrum has been to use public funds or oil price increases in a seemingly populist manner. Moreover, Ahmadinejad and his advisers may be iconoclasts on such issues as the presence of women in sports stadiums, satellite television, the wearing of the veil, and the freedom of young unmarried couples to meet in public areas. Finally, his devastating criticism of the enrichment of "the sons of the elites," and the corruption that prevailed during the 2005 and 2009 presidential campaigns, contributed to the trivializing of the republic and to the sidelining of Islamic ideology. At the same time, Ahmadinejad's nuclear policy satisfies nationalistic feelings, an integral part and still relevant heritage of the 1979 revolution.

Therefore, we must make sense of a conservative president, who, at times and on certain issues such as women, youth, the clergy, and local rural authorities, is more radical than even the reformists. For all these groups, he framed policies that provided an alternative (and not always a reactionary one) as compared with proposals promoted by the reformists, and, subsequently, the Green Movement. Surprisingly, Ahmadinejad has also shown himself to be a pragmatist. In October 2009, he argued for a nuclear compromise that was endorsed by the United States and which would have involved sending uranium out of the country for enrichment. This was vetoed by not only the Green Movement leadership but the Leader as well. Moreover, Ahmadinejad succeeded in reducing subsidies on flour, water, and diesel fuel, creating price spikes that, to date, have not provoked the kind of angry protests that followed the introduction of fuel rationing in 2007—despite a significant demonstration in February 2011. Neither Rafsanjani nor Khatami were able to achieve such structural adjustments to the Iranian economy. Of course, Ahmadinejad believes that the "Imam of the Age" (*Mahdi*) not only supports the plan to remove subsidies but also that He actually has been managing it. This combination of millenarianism, populism, and realpolitik has proven very costly for the Iranian economy and diplomacy. By the same token, it has served a purpose in destabilizing Ahmadinejad's special-interest opposition groups (thanks notably to the Green Movement's inability to support their claims and reframe them in a broader context). Such a combination allows him to rig elections, win through coercion, and rule with some measure of popular sympathy and a certain amount of support from institutions that he, himself, has never had much respect for.

Meanwhile, as long as Ahmadinejad remains president, the Green Movement will survive. In that sense, it seems that not only do they complement each other, but also that in all their rivalry, they are, in fact, dependent on each other for survival.

Notes

1. The day of Ashoura is the tenth day of Muharram in the Islamic calendar. It marks the climax of the commemoration of the martyrdom of Imam Husayn, the grandson of the Prophet, at Karbala, in 680.
2. Homa Katouzian, *Iranian History and Politics: The Dialectic of State and Society* (London and New York: Routledge, 2003).
3. These arrests have continued until the time of writing, more than one and a half years after the protests.
4. Charles Tilly, *La France conteste de 1600 à nos jours* (Paris: Fayard, 1986).
5. Seyyedeh Zahra Hosseini, *Da: Khaterat-e Seyyedeh Zahra Hosseini* (Tehran: Soureh, 1388/ 2009).
6. Also known in Persian as "*degar-andish*," this trait is attributed to those who literally think differently from the establishment, even if some continue to work within the system. It is worth mentioning that Farhad Ja`fari, who once mobilized the youth to vote against the establishment, has since become a supporter of Ahmadinejad. That's to say that being a "*degar-andish*" is no longer exclusive to reformists as it was once thought, during the mid-1990s.
7. Of course, the regime's internal political turmoil echoed the changes that had occurred following the end of the war against Iraq in 1988, and the death of Ayatollah Khomeini in 1989 as well as the difficulties it encountered in managing the consequences.
8. Gholam Hossein Karbaschi was accused of embezzlement, and Abdollah Nouri, of threatening national security following the closure of his newspaper, *Khordad*. This daily, whose title was both an allusion and tribute to the Persian calendar month when Khatami had got elected, was censured for having published a letter of Ayatollah Khomeini on the future of his successor-to-be, Ayatollah Montazeri, and for thereby challenging the official history of the Islamic Republic.
9. It was under Ahmadinejad that the most free-market law since 1986 was enacted, and was supported by the conservative right and opposed by the left. This law sought to limit the rights of worker representatives in factories and gave a free hand to the management.
10. This rise in the price of real estate in 2007, which is thought to have been partly planned by immigrants from the Gulf with their speculative investments in certain cities such as Mashhad or Shiraz, certainly facilitated the departure of Iranians from their country. With the price of real estate having increased tenfold, Iranians were able to invest abroad, often a condition for obtaining a residency permit or dual nationality, in places such as Dubai (until the eve of the economic crisis, in 2008).

11. In Shi`i Islam, every believer should, in theory, follow the teachings of a chosen *marja`*; in practice, however, such systematic allegiance is open to question. Moreover, the choice of *marja`* is often made at the family or local level, rather than at that of the individual.

12. This is the place where Imam Reza, the eighth Imam of the Twelver Shi`is, is buried.

13. The city of Qom houses the shrine of the sister of the eighth Imam, Hazrat-e Ma`sumeh.

14. The Shrine of Shahzadeh `Abdol`azim, in Rey, is one of the oldest in Tehran.

15. Shah-e Cheragh, in Shiraz, houses the tombs of two brothers who are the sons of Imam Musa Kazem, the seventh imam.

16. While the political class, at least on the surface, unified against the enemy during the war, the clergy, by contrast, did not hesitate to publicize their differences. The split between the "Society of the Combatant Clergy" and the "Association of the Combatant Clerics," remains the basis of today's political power struggle. Of course this division was initiated within the political leadership at the beginning of the Islamic Republic, in order presumably to better cope with a reluctant or even opposing traditional wing of the clergy.

17. *Mo'talefeh* is a conservative association made up of various religious groups among guilds inside the bazaar. Very active during the 1979 revolution, its members, later, became prominent actors in government and parliament. *Mo'talefeh* also has a strong representation in the Chamber of Commerce, and became a political party in 2003.

18. The people of Khorasan make their donations to the Imam Reza Shrine, Astan-e Qods, whereas the people of Tabriz do so to their local organization, *Mo'aseseyeh hemayat az mostamundan-e Tabriz* (The Association for the protection of the needy of Tabriz), in order to keep them in the province and to avoid donations from being sent to Tehran.

19. Subsequent to an agreement with the Hajj Pilgrimage Organization, the "Imam's Rescue Committee" has gained the right to take care of providing the pilgrims with both their material needs in Mecca and with gifts upon their return.

20. Kasra Naji, *Ahmadinejad: The Secret History of Iran's Radical Leader* (London and New York: I. B. Tauris, 2009).

21. *Basij* is a paramilitary corps, made up of volunteers. Its beginnings date back to the Iran-Iraq War and the need to strengthen the national defense, extending it to all social groups and classes. Their statute is as vague as their political opinions depending on their generation, their social groups, and the city they are based in.

22. Certainly, they officially joined the Revolutionary Guards in 2008, but in reality their institutional stature continues to evolve at the national level and is, in any case, dependent on the local context especially in Khorasan.

23. *Hojjatiyeh* was an association that was originally created in 1953 by Mahmoud Halabi to counter the influence of the Baha'is on the monarchy. From the outset, this movement had religious and even mystical dimensions. At the same time, the *Hojjatiyeh*—rationalists and devoted to science—recruited new members at universities and was thus far from advocating obscurantism.

24. He was thought to have played a role in the acceptance of the armistice of 1988, and of limited military expenditure in the early 1990s, when he was president.

25. Gholam hossein Nozari, the then oil minister, insisted also on the fact that the pension fund did not belong to NIOC, but to NIOC's employees, and that it constituted part of the private sector. http://www.etemaad.ir/Released/88–02–02/133.htm#141462.

26. http://www.naftnews.net/view-10123.html.

27. The investment for all these privatized companies in real estate properties in Dubai, before the crisis in 2008, cost too much to the national Iranian bank system (cf. my fieldwork in Dubai 2010).
28. Mounia Bennani-Chraibi and Olivier Fillieule, eds., *Résistances et protestations dans les sociétés musulmanes* (Paris: Presses de Sciences Po, 2003).
29. http://www.khabaronline.ir, May 18, 2009.
30. Said Amir Arjomand, "The Law, Agency, and Policy in Medieval Islamic society: Development of the Institutions of Learning from the Tenth to the Fifteenth Century," *Comparative Studies in Society and History* 41, no. 2 (April 1999): 263–293.
31. http://www.ksabz.net, November 1, 2009.
32. It is interesting to recall that Taher Ahmadzadeh initially declined the nomination, as Khorasan's governor, offered by the provisional government of Mehdi Bazargan in 1979. In fact, as one of the co-founders of the Center for the Diffusion of Islamic Truth, Taher Ahmadzadeh viewed the post as one that should be filled by the lieutenant of Astan-e Qods, who was then Vaez Tabasi, and he (Ahmadzadeh) undoubtedly would have expected to receive the nomination. Taher Ahmadzadeh ultimately had to accept the post of governor but without any illusions as to its real power in the face of the omnipotence of the *vaqf*. In any case, he was removed after Bazargan's resignation.
33. Chabahar is located in the southern part of the province of Sistan and Baluchestan, on the Sea of Oman.
34. Jean-François Bayart, "Jeux de pouvoir à Téhéran," *Politique internationale* 82 (Winter 1998–1999): 107–122.
35. Ali Rashidi, "The Process of De-privatization in Iran after the Revolution of 1979" in *L'économie de l'Iran islamique: Entre l'état et le marché*, ed. Thierry Coville (Tehran: Institut français de recherche en Iran, 1994), 37–68; Massoud Karshenas and M. Hashem Pesaran, "Exchange Rate Unification, the Role of Markets and Planning in the Iranian Economic Reconstruction" in *L'économie de l'Iran islamique*, 141–176; Zein Al Massawi, "Spéculation et marché noir: L'Etat au quotidien," *Peuples méditerranéens* 29 (octobre–décembre 1984): 85–90; Bernard Hourcade and Farhad Khosrokhavar, "La bourgeoisie iranienne ou le contrôle de l'appareil de spéculation," *Revue Tiers Monde* 31, no. 124, (octobre–décembre 1990): 877–898; M. Hashem Pesaran, "The Iranian Foreign Exchange Policy and the Black Market for Dollars," *International Journal of Middle East Studies* 24, no. 1 (February 1992): 101–121; Firouzeh Khalatbari, "Iran: A Unique Underground Economy" in *L'économie de l'Iran islamique*, 113–138; Thierry Coville, "La Banque centrale d'Iran et la politique de liberalisation économique," in *L'économie de l'Iran islamique*, 209–232; Y. H. Farzin, "Foreign Exchange Reform in Iran: Badly Designed, Badly Managed," *World Development* 23, no. 6 (1995): 987–1001; Sohrab Behdad, "From Populism to Economic Liberalism: The Iranian Predicament," in *The Economy of Iran: Dilemmas of an Islamic State*, ed. Parvin Alizadeh (London and New York: I. B. Tauris, 2000), 100–141.
36. It is unlikely, therefore, that the following flattering portrait of the directors of Astan-e Qods as depicted by Bernard Hourcade in the late 1980s would be still accurate: "Very simple in their beliefs and their comportment, they are greatly concerned with efficiency, and their moral power is the greater for not being ostentatious and for their preference for direct personal relationships over heavy administrative burdens. These hajjis (honorific title reserved for those who have completed the pilgrimage to Mecca) and bazaaris, totally imbued with Islamic culture, stand in contrast to the idea of what constitutes modern management." Cf. Bernard Hourcade, "Vaqf et modernité en Iran: Les agro-business de l'Astân-e qods de Mashhad," in *Entre l'Iran*

et l'Occident : Adaptation et assimilation des idées occidentales en Iran, ed. Yann Richard (Paris: Editions de la Maison des Sciences de l'Homme, 1989), 135.

37. The assessment of privatized firms' assets is one of the most controversial issues. Moreover, it happens often that buyers eventually are unable to honor their financial commitment. The privatization process involves many institutions at the cost of unsolvable straddling and competence conflicts, as it is always the case in the Islamic Republic.

38. It seems that many are anxious that the multiple exchange rates may be about to come back. Cf. Masoud Reza Zaheri, "The comeback of the multiple exchange rate systems," September 30, 2010, http://www.aftab.ir.

39. It is worth mentioning that the trade law which continues to be in vigor is that which was voted during the Pahlavi Monarchy in 1922 and partly revised in 1968. After the revolution and because of huge economic changes, a new project of trade law was planned during Mousavi's government, but it never reached the Parliament. See http://www.iraneconomist.com, April 12, 2009.

3

From "Reform" to "Rights": Mapping a Changing Discourse in Iran, 1997–2009

Negin Nabavi

In a special Nawruz supplement of the reformist daily *E'temad-e melli* published in March 2009 on the occasion of both the Persian New Year, as well as the thirtieth anniversary of the Islamic Republic, a series of open letters were published addressed to the future president, who was to be elected in June of that year.[1] Even though at this early stage, other than the incumbent, Mahmoud Ahmadinejad, the names of no other presidential candidates had been announced,[2] the point of this exercise was clearly to make public some of the demands that were talked about within reformist circles. Among these was a letter by Emadeddin Baqi, a reformist essayist, journalist, and human rights activist, raising the importance of the issue of human rights as a sign of the cultural maturity of any society, and asking that the future government establish a ministry for human rights. Arguing that human rights were not specific to any particular political faction, he wrote,

> In our world, one of the most important characteristics of successful development and culture consists of the level of respect paid to human rights (*hoquq-e bashar*)...The ideal state is one in which respecting people's rights is of utmost importance, and which people do not fear but like. [It is] one which builds trust by means of a just and precise implementation of the law, and creates equal opportunity for all, and where the rulers consider themselves the representatives of the people and [hold themselves] accountable to the public (regardless of whether the latter are supporters or opponents).[3]

While perhaps the most outspoken advocate of human rights,[4] Baqi was not the only one to bring attention to the question of rights. Others within the reformist circle, at this time, also raised similar questions. In the same supplement, for example, Mostafa Tajzadeh, another essayist, journalist, and a former adviser to Mohammad Khatami, highlighted the principle of citizens' rights and listed the different ways in which they should be adhered to by the next government.[5] Likewise, Jamileh Kadivar, a female essayist, political activist, and former parliamentarian, asked that the future president appoint a woman minister and in this way, respect women's rights at long last.[6] Women's groups, too, had been forthright with their demands for equal rights. Some three months before the presidential elections, a coalition of 42 women's groups, both secular and religious, reformist and conservative, had come together to form a "Convergence of Women" (*Hamgarayee-ye zanan*) calling for an end to discrimination against women in all aspects of law.[7] Last but not least, the question of human rights— encompassing the rights of citizens, women, and minorities— also featured in the campaign literature of the presidential candidates affiliated with the reformist camp, namely Mir-Hossein Mousavi and Mehdi Karroubi.[8] Each campaign issued a charter of human rights (*manshur-e hoquq-e bashar*), pledging that they would defend human rights in the event of getting elected.[9] This was the very first time in the history of the Islamic Republic that the question of human rights was receiving such public support by any presidential candidate.

In short, by 2009, it seems that what can be called a "discourse of rights" had supplanted that of reform, and gained some prominence among several sectors in society, as also evidenced by the high level of participation in the tenth presidential elections as well as the demands of the protestors in its aftermath in June of that year.[10] Yet few studies have commented on how this "discourse of rights" came to the foreground, what its origins were, and what, its relationship to the reformist discourse of 1997–2005 and the women's movement that constituted the domain in the Islamic Republic where the issue of "equal rights" had been articulated most effectively.[11] This chapter aims to explore the relationship between this "discourse of rights" and the reformist and women's rights discourse. More specifically, it will focus on how the "discourse of rights" gradually took shape, how it was influenced by the earlier discussions regarding what constituted "reform" and "reformism," and the extent to which it was informed by and further promoted and popularized by the women's movement. To this end, this chapter will examine the development of the major themes as they appeared in essays, articles, and round-table discussions in reformist publications that were primarily published in Iran.[12] It will cover an array of individuals, both religious and secular, men and women, who can be categorized broadly as "intellectual-activists" in view of the fact that they were first and foremost, concerned with the here and now, and addressing the ills of the nation.[13]

"Reform" and "Reformism": The Emergence and Shaping of a New Discourse

The reformist discourse of the 1990s was neither prepackaged nor its parameters well defined. Its origins, as is now widely recognized, lay primarily in the discussions carried out by religious intellectuals[14] (*rawshanfekran-e dini*) in two very different forums in the early to the mid-1990s. *Kiyan*, an independent monthly, centered around Abdolkarim Soroush, provided one focal point, and the Center for Strategic Studies, a think tank of sorts, affiliated with the office of the president, and directed by Mohammad Mousavi Khoeiniha, provided the other. Whereas *Kiyan* explored the question of the interrelatedness of religion and politics, and advanced a broad nonideological approach to Islam on a theoretical level, the Center for Strategic Studies investigated issues from a much more pragmatic perspective. Convened by a former revolutionary elite that felt increasingly disillusioned with the status quo, the discussions held at the Center, in particular in its "political office," were primarily to assess the chances of the development and political renewal of the Islamic Revolution.[15] Thus questions such as political structure, political culture, and behavior were of paramount concern, and it was in this context that the concept of *tawse'eh-ye siyasi* (literally political development, and a euphemism for "democracy")[16] was first coined by Saeed Hajjarian, a former deputy minister of intelligence turned reformist, and one who has generally come to be viewed as the theoretician of the reform movement par excellence.[17] The discussions at the Center, however, resulted in little more than "policy papers" that went largely unnoticed. In other words, while by the mid-1990s, the question of the need for a rethinking and reexamination of some key issues in society had been raised, it was still in its formative stages and restricted to the select few.[18] It was only with Mohammad Khatami's election victory in May 1997 that an opportunity was created for these discussions to be opened up to the society at large. On the one hand, a new vibrant press, which regarded its mission to be that of furthering the project of reform, began to flourish; and on the other hand, reformists were made to come face-to-face with the reality of the dualistic political structure that was the Islamic Republic. It was as a result of this combination of factors that for the first time, in the pages of the newly emerging press, the notion of "reform" was provided with an opportunity to be discussed, developed, and critiqued extensively from a variety of perspectives. It is this discourse, as reflected in the writings of journalists or secondary intellectuals in the early years of Khatami's presidency that I would like to focus on in this first part of the chapter.

Central to this discourse, in these early years, was the question of how to define reform itself. Most agreed that Khatami's election had provided a new beginning and a new hope for a better life. In the words of Morteza Mardiha, an essayist and contributor to the reformist dailies such as *Jame'eh*, *Neshat*, and *Tus*, the Second of Khordad (May 23, 1997), the day that Khatami was elected president for the first time, was the chance to resume ordinary life, "to eat, sleep, joke, talk, love, read, protest, have no fear and thus live."[19] The Second of Khordad signified "an end to the respectability of the age of epic, and the arrival of the time for love and co-existence."[20] Yet, for all this idealism and optimism, there was a general recognition that reform was an abstract idea without much of a track record or successful precedent in past Iranian history or political culture. Hence, the columns that were devoted to defining "reform" tried to do so by comparing and contrasting it to something that Iran had had much experience of in its modern history, namely revolutions. Mardiha, for example, wrote:

> Revolutions are in search of novelty. They don't accept ready-made prescriptions, but regard themselves as blueprints for others to follow. Reform [by contrast] tends to be less concerned with innovation (*naw-avari*). It seeks to learn from the experience of others, it recognizes the need to study and examine…Revolutions are proud and self-obsessed (*khod-shifteh*). They take things easy and make big plans but reform is modest and open to criticism (*enteqad-pazir*). When faced with problems, it [reform] thinks and looks for solutions. Understanding the complexities of reality slows the pace of reform and limits the parameters of its actions.[21]

In other words, reform was defined as everything that revolution was not. If, for instance, revolutions undid the old order and brought about sudden change, reform would be necessarily gradualist. If revolutions were movements full of passion and radicalism, reform would have to be cautious and encourage compromise. Finally, if revolutions demanded unity, reform would have to allow for a multiplicity of voices.[22] As Mardiha elaborated on this same theme in another article, "tearing down [everything] completely in order to build afresh is a quixotic gamble. It is not a wise course of action. [We need to] enter an age which is no longer the age of revolutions; but that of cautious calculations, the recognition of reality and its steady reform."[23]

Mardiha was not the only one to define reform in distinction from revolution. Others, too, pointed to different aspects of this contrast to come up with their own definitions of what constituted reform. Emadeddin Baqi, for example, similar to Mardiha, saw the primary difference between revolutions and reform in the different approaches that they took to the past. In his words, while "revolutions looked to the past, and on the basis of fighting the past, became intent on wiping out the present circumstances in order to move forward, reform just looked to the future…without wanting to make the past into a setting for punishments or executions."[24] Abbas Abdi, another prolific essayist and activist,[25] expanded on their contrasting nature: in his view, whereas revolutions tended to be violent, erratic, and unpredictable with a momentum of their own, reform could only take place through nonviolent and lawful means.[26] In other words, while he believed that reform and revolutions shared the goal of seeking change, what distinguished them was the manner in which each went about doing so. Revolutions did so by means of confrontation and defiance, even if it meant breaking the law; and reform, through reaching compromise, working within the system, and respecting the law.

In short, for essayists and thinkers such as Mardiha, Baqi, Abdi, and Hajjarian, reform was the most cost-effective way to bring about change in the political domain. It was therefore no surprise that respect for the rule of law constituted one of the major mottoes of reformists. Defending the rule of law, while ostensibly conservative, according to Abdi, was actually a progressive act since this had been a long-lasting problem in Iranian history that had never been overcome.[27] Laws, explained Hajjarian, were essential since they ensured institution building on the one hand, and prevented violent action on the other.[28] Laws were indispensable, argued Mardiha, because they were what protected freedom and democracy from falling into chaos. In short, a major component of this reformist talk was confidence in the ability of existing laws to bring about the needed political changes. The key, therefore, was to make sure that these laws were implemented properly. In an interview years later, Abdi reiterated the importance of laws in his understanding of the reformist perspective: "The aim [of reform] was not to limit the power of *Velayat-e faqih* (the rule of the jurist), but rather to make it accountable and answerable to the law."[29] Reformism, therefore, implied the idea, in Baqi's words, that "it was possible neither to accept the status quo nor to oppose the revolution."[30] In other words, the objective was not to dismantle the political system, but rather to modify it from within through political development.

It was in this context that the concept of civil society (*Jame'eh-ye madani*) and institution building became one of the key components of the discourse of reform and the subject of much discussion. Originally a campaign slogan in the 1997 presidential elections, in subsequent years a range of opinions developed as to what civil society entailed, and the prerequisites that were necessary for its emergence. However, the general view was that civil society was a key factor, a panacea of sorts in bringing about a "more balanced relationship between the rulers and the ruled,"[31] and thus necessary for political development. In the words of Abdi, for example, civil society acted like an "anchor" (*langargah*) without which, the gap between state and society would widen to such an extent as to become dangerous. In other words, inasmuch as civil society consisted of mediating institutions, it was one way of ensuring societal stability, and preventing sudden, unexpected change.[32] It is not my intention, here, to analyze the civil society debate in detail,[33] but suffice it to say for our purposes, that over time, the concept of "civil society" came to be considered too abstract and theoretical to win over public opinion. As a result, the discussion that had begun with much enthusiasm, lost its pervasiveness, and was replaced by other more accessible aspects of the reformist discourse, such as that of "rights," as will be discussed further below.

The principles of nonviolence and lack of confrontation were, therefore, central to the reformist outlook. If a former revolutionary like Abdi, for example, who incidentally, had been one of the radical students that had taken over the US embassy in 1979, had had such a change in viewpoint—that he called himself a "conservative revolutionary"[34] in 1998—it was not only because he had been sobered by age, but also because he was responding in part to a new view of Iranian history that many within the reformist camp had come to share. In an interview with *Rah-e naw* weekly in April 1998, he hinted at this historical perspective:

> A consensus is gradually taking shape concerning Iran. All consider our lack of political development to be a result of the lack of civil institutions, [as well as] political instability, violence, revolution and suppression. All have reached the conclusion that in reality the solution to Iran's problems cannot be achieved through the elimination of others or violent confrontation against the state.[35]

According to this view, the course of the twentieth century history in Iran had been characterized by two factors; volatility and the several abortive attempts at curtailing authoritarian rule. While there had been no shortage of upheavals, there had been little in terms of concrete political gains. The way ahead, therefore, it was argued, was to move away from these recurrent patterns, to try to avoid turmoil and instead, bring about political change through slow, modest, and measured steps. When put in this historical perspective, reformists, by and large, considered their own goals as not that different from those of the constitutionalists in the early part of the twentieth century, at least in the initial stages when extremism had not yet taken over, and the aim was to move beyond autocracy toward a more representative form of government. As a result, from 1998 onward, public debates about the constitutional revolution as a point of reference and legitimizing precedent for the reformists, gained more popularity in the reformist circles, paradoxically superseding the official historiography of the Islamic Republic which had otherwise considered June 1963, and Ayatollah Khomeini's speech against the Shah's White Revolution, as signaling the start of the struggle that was to lead to the Islamic Revolution.

In keeping with this view of history, the role of the intellectual in introducing reforms was also reassessed. According to Hajjarian, for example, since reform was not a top-down process, it could only be achieved through a process that involved the grassroots as well as the elite simultaneously. That is, while there had to be pressure from below in the form of mass mobilization and public opinion, there had to be negotiation at the top. In such a context, intellectuals were in a unique position to give voice and articulate the demands made by the people. For this to happen, however, intellectuals had to change their habit of confronting the state and learn, instead to negotiate and compromise with power. In his words, "the calamity of our intellectuals has been that they worry too much about becoming associated with the system (*dastgahi shodan*). They have always wanted to stand outside the state and confront it. One of the implications of the Second of Khordad was that there is no reason to stand outside. In order to succeed, one must get one's hands dirty."[36]

In short, reform, as was understood in the late 1990s, was a reaction to what had been perceived as failures of the past. It represented recognition of the fact that political change was necessary, but that there were no quick fixes. Whether it advocated compromise, respect for the rule of law, gradualism, and nonviolence, it did not constitute a political program. At one level, reform was liberalism at its best, with no specific paradigm, and few set rules; at the other, its aim was to encourage greater political openness, tolerance, and transparency in the least disruptive way, although it was not quite clear how one would enable the other.

While most in the reformist camp agreed on the broad outlines of the idea of reform as delineated above, certain differences began to emerge from the outset with regard to the details and practicalities involved. There was no consensus, for example, over the extent to which reform was a process as opposed to a political project. In other words, was reform primarily a means to an end, or was it a goal in itself? Many believed in the principle that "in politics, the means [was] as important if not more important than the aim."[37] Mohammad Quchani, a journalist and editor of a number of reformist dailies, put the idea succinctly when he wrote, "A century of unsuccessful pursuit of freedom has resulted in us finally learning that the means have to be commensurate with the ends. One cannot go in search of sacred aims with tainted means."[38]

Over time, however, as attempts at reform were frustrated and thwarted by hard-line factions within the system, using the very same laws that the reformists had so cherished, in order to curtail their maneuvers, shut down their newspapers, and arrest several major figures from their ranks, a growing number of reformists began to criticize this emphasis on method as opposed to ends. Baqi, for example, characterized this overly reverential attitude to process as being tantamount to "considering as principle that which was [meant to be] a means to an end, but that same means becomes sacred in itself. [It becomes] an end, and you sacrifice everything for this means."[39] Hamidreza Jalaeipour, similarly, faulted this tendency and attributed it to the failure of the reformists:

> [For the reformist movement] the method of struggle is more important than the aim of the struggle. I think that one of the reasons behind the weakness and inefficiency of this movement is this very reason that they [reformists] are committed to a series of methods and have their hands tied, whereas the opposing side is not in the least bit committed to these methods, and has all the means to assert control.[40]

With the passage of years, as Khatami's presidency proved too ineffective vis-à-vis the entrenched theocratic political system, and as promises of political reform seemed to wane, many more critiques and differences of opinion as to what "reform" entailed and how it should have been implemented and put into practice, came to the fore. In fact, by the beginning of Khatami's second term, many reformists began to cast doubt on the viability of reform in the way that it had been defined. In a series of roundtables and articles that appeared in reformist journals, reformists criticized the movement for having been too elitist, and too theoretical. They faulted it for not having reached out or sought consensus over strategy, and for having been too cautious and unwilling to risk changing strategies to adapt to changing times.[41] In retrospect, some argued, that had reformists paid more attention to strategy and approached reform more as a political project with a specific aim rather than a process, then perhaps reforms would have been more effectual.[42] It was therefore no surprise that by the time of the 2005 presidential elections, differences among reformists had deepened to such an extent that they lost not only any semblance of consensus over their preferred goal, but they also labeled their divergences in approach somewhat disparagingly in terms of "state reformists" (*eslahtalaban-e hokumati*) and "non-state reformists" (*eslahtalaban-e birun az hokumat*), with the latter questioning the possibility of "reform from within" altogether, and arguing instead for the boycott of the elections.

It was in such a context that a new discourse began to gain prominence. While it has generally been recognized that "the political failure of the religious reform movement" resulted in a loss of appeal of the reformist discourse, giving rise to a "competing secular discourse with modernity as its focal point,"[43] as will be discussed in the next section, the "discourse of rights" was neither entirely secular nor entirely religious. It had grown out of the reformist discourse, but what made it feasible and perhaps even lent it greater currency was the fact that it shared points of commonality with the rights-oriented discourse of the women's movement that had proven relatively successful in attaining some of its goals.

Civil Rights, Human Rights, and Women's Rights

The concept of "rights" was very much part and parcel of the reformist discourse from the outset. It had featured as a key component in Khatami's vision of civil society, which as mentioned earlier, had constituted a popular campaign slogan in 1997. "Our civil society," as he put it, "is not a society where only Muslims have rights and are considered citizens of the system, but it is a society where every human being has rights in the framework of law and order, and defending his rights, is among the duties of the state."[44] This idea of an inclusive society where people, regardless of their faith, were protected by the law was also extended to the "rights of dissidents" (hoquq-e mokhalefan). As was argued in a series of articles published in Rah-e naw, already in 1998, "rights of dissidents" was not an abstraction, but a necessity; not only would dissident voices invigorate the politics of any society, as Abdi argued, but they would also help bring attention to the shortcomings of society, which would in turn have to be addressed by the powers that be.[45] In a similar vein, the editorial of the same issue of Rah-e naw contended that ensuring the "rights of dissidents" was what distinguished a democratic from an autocratic system of rule. It would further reduce the chances of a sudden and violent change of government and thus bring about a unity of purpose and greater harmony between different viewpoints, and therefore, stabilize the ruling system.[46]

In later years, the question of the "rights of dissidents" was broadened to that of human rights. Baqi serves as a good case in point of this shift in emphasis.[47] He, too, had advocated for tolerance of opposing views, arguing that "freedom [would] only be institutionalized in our society when...the culture of the rights of dissidents becomes accepted, officially recognized and implemented."[48] Furthermore, upon his release from prison in 2002, following a three-year stint, Baqi emerged as an outspoken proponent of individual rights. He set up the "Association for the Defense of the Rights of Prisoners," (Anjoman-e defa' az hoquq-e zendaniyan) with the aim of bringing attention to the marginalized in society, in particular criminals who were overlooked even more than political prisoners. Later, he established a second association, called "Guardians of the Right to Life" (Pasdaran-e haqq-e hayat), so as to defend the rights of those who had been sentenced to death, and to argue for an end to the death penalty. Starting in late 2003, however, Baqi's writings focused increasingly on human rights. In an interview in 2009, he explained that if he had turned his attention to human rights issues, it was because in prison, upon thinking over his own actions along with that of the reformers in general, he had concluded that "in the reform period, we [reformists] had been afflicted with elitism and had distanced ourselves from the social domain."[49] In other words, engaging in human rights was one way of engaging with society and compensating for those aspects that he considered to have been neglected by reformists. In this sense, as he put it in the same interview, "prioritizing human rights over democracy meant deepening the roots of reform."[50]

The appeal of human rights, therefore, lay in the fact that it did not suffer from the disadvantages of "reformism" and thus had the potential to impact society in the way that reform never could. There were two interrelated aspects to this: the first was the fact that in comparison to reform, human rights was thought to be much more tangible and accessible to a broad group of people in society. From Baqi's point of view, since the Universal Declaration of Human Rights (to which Iran was a signatory) consisted of a range of rights that were "inherent to all human beings [including] the right to life, the right to health, the right to justice, the right to freedom from torture, the right to equality before the law...the right to marry and to set up a family..."[51](and so on), human rights affected ordinary people from all walks of life, and thus represented one way of broadening the project of reform, and reaching out to many more sectors of society. Similarly, because human rights was more specific in its demands, it was more easily understandable, less abstract, and thus by definition, would not be limited to a select group of proponents. Second, Baqi went to great lengths to make the case that demanding human rights as a principle went beyond politics. In his view, human rights constituted a moral issue, not a political matter. It belonged to all human beings, irrespective of faith, ideology, or even social position so that the rulers were as entitled to these rights as the ruled.[52] As he put it in another article, "the difference between a political activist and a human rights activist is in the fact that the political activist takes part in the contest to gain power, and to this end, defends a specific candidate [in the elections], whereas the human rights activist has to defend the principle of free and fair elections."[53] In this sense, human rights was as much part of the moral obligations of the state as it was of the human rights activist. Demanding human rights, therefore, was thought to represent a peaceful way of gaining the trust of society without alienating the state. Although he did not doubt that seeking human rights would be as challenging as fighting for political development and democracy had proven to be, these two advantages meant that the state could ill afford to suppress human rights the way it had the reform movement.

Last but not least, as a lay "religious intellectual" (*rawshanfekr-e dini*), Baqi did not see any incompatibilities between Islam and human rights. In his view, the main point of commonality lay in the fact that both had concern for the protection of human dignity.[54] If there were points of friction, he argued, they need not be long lasting, since a rereading and reinterpretation of *fiqh* (Islamic jurisprudence) could easily resolve this tension, as had been shown by Ayatollah Hossein-Ali Montazeri's *fatwa* regarding the rights of nonbelievers.[55] In fact, human rights had the potential of reconciling tradition with modernity. In his words, "human rights have their source in mysticism, tradition and earlier religions. It is only in the modern era that they have taken on a humanistic expression and become rational and secular."[56]

Demanding human rights was, therefore, one avenue that could be pursued by former reformists like Baqi who had become disillusioned with the project of reform. Now that defending the rule of law as defined by the constitution seemed impractical, aspiring to universal values was an attempt to rise above politics rather than become hostage to it as had been the case with reform. The universality of human rights would allow activists to bypass the state while at the same time holding it accountable to international standards.

At the same time, there were other developments, too, that may have played a part in boosting the human rights cause. Among them was the awarding of the Nobel Peace Prize in October 2003 to Shirin Ebadi, a human rights lawyer, women's right activist, and one of the founders of the "Center for the Defense of Human Rights" (*Kanun-e modafe'an-e hoquq-e bashar*). This event served as proof that such efforts would not go unnoticed by the international community. Another factor that may have had an impact even if it has not received as much attention in this context was the women's movement. In fact, one could argue that if the human rights discourse gained increasing prevalence by 2009, it was in part due to the women's movement and its success in making a case for the notion of equal rights and gender justice. Even though in the early years of the reform movement, many of the reformists (including Baqi) did not consider women's rights as significant enough to deserve separate attention,[57] evidence suggests that in later years, the women's movement provided an alternative paradigm[58] for social movements, in general, and the reform movement in particular. After all, in the years that the reform movement was considered "dead," the movement that continued to demand change in terms of reform and rights, was that of women.

Even though the challenges that women faced were quite different from that of the reformists, they did share a number of commonalities. Among them was the fact that the women's movement, like that of the reformists, was decentralized; it had no obvious leadership and consisted of diverse groups with a range of understandings and views. Furthermore, it was committed to bringing about change in a nonviolent manner, through the transformation of mindsets, by raising awareness among both men and women about the level of discrimination and gender biases present in society at large.

At the same time, the two movements were distinct in a number of ways. In view of the fact that among the most important obstacles that women had to contend with since the onset of the 1979 revolution, was the politicization of the "woman question," and the equating of women with symbols of authentic culture, women activists had concluded that one way to effect change, was to distance their demands from politics, and to present women's grievances in terms of social and legal ills that had to be addressed. The importance for women to maintain their independence from the state was being talked about by essayists and women's rights activists like Mehrangiz Kar already in 1995.[59] In a similar vein, since another long-term hurdle for women had been that of patriarchy in general and inequality in family law in particular, the women's movement had become "rights oriented"[60] from the outset. That is, its aim was focused primarily on demanding equal rights for women and a change in discriminatory laws from early on. As Ebadi put it in an interview with *Zanan* monthly in 1997, "we must all, in unison, announce that the equality of all peoples is good and that oppressing a number of human beings on the basis of gender, race or religion is wrong."[61]

Such straightforward and unequivocal public positions together with the fact that women's activism had managed to adapt to changing circumstances and take different shapes at different times in the 30-year history of the Islamic Republic, had enabled women to maintain a defiant presence in all spheres of public life in spite of the many restrictions imposed on them. A recent example of a novel approach was the "One Million Signatures Campaign." Officially launched by a group of women in summer 2006 (following two demonstrations in 2005 and 2006 that had been broken up by security forces), at a time when in the words of one of its founding members, Noushin Ahmadi Khorasani,[62] "the most reactionary and repressive elements of the Islamic Republic were riding high after an interval of still-born reformism under Khatami,"[63] the aim of this movement was ostensibly to collect one million signatures in support of putting an end to discriminatory laws regardless of the government in power. However, the bigger goal was to raise consciousness of both women and men at a more fundamental level. In Ahmadi Khorasani's words again, "the past thirty years have shown that private debates over theory are not going to be enough to bring about a broad societal opening or a process of concrete reform. Without seeping into the fabric of daily life, philosophical discourses cannot—and for years have not been able to—have a practical influence on the real life circumstances with which Iranian women must deal."[64] The "One Million Signatures Campaign" could, therefore, be viewed, in part, as a reaction to what they had considered to be the failures of the reform movement. In this attempt to distance themselves from abstractions, the campaign activists built on the past achievements of the women's movement by continuing to focus on "concrete problems and shared pains inflicted by unfair laws,"[65] while at the same time adopting a new approach of taking their demands to the streets, all so as to mobilize and involve a larger number of ordinary men and women for the cause of equal rights. In doing so, they succeeded in popularizing the discourse of rights. According to Ahmadi Khorasani, the Campaign was to "breathe a spirit of broad popular participation with its conviction that since all must live under the laws, all may have a say in pointing out to both the authorities and the general public how these laws may be made better."[66]

The "One Million Signatures Campaign" was not the only movement that adopted a focused, pragmatic, and nonideological approach to changing discriminatory laws against women. Other grassroots women's initiations also emerged from 2006 onward, among them, "the Stop Stoning Forever Campaign"; "the Women for Equal Citizenship Campaign"; "the Women's Access to Public Stadiums Campaigns"; "the National Women's Charter Campaign"; and "the Mothers for Peace,"[67] each focusing on a specific issue constituting part of the larger struggle for equal rights.

One may therefore argue that the women's movement had given rise to a new paradigm with certain advantages: their focus on concrete demands such as equal rights irrespective of the government in power, together with their flexibility in terms of tactic meant that, contrary to the earlier efforts of the reformists, they did not get stuck on definitions and allowed for a divergence of approaches, collapsing the secular/ religious dichotomy in the process. This pragmatic and nonideological approach had much in common with the human rights discourse—it, too, was an attempt to rise above politics, and persist with trying to foster change peacefully. To that extent, and the fact that women had managed to gain some recognition for their cause, the women's movement contributed to the promotion of the human rights cause and played a significant part in enabling a general discourse of rights to supplant that of reform by 2009.

The highly polarized political environment that has dominated the country since June 2009, together with the subsequent brutal crackdowns, has closed all doors to any form of dissent and alternative expression, and instead revived a hegemonic state discourse that views "human rights" as a tool of foreign intervention and what has been called a "velvet revolution" or "soft subversion" (barandazi-ye narm). However, in view of what has been argued above, one can say that the shift in discourse from "reform" to "rights" marked a shift in the mindset, not only of reformists but also of large sections of the population, as evidenced by the popular demonstrations both on the eve as well as in the immediate aftermath of the tenth presidential elections. It, furthermore, represented the convergence of principles espoused by both the women's movement, in all its diversity, as well as disillusioned reformists looking for ways to promote social change in a matter-of-fact and peaceful manner. While the future is uncertain, it would not be unreasonable to imagine that in the event of a slight opening in the political situation, the human rights discourse would once again come to the fore as a principal avenue for bringing about peaceful political and social change.

Notes

1. E`temad-e melli: si sal, si khatereh, 1357–1386 (E`temad-e melli: thirty years, thirty memories, 1978–2007), special Nawruz issue, spring 2009.
2. According to the laws of the Islamic Republic, the Guardian Council announces the approved names of the candidates some three weeks (between 20 and 23 days) before the presidential elections, at which time the candidates can officially begin their campaigning.
3. Emadeddin Baqi, "Vezarat-e hoquq-e bashar ta'sis konid" (Establish a ministry for human rights), E`temad-e melli: si sal, 109.
4. For a detailed background of Emadeddin Baqi, see Fatemeh Kamali Ahmad Sara'i, "Zendegi-nameh-ye Emadeddin Baqi," Emadbaghi.com, 26 Aban 1383/ November 16, 2004, http://www.emadbaghi.com/archives/000370.php
5. Mostafa Tajzadeh, "Ancheh nabayad anjam dahid" (That which you must not do), E`temad-e melli: si sal, 112–113.
6. Jamileh Kadivar, "Tabu-ye vazir-e zan ra beshkanid" (Break the taboo of [having] a woman minister), E`temad-e melli: si sal, 100.
7. See Nayereh Tohidi, "Tohidi: Women and the Presidential Elections: Iran's New Political Culture," Informed Comment, September 30, 2009, http://www.juancole.com/2009/091/tohidi-women-and-presidential-elections.html; See also the chapter by Fatemeh Sadeghi in this same volume.
8. While Mir-Hossein Mousavi issued a general charter of human rights, Karroubi released separate statements on citizens' rights, the rights of minorities and women, and human

rights. Neither Mahmoud Ahmadinejad, the incumbent, nor Mohsen Rezaei, the candidate of the conservative camp paid much attention to the question of human rights.

9. On the first anniversary of the Green Movement, in June 2010, a "Green Movement Charter" was also published, which listed "defending human dignity and human rights, regardless of ideology, religion, gender, ethnicity and social position" as among its values and priorities. See Nader Hashemi and Danny Postel, eds., "The Green Movement Charter," in *The People Reloaded: The Green Movement and the Struggle for Iran's Future* (New York: Melville House Publishing, 2010), 339–340.

10. Some have argued that what drew the large numbers of people to take part in June 2009 presidential elections may have been in part the "new pledges regarding human rights and citizens' rights." See Hossein Baqerzadeh, "Mahv-e eslahtalabi az gofteman-e siyasi" (The elimination of reformism from the political discourse), *Iran-e emrooz*, 13 Mordad 1388/ August 4, 2009, http://www.iran-emrooz.net/index.php?/politic /more/19024/. For a selection of articles on the Green Movement and the protests that followed the tenth presidential elections, see also Nader Hashemi and Danny Postel, eds., *The People Reloaded: The Green Movement and the Struggle for Iran's Future*.

11. For an account of how the question of women's rights has percolated even into conservative circles, see Nazanin Shahrokni, "All the President's Women," *Middle East Report* 39, no. 4 (Winter 2009): 2–6.

12. Many of these articles are also available either in print as part of "collected essays" or on personal websites set up by the authors.

13. For a definition of "intellectual-activists, see Mehran Kamrava, *Iran's Intellectual Revolution* (Cambridge, UK: Cambridge University Press, 2008), 122.

14. Religious intellectuals (*rawshanfekran -e dini*), also known as *naw-andishan-e dini*, have often been divided into two categories: those whose writings tend to be more theoretical and philosophical and thus not as accessible to the general public, and those essayists/ journalists whose writings address primarily the concerns of the here and now. See, for example, Kamrava, *Iran's Intellectual Revolution*, 122.

15. For an account of the personalities and activities at the Center, see Ali Mirsepassi's interview with Alireza Alavi-Tabar. Ali Mirsepassi, *Democracy in Modern Iran: Islam, Culture and Political Change* (New York: New York University Press, 2010), 125–147.

16. In a speech that he gave to the Participation Front Party (*Hezb-e mosharekat*) in February 2005, Hajjarian explained the background for the coining of the phrase, *tawse'eh-ye siyasi*. Since, in the early days of the 1979 revolution, Mehdi Bazargan had insisted on the name, the "Democratic Islamic Republic of Iran" as opposed to the "Islamic Republic," a sort of sensitivity if not hostility had developed among the groups within the power structure toward the word "democracy." As a result, the word "democracy" was avoided in much of the official literature of the Islamic Republic and so, Hajjarian and his colleagues preferred to use a generic term such as *tawse'eh-ye siyasi* (political development) or *naw-sazi-ye siyasi* (political renewal.) "Hajjarian: eslahtalaban dar teori aqab mandehand" (Hajjarian: the reformists are lagging behind in theoretical thinking), *Sharq*, 29 Bahman 1383/ February 17, 2005.

17. Hajjarian became the target of an assassination attempt in March 2000, which left him severely disabled. This assassination attempt was widely seen as a warning by the hard-liners to the reformists that the latter's "mandate would not translate into effective political power." See Günes Murat Tezcür, *Muslim Reformers in Iran and Turkey: The Paradox of Moderation* (Austin, TX: University of Texas Press, 2010), 131.

18. Hajjarian did discuss some of these ideas in a number of articles that he published in the daily *Asr-e ma*, in 1994–1995. For more, see Hajjarian, *Jomhuriyyat: afsunzeda'i az qodrat* (Republicanism: the demystification of power) (Tehran: Tarh-e Naw, 1379/ 2000.)

19. Seyyed Morteza Mardiha, "Bogzarid zendegi konam" (Let me live), in *Ba mas`uliyyat-e sardabir: moqadameh-i bar projeh-ye eslah* (With the responsibility of the editor: an introduction to the project of reform), ed. Seyyed Morteza Mardiha (Tehran: Jame`eh-ye Iraniyan, 1379/ 2000), 26.

20. Ibid., 29.

21. Mardiha, "Enqelab va eslah" (Revolution and Reform), in *Ba mas`uliyyat-e sardabir*, 123.

22. See Mardiha, "E'telaf, janeshin-e ettehad" (Coalition, the successor to unity), in *Ba mas'uliyyat-e sardabir*, 124.

23. Mardiha, "Cheguneh enqelab konim" (How should we rebel?), in *Ba mas'uliyyat-e sardabir*, 198.

24. Emadeddin Baqi, "Hadaf-e tarahan-e terror barchidan-e dawlat-e Khatami va hazf-e jebheh-ye dovvom-e khordad bud" (The aim of the planners of the terrorist attack was to bring down Khatami's government and eliminate the Second of Khordad Movement), in *Goft-o-gu ba Saeed Hajjarian: bara-ye tarikh* (A conversation with Saeed Hajjarian: for the record), ed. Emadeddin Baqi (Tehran: Nashr-e Ney, 1379/ 2000), 129.

25. For a detailed background on Abbas Abdi, see Abbas Abdi, "Heyf va sad heyf," (A pity and a hundred pities), *Ayandeh*, spring 1384/ 2005, http://ayande.ir/2006/04/01 /post_11.

26. Abbas Abdi, "Eslahat-e mored-e niyaz-e emruz-e ma eslahat-e raveshi ast" (The reforms that we need today are reforms in method), in *Eslahat va porseshha-ye asasi: majmu`eh maqalat* (Essential reforms and questions: collected essays), ed. Mohsen Armin (Tehran: Zekr, 1380/ 2001), 185.

27. In his words, "Defending the rule of law, on the surface, is a wholly conservative matter. Law, in itself, means conservatism. But in the context of Iran, this is completely revolutionary." See Abdi, "Negahi jame`eh-shenakhti beh vaqe`eh-ye dovvom-e khordad: dar goft-o-gu ba Abbas Abdi" (A sociological look at the event of the Second of Khordad: in conversation with Abbas Abdi), *Rah-e naw*, no. 1, 5 Ordibehesht 1377/ April 25, 1998, 19.

28. See Hajjarian, "Chera qanun-gera'" (Why turn to law?), in *Jomhuriyyat: afsunzeda'i az qodrat*, 69.

29. Abdi, "Heyf va sad heyf."

30. Emadeddin Baqi, "Eslahat bedun-e hazineh momken nist: goft-o-gu ba ruznameh-ye E`temad-e Melli" (Reforms are not possible without [incurring] costs: in conversation with the daily E`temad-e melli), part one, *Emadbaghi.com*, 19 Bahman 1387/ February 7, 2009, http:www.emadbaghi.com/archives/001016.php

31. Kamrava, *Iran's Intellectual Revolution*, 141.

32. Abdi, "Negahi jame`eh-shenakhti beh vaqe`eh-ye dovvom-e khordad," 18.

33. Much has been written on the civil society discourse in Iran in both Persian and English. See, for example, Mehran Kamrava, "The Civil Society Discourse in Iran," *British Journal of Middle Eastern Studies* 28, no. 2 (2001): 165–185; Asghar Schirazi, "The Debate on Civil Society in Iran," in *Civil Society in the Middle East*, ed. Amr Hamzawy (Berlin: Verlag Hans Schiler, 2002), 47–83; Mohsen Armin et al., *Nesbat-e din va jame`eh-ye madani* (The relationship between religion and civil society) (Tehran: Zekr, 1379/ 2000).

34. Abdi, "Negahi jame`eh-shenakhti beh vaqe`eh-ye dovvom-e khordad," 19.

35. Ibid.

36. Saeed Hajjarian, "Dovvom-e Khordad: bimha va omidha, payamha va cheshmanda-zha, dar goft-o-gu ba Saeed Hajjarian" (The Second of Khordad: fears and hopes, messages and expectations, in conversation with Saeed Hajjarian), *Rah-e naw*, no. 5, 2 Khordad 1377/ May 23, 1998, 18.

37. Behruz Nazer, "Dar nafy-e radikalism beh onvan-e ravesh" (In refuting radicalism as a method), *Rah-e naw*, no. 5, 2 Khordad 1377/ May 23, 1998, 7.
38. Mohammad Quchani, "Dovvom-e Khordad: ham estrateji, ham taktik" (The Second of Khordad as both strategy and tactic), in *Bazi-ye bozorgan: Vaqaye`-negari-ye jonbesh-e eslahat-e demokratik dar Iran* (The Elite's game: Chronicling the democratic reform movement in Iran), ed. Mohammad Quchani (Tehran: Jame`eh-ye Iraniyan, 1379/ 2000), 234.
39. Emadeddin Baqi, "Chera eslahat?" (Why reforms?), in *Jonbesh-e eslahat-e demokratik dar Iran: enqelab ya eslah* (The Democratic reform movement in Iran: revolution or reform) (Tehran: Nashr-e Sara'i, 1383/ 2004), 415–437.
40. "Jame`eh-shenakhti-ye siyasi-ye eslahat: ru dar ru, Khashayar Deyhimi va Hamidreza Jalaeipour" (The political sociology of reforms: face-to-face, Khashayar Deyhimi and Hamidreza Jalaeipour), *Aftab*, no. 18, Shahrivar 1381/ September 2002, 6.
41. Kamrava, *Iran's Intellectual Revolution*, 34.
42. "Ekhtelafat dar keshvar jedi ast: Entekhabat dar goft-o-gu ba Khashayar Deyhimi" (The differences in the country are serious: the elections, in conversation with Khashayar Deyhimi), *Roozonline*, 10 Azar 1387/ November 30, 2008, http://www.roozonline.com.
43. Kamrava, *Iran's Intellectual Revolution*, 34. See, also, Ali Gheissari and Vali Nasr, *Democracy in Iran: History and the Quest for Liberty* (Oxford, UK: Oxford University Press, 2006).
44. Mohammad Khatami, "Jame`eh-ye madani az negah-e Eslam" (Civil society as seen by Islam), in *Nesbat-e din va Jame`eh-ye madani* (The relationship between religion and civil society), ed. Mohsen Armin (Tehran: Zekr, 1378/ 1999), 181.
45. Abbas Abdi, "Seda-ye mokhalefan bayad saf shavad" (The voice of the dissidents must be made clear), *Rah-e naw*, no. 6, 9 Khordad 1377/ May 30, 1998, 3.
46. "Azadi-ye mokhalefan" (The freedom of dissidents), *Rah-e naw*, no. 6, 9 Khordad 1377/ May 30, 1998, 2.
47. Another reason for focusing on Baqi here is that his website www.emadbaghi.com has made available and organized his writings on "human rights" in a chronological fashion throughout the years.
48. Emadeddin Baqi, "Azadi az an-e kist?" (To whom does freedom belong?), *Hoquq-e mokhalefan: tamrin-e demokrasi bara-ye jame`eh-ye irani* (The rights of dissidents: An exercise in democracy for the Iranian society) (Tehran: Nashr-e Sara'i, 1379/ 2000), 24.
49. Baqi, "`Eslahat-e bedun-e hazineh momken nist," part two, *Emadbaghi.com,* February 9, 2009, http://www.emadbaghi.com/archives/001017.php#more.
50. Ibid.
51. Baqi, "Eslah-talabi-ye sadeqaneh, eslah-talabi-ye riyakaraneh" (Honest reformism, deceitful reformism), *E`temad-e melli*, 28 Dey 1387/ January 17, 2009, http://news.gooya.com/politics/archives/2009/01/082582.php.
52. Baqi, "Akhlaq va siyasat: hoquq-e bashar, hoquq-e shahrvandan, hoquq-e zamamdaran" (Morality and politics: human rights, citizens' rights, rulers' rights), *Hammihan*, 3 Tir 1386/ June 24, 2007, http://www.emadbaghi.com/archives/000914.php.
53. Baqi, "Gozashteh: chah ya cheragh-e rah-e ayandeh?" (The past, the ditch or the light of the future path), *Emadbaghi.com,* Khordad 1388/ June 2009, http://www.emadbaghi.com/archives/001053.php.
54. Baqi, "Jonbesh-e hoquq-e bashar: sokhanrani va porsesh va pasokh dar jam`-e sardabiran-e servisha-ye khabargozari-ye jomhuri-ye eslami-ye Iran" (The Human Rights Movement: a speech together with questions and answers in a gathering of the editors of the news agencies of the Islamic Republic of Iran), *Emadbaghi.com*, 24 Tir 1383/ July 14, 2004, http://www.emadbaghi.com/archives/000176.php.

55. Ibid. Based on his reading of the Quran and the hadiths, Ayatollah Montazeri issued the opinion that all human beings, whether Muslim or non-Muslim, by virtue of being human, had dignity and thus were entitled to civil rights. See Baqi, "Hoquq-e bashar ya hoquq-e mo'menan: taqrirat-e dars-e feqh –e hazrat-e ayatollah 'ozma Montazeri piramum-e hormat-e ensan" (Human rights or Muslims' Rights: an exposition of the Grand Ayatollah Montazeri's lesson in fiqh on the subject of human dignity), *Emadbaghi.com*, 11 Azar 1382/ December 2, 2003, http://www.emadbaghi.com/archives/000119.php. In 2008, this opinion was reflected in Montazeri's unparalleled decree regarding Baha'is, where he said that Baha'is "had the right to citizenship in Iran and must [be able to] benefit from Islamic compassion which is stressed in the Quran and by religious authorities." See http://www.bahai-egypt.org/2008/05/ayatollah-montazeri-decrees-Bahais.html.

56. Baqi, "Jonbesh-e hoquq-e bashar" (The Human Rights Movement), *Emadbaghi.com*, 27 Esfand 1382/ March 17, 2004, http://www.emadbaghi.com/archives/000101.php.

57. In 1999, the women's monthly *Zanan* invited a number of religious intellectuals to discuss their views regarding the "woman question," whether they officially recognized the existence of such an issue, and if so, what solutions they proposed to resolve it. For Emadeddin Baqi's standpoint, see Emadeddin Baqi, "Mas'aleh-ye zanan: kodam mas'aleh?" (The woman question: what question?) *Zanan*, no. 57, Aban 1378/ October–November 1999, 23–25. For a comprehensive review of the writings of religious intellectuals regarding the question of women, see Farideh Farhi, "Religious Intellectuals, the 'Woman Question,' and the Struggle for the Creation of a Democratic Public Sphere in Iran," *Intellectuals in Post-Revolutionary Iran*, ed. Ahmad Ashraf and Ali Banuazizi, special issue, *International Journal of Politics, Culture and Society* 15, no. 2 (winter 2001): 315–339.

58. See Fariba Adelkhah's chapter in this same volume.

59. Mehrangiz Kar, "Aya hoquq-e zan yek maquleh-ye siyasi ast?" (Is women's rights a political topic?), *Zanan*, no. 23, Farvardin-Ordibehesht 1374/ March–May 1995, 22–26.

60. Nayereh Tohidi, "The Women's Movement and Feminism in Iran: A Glocal Perspective," in *Women's Movements in the Global Era: The Power of Local Feminisms*, ed. Amrita Basu (Boulder, CO: Westview Press, 2010), 378.

61. "Mohemtarin masa'el-e zanan-e Iran chist? Miz-e gerdi ba sherkat-e Shirin Ebadi, Alireza Alavitabar va Nahid Moti'" (What are the most important problems of Iranian women? A round-table with Shirin Ebadi, Alireza Alavitabar and Nahid Moti'), *Zanan*, no. 34, Ordibehesht 1376/ May 1997, 18.

62. In addition to being one of the founding members of the "One Million Signatures Campaign," Noushin Ahmadi Khorasani was also the publisher and editor of a number of now-banned women's journals such as *Jens-e Dovvom* (Second Sex), *Fasl-e Zanan* (Women's Season), and the blog *"Madreseh-ye feministi"* (the Feminist School).

63. Noushin Ahmadi Khorasani, *Iranian Women's One Million Signatures: Campaign for Equality, the Inside Story* (Washington, DC: Women's Learning Partnership, 2009), 43.

64. Ibid., 46.

65. Ibid., 47.

66. Ibid., 47.

67. In order to reflect the activities of these new campaigns, a new website called *Meydan-e Zanan* was founded, also, in summer 2006. See http://www.meydaan.org/aboutus.aspx.

4

The Sacred in Fragments: Shi'i Iran since the 1979 Revolution[1]

Babak Rahimi

February 2009 marked the thirtieth anniversary of the Iranian Revolution of 1979, a popular upheaval that has been primarily identified as an "Islamic" revolution. Although not entirely a religious phenomenon, the revolutionary spirit that galvanized an overwhelming majority of Shi'i Iranians to rise up against the Pahlavi regime installed the only Islamic state in modern history.[2] As a witness to the revolution, the late Michel Foucault described this "spirit" as a new kind of subjectivity, "Something other than the desire to obey the law more faithfully," and, for the revolutionaries, a "desire to renew their entire existence by going back to a spiritual experience that they thought they could find within Shi'ite Islam itself."[3] In many ways, though, the 1979 revolution did not solely mark a crystallization of a new revolutionary theocratic republic based on a mere "spiritual experience," but also the transformation of Iranian Shi'ism into a new (inter)subjective force of religiosity in opening up a new conception of the sacred and profane, or as Foucault would call it, a new "political spirituality."[4] By and large, the 1979 revolution marked a renewal of Shi'i Iran, a reinvention of tradition in light of modern imaginaries of self and reality with the aim to create a new form of modernity.[5]

In historical terms, Twelver Shi'i Islam has maintained a distinct religious culture and hierocratic order in a country known for the strong presence of mysticism and a poetic taste for the sublime.[6] With the establishment of the Safavid dynasty in 1501, Shi'ism emerged as the official religion of the state and a source of legitimacy for imperial authority in early modern Iran. Although it took many years for the country to acquire a Shi'i character, the ascendency of the clerical institution, particularly under Shah Abbas I (1587–1629), involved the formation of a complex fusion of theological legalism and popular piety with clerics playing the leading role as guardians of religious texts and practice in the propagation of Shi'ism in the everyday life of early modern Iranian society.[7] With the collapse of the Safavid Empire in the early eighteenth century, the clerical establishment gradually gained (relative) autonomy from the state and evolved into an alternative source of legitimacy, at times competing with the monarchy for resources and power. By the nineteenth century, Shi'i Iran had developed an entirely nationalized religion, with distinct Persian cultural traits, largely associated with sites of ritual performances (e.g., *ta'zieh* ceremonies), cultures of sociability, pious associations (*hey'at*), and clerical and bazaar networks based in cities like Isfahan, Mashhad, and Qom. By virtue of its theological disposition based on revolutionary aspirations against entrenched power, by the 1960s, a new religious opposition led by Ayatollah Ruhollah Khomeini (d. 1989) rearticulated Iranian Shi'ism in the form of a new radical ideology, with martyrdom as a major ethos of political action. The 1979 Islamic Revolution marked an attempt, to use Foucault's language, at self-constitution as a way to create a new order based on a new vision of political spirituality.

What follows is an attempt to provide a broad account of the transformation of Shi'i Iran since the 1979 revolution. The main claim is that, as a complex set of discourses and practices, postrevolutionary Shi'i Iran has undergone significant changes that essentially involve a rethinking of the Islamic Republic's theocratic underpinnings and, moreover, innovatively rearticulate Shi'ism beyond an ideology of political spirituality that involves the consolidation of clerical rule through mundane governance. Such subjective processes have led to the emergence of competing Shi'i Islams, generating new dynamic discourses and practices in the context of state and society relations. Paradoxically, however, with the increasing centralization of Shi'ism under the Islamic Republic, contemporary Shi'i Iran has undergone a relative decentralization of authority, a fragmentation largely due to the formation of competing centers of spiritual authority in response to the consolidation of the Islamic Republic and its official ideology.

As dominant trends since the outbreak of the revolution, I maintain that these transformations have consisted of six historical phases: (1) "Khomeinist" (1979–1989); (2) "statist" (1989–1997); (3) "reformist" (1997–2003); (4) "the Najaf spring" (2003–present); (5) "neo-Khomeinist" (2005–2009); and, finally, (6) "the Green Wave" (post-June 2009). In the course of these historic phases, this study argues that the final stage ("the Green Wave") inaugurated a new conception of Shi'i "political spirituality,"[8] articulated by dissident clerics like Ayatollahs Montazeri (d. 2009) and Sane'i, in which *mashru'iyyat* (legitimacy) is sharply distinguished from worldly power (*hokumat*). This new discourse radically undermines the basis of theocratic rule in the period of Occultation, during which the Shi'i community awaits the return of the Hidden Imam, who will bring justice to earth. More importantly, however, it fuels and accelerates the formation of a new and vibrant Shi'i Iran, in its many manifestations, that involve ongoing contestation over doctrines, scriptures, and practice.

The "Khomeinist" Phase

In the wake of the 1979 Iranian Revolution, Shi'i Islam saw the triumph of a major radical movement led by activist clerics with a revolutionary agenda of establishing an Islamist political order. By 1979, the victory of the revolution gave the revolutionary clerics, led by Ayatollah Khomeini, the opportunity to establish a new regime and institutionalize a radically new concept of Shi'i authority, an ideological mix of populism and clericalism under the charismatic leadership of Khomeini, labeled "Khomeinism" by Ervand Abrahamian.[9] These clerics ardently propagated Ayatollah Khomeini's "Islamic government," arguing that the royal institution was illegitimate and that just government should be the responsibility of the clerics. In many ways, the institutionalization of the political ideology of *velayat-e faqih* or the "guardianship of the jurist" brought to the fore a new interpretation of Shi'i government that assigned ulama the responsibility of ruling on behalf of the Twelfth Imam, whose eventual return is believed to culminate in the establishment of divine justice on earth.[10] With the authority to participate in the political decision-making process, new radical clerics emerged to establish the first theocratic power in Shi'i Islamic history, hence breaking away from the traditionalist quietist school of thought dominant within Shi'ism for centuries.

As militant clerics gradually took over power in 1979–1980, the transition from monarchy to the Islamic Republic entailed a major challenge of legitimacy. During the first nine years following the revolution, the Islamic Republic wrestled with the ideological question of how best to institutionalize the different branches of Islamic government. While struggles between pragmatists and ideologues over state management continued to make headlines, the Iran-Iraq War (1980–1988), perceived as a Western aggression led by a corrupt Arab government, enabled the revolutionaries to further radicalize their position. Such radicalization became partly evident in the training and promotion of a number of militant clerics within the newly established Islamist state. "Khomeinist" clerics not only participated in the legislative processes and the judiciary, but also formed powerful unelected institutions such as the Guardian Council that functioned as a watchdog over elections and the parliament, ensuring that ultimate political control would remain with the pro-Khomeini ulama.[11] The new constitutional politics evolved largely around an ideological discursive struggle (and hence, not only a symbolic and philosophical discursive frame) to convince the Iranian public (and the clerical establishment) of the institutionalization and, accordingly, legitimation of the theocratic republic as a modern manifestation of an indigenous political system, led by *rawhaniyat* or clergy who best knew how to run the country. While Khomeini's leadership based on the doctrine of *velayat-e faqih* provided considerable power to the clerics, the new theocracy added a new center of authority to the traditional multiple cores of Shi'i authority. The fragmentation of authority laid the foundation for a forthright separation between traditional Shi'i centers in Iran and beyond (Najaf), and Tehran, with Khomeini as the head of a postrevolutionary Shi'i state. However, the institutionalization of a theocratic political system, articulated in the new constitution, met with a range of internal opposition. The first group was composed of Shi'i lay intellectuals like Mehdi Bazargan (d. 1995), Abol-Hasan Bani Sadr, and Ibrahim Yazdi, and clerics like Seyyed Mahmoud Taleqani (d. 1979) who saw certain despotic tendencies in the newly established Islamic Republic. For Taleqani, a socialist-leaning cleric with a modernist interpretation of Qur'an and legal tradition, an unaccountable revolutionary order could lead to a "return to despotism."[12] In the early years of the revolution, this first group, who was influenced by the ideas of Islamic modernists like Jamal-al-Din al-Afghani (d. 1897) and Mirza Reza-Qoli Shariat Sangelaji (d. 1944) in an attempt to modernize Shi'ism, was gradually sidelined within state institutions. A greater challenge however, came from the quietist clerics, who saw the formation of the new Shi'i theocracy as a danger to the *hawzeh* (theological seminaries based in Isfahan, Mashhad, and Qom) and, essentially, the integrity of the clerical establishment, which for centuries had sought to remain independent from state corruption and worldly power. Clerics like Baha' al-Din Mahallati (d. 1981), Sadeq Rohani, Morteza Ha'eri Yazdi (d. 1985), and Ahmad Zanjani expressed concern about the dangers of the new theocracy and the secularization of religious authority to the institution of *marja'iyyat* (sources of emulation).[13] One of the most prominent of all the quietist clerics, Ayatollah Mohammad Kazem Shariatmadari (d. 1986), a pro-constitutionalist senior Shi'i cleric, publicly opposed the referendum supporting Khomeini's constitution. He argued that Khomeini's radical new reinterpretation marked a deviation from true Shi'ism, an objection that was shared by the Grand Ayatollah Abdol-Qasem Khoei (d. 1992) in Najaf, who had famously sent an "agate ring with a special prayer" to the Shah in 1978 to show his contempt for Khomeini.[14]

In response to Shariatmadari's defiance, and the subsequent clashes between his followers and the pro-Khomeini militants in Tabriz, in December 1979, the regime immediately stripped Shariatmadari of his religious authority and placed him under house arrest until his death in 1986. This was a major affront to a clerical establishment that had never before seen such a high-ranking jurist deposed by another cleric.[15] Ayatollah Hossein Qomi (d. 1999), another dissident cleric, was put under house arrest, and Ayatollah Ali Tehrani, who was Khomeini's former pupil and a member of the Islamic Revolution Council, fled to Iraq, where he worked for a Persian-language radio program funded by the Baathist regime.[16] In addition, the takeover of Qom, the country's religious scholarly center, by state-sponsored activist clerics based in Tehran caused many non-Khomeinist ulama to keep quiet in fear of retribution, hence allowing the state to successfully contain dissident senior clerics and their followers. These attacks also followed Khomeini's 1984 ban of the apolitical *Hojjatiyyeh* association, a Shi'i civic organization with a messianic outlook, some of whose members denied the authority of Khomeini as the deputy of the Hidden Imam.[17] The marginalization of the religious association of *Hojjatiyyeh* helped diminish millenarian expectations, and the ideological position of those who opposed the idea that the Islamic Republic represented the only alternative to the awaited Mahdi.

Finally, the *velayat-e faqih* as a political system was effectively consolidated with the appropriation of various religious ceremonies, especially the annual Muharram rites performed in commemoration of Imam Husayn's martyrdom in 680 C.E. in Karbala, Iraq. During the early revolutionary period and particularly during the Iran-Iraq War, the ceremonies not only produced cultural sites of ideology to bolster state legitimacy, but also constructed a powerful set of visual and narrative technologies that innovatively identified the story of Husayn and his self-sacrifice with the cause of justice and the newly established Islamist state, perceived as an underdog facing powerful internal and foreign foes. Whether on the bloody battlefields of the province of Khuzestan or the busy streets of Tehran, the staging of Muharram performances promoted a way of thinking and practicing Shi'ism that was essentially about the theology of salvation through suffering. This honorific ethos served as a new model of selfhood for the revolutionary-warrior society led by Khomeini, creating the credence that the Islamist state was something that transcended the particular individuals who governed it. The images and tales of self-sacrifice, particularly on display at the war fronts, became a staple of the state's propagation of an official Shi'ism, fostering doctrinal cohesion and reawakened solidarity among the Shi'i revolutionaries for the early years of the Islamic Republic.[18]

The Statist Phase

In contrast to the early years of the revolution, as political pragmatism came to the forefront after the Iran-Iraq War, the centralization of Shi'i Iran became manifest beyond a mere ideological process. The term "statist" here refers to a process of bureaucratization through which the charisma-dominated political order under Ayatollah Khomeini underwent a dramatic process of rationalization of power. Following the death of Khomeini and the election of Akbar Hashemi Rafsanjani in 1989, this process was initiated by pragmatist clerics, who aimed to strengthen state control over the public sphere for the purpose of establishing a functioning bureaucratic state and a realist foreign policy in the postwar period. On the legal-institutional level, the push for state centralization primarily involved major constitutional amendments that not only broadened the juridical and political power of the guardian jurist, with the absolute mandate to rule, but also the ability to qualify for the post without being a *marja'* or source of emulation.[19]

Constitutional reform was prompted by the belief that a smooth process of succession could inherently serve as a stabilizing force. However, the separation of the position of *marja'* and *faqih* (jurist) set the stage for the destabilization of Shi'i authority. The August 1989 appointment of mid-level ranking cleric Seyyed Ali Khamenei to the position of Leader introduced a major transformation in the classical function of Shi'i juristic authority that previously had only recognized the most learned *mujtahid* or jurist as the spiritual head of the community. First, the constitutional separation of the *marja'* from the political leadership set into motion a latent *secularization* of the Islamist state that generated a rift between state power and spiritual authority.[20] Although this separation somewhat lessened when Khamenei was officially declared a *marja'* by the Association of Scholars of the Seminary of Qom (*Jame'eh-ye Moddaresin-e Hawzeh-ye 'Elmiyyeh-ye Qom*) in 1994, along with six other high-ranking clerics, a rift between state power and hierocracy began to gradually widen over questions of religious authority, public leadership, and the ability to interpret matters related to spiritual and worldly affairs.[21] The routinization of Khomeini's charismatic authority into a "secularized" clerical rule under Khamenei therefore set the parameters for the formation of multiple spheres of spiritual authority. By and large, it identified the authority of Khamenei as both a political and a religious leader over all other high-ranking clerics, whose authority only pertained to the spiritual realm of public life.

The second transformation became evident with questions over the scholarly qualification of the newly selected leader of the Islamic Republic. Before he assumed leadership, Khamenei was known as a *Hojatoleslam* (proof of Islam), a clerical rank that lacks religious authority to exercise *ijtihad* or legal rulings based on independent judgment. The appointment of Khamenei not only angered many traditional clerics based in Iran and Iraq, but also undermined the consensus-based selection of religious authority within the clerical establishment, which ultimately recognized the ability and freedom of an ordinary Shi'i Muslim in determining his or her religious leader. While a number of high-ranking clerics like Ayatollahs Mohammad Reza Golpayegani (d. 1993) and Abdol-Qasem Khoei refused to recognize Khamenei publicly as a *marja`*, in 1997, Ayatollah Hossein-Ali Montazeri, once the designated successor to Khomeini and a principal figure amongst the most revolutionary clerics in the early years of the Islamic Republic, ridiculed Khamenei's religious credentials and questioned his ability to issue religious rulings. Despite the resistance of leading clerics, Khamenei was finally granted a degree of *ijtihad* with the help of Ayatollah Mohammad Taqi Bahjat (d. 2009).[22]

By the early 1990s, the conflict between statist clerics and traditional *maraje`-e taqlid* (sources of imitation) led to renewed concerns over the future compatibility of the two forms of authority. With the deaths of Ayatollah Khoei and Ayatollah Golpayegani in 1992 and 1993, respectively, however, the state unleashed its most aggressive effort to centralize the traditional clerical establishment. The first move was to coerce the Khoei and Golpayegani Foundations to recognize Khamenei as a *marja`* and pay him religious taxes.[23] Later in December 1994, the state-funded *Jame'eh-ye Moddaresin-e Hawzeh-ye `Elmiyyeh-ye Qom* (Association of Scholars of the Seminary of Qom), which earlier had played a role in advancing "Khomeinist" ideology in traditional seminaries throughout the country, released a list of high-ranking clerics that excluded the names of a number of *marja`* that the state saw as potential threats.[24] The names of Ayatollah Montazeri and Sistani, who had succeeded Ayatollah Khoei in Najaf, were not featured on this list, underlining a deliberate attempt by the state to exclude clerics considered a potential threat to the clerical regime.

By the mid-1990s, the state accelerated the marginalization of traditional clerics. By centralizing the complex financial and educational systems within the seminary structure, customarily managed by the high-ranking clerics and their associations, it brought the traditional institutions under the supervision of a newly named "Management Center of the Seminary" (*Markaz-e modiriyyat-e Hawzeh-ye `Elmiyyeh-ye Qom*), an institution accountable only to Khamenei.[25] Accordingly, along with the important task of monitoring religious financial transactions, the "Management Center" played a critical role in supervising and limiting the activities of clerics (especially those of lower ranking status), who would engage in "non-Khomeinist" conceptions of Shi'i authority. The objective was to promote a like-minded body of clerics whose devotion and loyalty would be to Khamenei and the doctrine of *velayat-e faqih*, although that attempt ultimately failed. In a way, the growth of pro-state clerics under the leadership of Ayatollah Mesbah Yazdi in Qom can be credited to the mid-1990s centralization of the seminaries. Such ascendency was partly due to state financial support in the bureaucratization of the curriculum of the seminaries, and also as a result of the propagation of a "Khomeinist" version of Shi'ism, which identifies the sources of political legitimacy in religious doctrines, giving primacy to the execution of sacred laws to ensure that society matures according to Islamic guidelines.

As a new power structure emerged with state-building measures to exert control over the *hawzeh* in Qom, a number of intellectual trends also began to articulate a new way of thinking that undermined the foundation of the Islamic Republic. In the early 1990s, Shi'i intellectuals like Mashallah Shamsolva'ezin and Abdolkarim Soroush posed a direct challenge to state authorities by arguing that no single group or individual maintained the divine right to monopolize spiritual authority. As a philosopher of science, Soroush famously asserted that religious knowledge was relative, and Islam was flexible in shifting historical and social settings. More importantly, he argued that religion should be devoid of ideology, which denies human thought and could eventually lead to dictatorship.[26] On the clerical side, Hojatoleslam Hasan Yousefi Eskhevari, a midranking cleric, followed Soroush by proposing the notion of "religious democracy," challenging the theocratic position that Islam should be the only source of legitimacy and that during the period of Occultation true authority lies with the clerics.[27]

The early 1990s also saw the rise of "Islamic feminism." Advanced by figures like Zahra Rahnavard, Shahla Sherkat, and A'zam Taleqani, this new discourse promoted gender consciousness in a male-dominated Shi'i society, questioning some of the patriarchal structures within the Islamic Republic and their ideological conceptions of motherhood and the authentic woman. The publication of popular journals like *Zanan* (Women) and *Jens-e Dovvom* (The Second Sex) reinterpreted Shi'i Islamic thought in light of a feminist agenda, at times bluntly questioning some of the patriarchal positions of the "Khomeinist" state.[28] Despite state clampdowns on dissident activity, the new wave of religious reformist thinkers led to the education of a new class of Shi'i students, intellectuals, and seminarians, leading the charge for reforms in the post-Rafsanjani period.

The Reformist Phase

By the mid-1990s, a loose coalition of dissident Shi'i clerics, seminary students, university students, intellectuals, and middle-class professionals gradually formed a movement to challenge the status quo. The presidential elections of 1997, won by the reformist cleric Mohammad Khatami, gave momentum to this new coalition. With Iran's demographic makeup rapidly undergoing change, largely in response to urbanization, bureaucratization, and diffusion of new technologies in everyday life, a new generation—mostly born after the revolution—embraced the new alliance. While the previous phases marked a period of centralization of Shi'ism through ideology and state building, in response to such measures, the reformist phase unleashed a series of reflexive rational-critical and countercultural processes through various discourses and practices that assigned new meanings and interpretations to sociability and religiosity.

The impact of the reformist movement on Shiʻi Iran can be described in many ways, but one prominent feature was the escalation of political rivalry between reformists, who sought to limit the absolute authority of the Leader and the conservative clerics, aiming to maintain political hegemony through political repression and manipulation of the electoral process. The late 1990s became the high point of political factionalism in the post-Khomeini era, which, in turn, helped release Iranian civil society from the tight monopoly of conservatives, especially in the legislative branch of government. On the societal level, the younger generation shaped new public spaces of sociability, which also included ritual spaces of interaction like the annual Muharram ceremonies, during which men and women sensually intermingled and donned fashionable clothing, creating sites of misrule in the course of mourning processions.[29] The carnivalesque culture of postwar Shiʻi rituals characterized a type of politics of subversion that took place in the everyday lived experiences of embodied actors, rejecting the official code of ritual conduct endorsed by the state. Yet, in a political sense the reform period also brought to life an intellectual movement that emphasized the rule of law and civil society (*Jame'eh-ye madani*) as prerequisites of an enlightened religious society, in contrast to Islamic governance (*hokumat-e eslami*), which was a key slogan of the 1979 revolution.[30] It promoted a political community in which reformist clerics played a critical role in democratizing the religious debate and opening a new understanding of Islam in terms of pluralism and inclusion.

Grand Ayatollah Montazeri emerged to represent the most defiant voice as a primary intellectual spokesperson for the dissident clerics. As a follower of Khomeini who had supported the revolutionary theology of clerical guardianship, Montazeri had been considered a principal figure and amongst the most revolutionary clerics in the Iranian government in the 1980s, with his statements being viewed as second in importance to those of Khomeini. However, in one of the most dramatic episodes in postrevolutionary history that threatened the stability of the Islamic Republic, Montazeri was forced out of his position as the designated heir to the office of guardian-jurist by Khomeini on March 28, 1989.[31] Following his forced resignation, Montazeri became the most vocal critic of the regime within the clerical establishment. In his later works and sermons, Montazeri boldly defended a conception of spiritual authority with strong elements of democratic principles of human rights. In the 1990s, Montazeri began to challenge the absolutist notion of Islamic governance, and advocated a democratic Islamic Republic based on the notion of *Velayat-e Entekhabi-e Moqayyadeh* (elected conditional rule), a type of Shiʻi clerical authority that had a limited scope of power and was accountable to the people through the electoral process.[32] In 1999, he published a book entitled *Hokumat-i Mardomi va Qanun-e Asasi* (Democratic Government and Constitutionalism), in which he bluntly rejected the absolutist conception of clerical rule and criticized the Guardian Council's factional politics in disqualifying certain candidates from running in elections.

Toward the end of Khatami's first term as president, Montazeri publicly defended a new model of clerical activism for the younger, mid-level dissident ulama that eventually followed the grand ayatollah's lead into a discursive battle-field of redefining political power in light of a new understanding of spiritual authority. In December 2000, Montazeri shocked the conservative establishment when he posted his 600-page memoir on his official website,[33] publicly questioning some of the early policies of the revolutionary period in the 1980s under the guidance of Ayatollah Khomeini, hence, implicitly criticizing the absolutist political system of "guardianship of the jurist." With the use of new technology, Montazeri advanced the propagation of an alternative Shi'i jurisprudence and explored various theological issues using cyberspace as a new means of communication for the ayatollah to express his personal views on current affairs and politics.[34] Following Montazeri's new conception of theocratic democracy, mid-ranking clerics such as Mohsen Kadivar and Mohammad Mojtahed Shabestari also proposed their new hermeneutics of theology, known as "dynamic jurisprudence" (fiqh-e puya), as a new discourse of Islamic reformism, aimed at reinterpreting sacred law in a modernist light.

In the early 2000s, amid simmering tensions between conservatives and reformists, Montazeri's activism represented the most ostensible manifestation of a dissident voice in virtual space, challenging online the authority of the Leader and his security forces that monitored and harassed most of the activities of the more independently minded Shi'i jurists of Qom. With the heavy state censorship of print media, the Internet became an alternative forum for reformist ulama to publish their works for a young educated public, mostly born after the 1979 revolution.[35] Meanwhile, weblogs of the reformist vice president, Mohammad Reza Abtahi,[36] came to represent a new form of clerical presence in the blogosphere, interactively discussing and debating various topics ranging from politics to religion. Along with a growing body of technologically savvy Iranian bloggers, clerics like Abtahi presented a busy online community, "making Persian one of the leading languages in the blogosphere, and increasing the share of Persian material online."[37] Blogs also provided communicative platforms for Shi'i women, especially of the younger generation, to reconstruct multiple identities of both religious and nonreligious orientation, effective relationships, and experiential realities within lived existence that carved out new interpretive spaces of self-disclosure and sociability in virtual space.[38] Meanwhile, Islamic feminism expanded, led by figures like A`zam Taleqani, with calls to rethink the Qur'an from a woman's perspective.[39] In many ways, the configuration of Shi'i Iran during the reformist phase emanated from highly innovative discursive practices that involved major subjective transformations in how the sacred and profane could be reinterpreted in politically charged ways.

The political uses of the Internet did not go unnoticed by the regime. In response to various challenges posed by the Internet, the conservative establishment, in particular the judiciary, introduced tougher measures to assert control over cyberspace. Between 2001 and 2003, a censorship regime of filtering net activity, surveillance tactics, and arresting web designers and bloggers was enacted, while dissidents of various political leanings continued to navigate around the restrictions through proxies and antifilter technology, posting their works for the growing virtual reading public. In fact, the regime also proactively used the Internet to propagate its ideology and publicize the ideas of key figures in the government, including the Leader. However, by 2003, reformist clerics saw another side to the efficacy of the Internet as a transnational forum of communication: the reemergence of quietist theology from the wreckage of another Shi'i scholarly center, Najaf, represented by Grand Ayatollah Ali Sistani.

The Najaf Spring

With the collapse of Saddam's regime in 2003 and the subsequent revival of Najaf representing the center of quietist orthodoxy, Shi'i Islam underwent a new development.[40] While reformist clerics and lay intellectuals continued to reinterpret Shi'ism in Iran in a democratic light, Ayatollah Ali Sistani, the most revered Shi'i cleric in the world, based in the Iraqi city of Najaf, emerged as a leading quietist senior cleric to offer an alternative model of leadership. With an expanding religious network and a tight social organization operating on a global basis, coupled with adherence to a Shi'i democratic tradition dating back to the Constitutional Revolution in the early part of the twentieth century, Sistani's influence over Iraqi democratic politics began to serve as a model for many Iranian reformists who rejected Khomeini's ideology of clerical hegemony. This historical phase brings to light an alternative interpretive tradition of Islamic governance advocated by Sistani that carries the quietist ideal of clerical involvement within the limits of serving the community's interest, rather than promoting clerical control over the state apparatus.[41] Sistani's post-Baathist politics emerged based on the promotion of the electoral and legislative processes, with the aim of expanding pluralism and citizen participation. Sistani has also been a major advocate of the accountability of government and the formation of legitimacy based on the ideals of popular sovereignty as a way to challenge the Coalition Provisional Authority's insular plans for the promotion of a top-down model of democratization for Iraq.[42]

In many ways, Sistani's position on the institutionalization of democratic politics in Iraq resembles the democratic views of Ayatollah Mohammad-Hossein Na'ini (d. 1936), who, almost a century earlier, had defended a constitutionalist concept of Shi'i governance against arbitrary rule. Sistani had also been the model of a traditional cleric, especially during his pre-2003 leadership period, when he refrained from any involvement in state affairs.[43] According to this tradition, the role of the ulama is limited to guiding the Muslim community while securing a social contract between the ruler and the ruled and promoting a just society grounded on Islamic principles. He is responsible for advancing the cause of justice against oppression, which best describes a despotic regime that is guided by the personal ambition of the ruler, while his guidance includes an effort to guard the community from arbitrary power by warning the rulers of their contract with the citizens and of their duty to rule with justice. Sistani's role in the democratization of Iraq, in this sense, has been the promotion of a type of government that protects citizens from arbitrary power, and the advocacy of a social contract approved and institutionalized by the elected officials representing the people. In contrast to Na'ini, Sistani has not endorsed "a council of guardians to scrutinize the bills that would be introduced in the assembly," a move that demonstrates his dislike for an official clerical institution operating within the state apparatus.[44]

As the most senior of the Shi'i clerics, Sistani controls a large number of the Najaf seminaries, and enjoys a large following among students not only in Iraq but also further afield, in countries such as Iran, Lebanon, and Syria. These seminaries are funded through religious taxes and since April 2003, have expanded financially with the influx of foreign capital (particularly from Britain, Kuwait, and Iran) to the southern regions of the country.[45] Since the 1990s, Sistani has led one of the most advanced transnational networks in the region through the digital information superhighway. Equally important to Sistani's power is the fact that he is among the most preeminent and best financed of the ayatollahs remaining in Najaf, and—by extension—in other parts of Iraq and Iran. Since 2003, a number of reformist clerics and Shi'i activists in Iran have not only created new sites through Sistani's "Ahl al-Bayt Global Information and Media Center in Qom," but also rearticulated their oppositional discourses against the Islamic Republic in light of Sistani's advocacy of democracy in post-Baathist Iraq. What Sistani has been able to do in Iraq in a matter of a few years, as Ali Reza Behehshti, a leading reformist intellectual and senior adviser to the failed 2009 presidential candidate Mir-Hossein Mousavi, describes, "is what we have been trying to achieve in Iran since the Constitutional Revolution of 1906."[46]

The "Neo-Khomeinist" Phase

While quietist Shi'ism began to gradually expand in Iraq and beyond under the leadership of Sistani, by early 2000, Iran saw the ascendency of a new political force: "neo-Khomeinism." At the heart of this new movement lay the drive for revolutionary zeal and a pledge to Khomeini's original mission of establishing a just Islamic society prior to the return of the promised Mahdi. The late Fred Halliday famously described such revolutionary fervor as "a second reassertion of militancy and egalitarianism that rejects domestic elites and external pressure alike," a revival of populism advanced by the new guard with nostalgia for revolution and war, martyrdom and support of the destitute.[47] In many ways, then, what distinguishes the "neo-Khomeinists" from other Shi'i factions in the postrevolutionary period is the former's emphasis on the collective memory of the war years, a period marked by self-sacrifice, devotion to God and piety in the face of the inevitability of martyrdom on the front lines of the conflict with Iraq. The middle-aged hard-liners of nonclerical background in the new movement were primarily veterans of the Iran-Iraq War. This is the generation that had entered universities during Rafsanjani's presidency (1989–1997) and maintained official positions in the state bureaucracy during the reform period (1997–2005).[48] Unhappy at state incompetence over issues related to corruption and social justice, the new hard-liners, who maintained close ties with the Revolutionary Guard and intelligence forces, broke away from the established conservative factions and formed a new political front with the aim of reviving the populist revolutionary spirit of the early republic.

The "neo-Khomeinists" first entered the political scene during the conflict simmering between reformists and conservatives in the period of 1997–2005. For the most part, the young hard-liners, many of whom shared technocratic credentials as well as a deep belief in the populist-theocratic foundation of the Islamic Republic, saw the reform movement as a major threat to the establishment and formed a tight coalition in order to gain political influence over several key instruments of power. The new alliance, the Iranian Islamic Developers Coalition (*E'telaf-e Abadgaran-e Iran-e Eslami*), enjoyed the backing of several hard-line religious associations with links to the military-security complex.[49] As the young conservatives gained increasing political clout during the 2004 parliamentary elections, largely due to the support of the Guardian Council, they also saw the 2005 presidential elections as an opportunity to further advance their position. The electoral victory of the "neo-Khomeinist" Mahmoud Ahmadinejad represented a significant takeover of elected institutions, with the aim of monopolizing power amid ongoing factional politics.

The "neo-Khomeinists" began to advance a version of Shi'i political authority that was nonclerical and yet populist in spirit; they saw political authority less in statist terms and more in the form of charismatic authority led by figures who were detached from worldly interests and keen on bringing about social justice, hence, reviving the original revolutionary spirit best articulated by Khomeini. In their view, the pragmatism of the old guard, led by figures like Rafsanjani, had only produced an increasingly corrupt state, a politics of the status quo that benefited the rich who ruled in the name of Islam. The key was to empower a new revolutionary elite to manage and control the government. Ahmadinejad would represent just such a new revolutionary elite.

As the sixth president of the Islamic Republic, Ahmadinejad's meteoric rise to power combined the support of Leader Khamenei and the military-intelligence complex that viewed the popularity of the reformists as a threat to the political establishment. As the mayor of the capital city, Tehran, in 2003–2005, Ahmadinejad had worked closely with the Iranian Revolutionary Guards Corp (IRGC), supporting the Guard's economic and industrial expansion.[50] However, it was Ahmadinejad's appeal to millennial expectations of the revolutionary return of the Mahdi that attracted many from the hard-line factions to his side. Though the 1979 revolution was replete with millenarian symbols and themes, Ahmadinejad's public show of millennial expectation expressed a shared desire by hard-liners to return to preparing the way for the Mahdi, believed to be in hiding until the End of Time. Likewise, his populist rhetoric called for a new Islamic vision of politics resurrecting the Shi'i revolutionary model of action. The promotion of millenarian narratives and construction (or expansion) of holy spaces such as the popular Jamkaran mosque, believed to be a site of miracles and mysteries of the Hidden Imam, marked a resurgence of popular Mahdism.[51]

In clerical circles, too, apocalyptic millenarianism saw a spasm of revival. Unlike quietist millenarianism, charismatic Mahdism, with its emphasis on a looming cosmic battle between good and evil, advances the notion of an immediate return of the Hidden Imam. A new class of clerics promoted the new messianic trend and received the patronage of key clerical figures, in particular Ayatollah Mohammad Taqi Mesbah Yazdi. As the director of the Imam Khomeini Education and Research Institution in Qom, Ayatollah Mesbah Yazdi, who is also known as Ahmadinejad's spiritual guide, has led the way in training seminarians and nonclerical politicians in Qom and Tehran.[52] In the late 1990s, Mesbah Yazdi also helped in the revival of the messianic *Hojjatiyyeh* School, and, as one of its original founders, argued in favor of an absolutist authority in the concept of "Imamate" in an attempt to diminish the republican tendencies of the Islamic Republic.[53] Likewise, in his defense of an absolutist clerically dominated political order, Mesbah Yazdi's rigid interpretation of Shi'i texts formed a counterdiscourse to the reformist conception of religious democracy.[54] By separating legitimacy from popular will, Ayatollah Mesbah Yazdi came to express the most antidemocratic trend in the clerical establishment, a tendency that aimed to apply millenarian belief in the legitimation of an absolutist conception of clerical rule. During Khatami's second term as president (2001–2005), the millenarian movement led by Mesbah Yazdi further expanded through the religious segment of Iranian society through "selective mosque networks and Islamic associations."[55]

In a pattern that would prove all too familiar to postrevolutionary religious politics, the ascendency of the neo-Khomeinists between 2004 and 2009 hardly overshadowed the political and religious scenes. Amid this steady rise to power during the first term of Ahmadinejad, a number of dissident clerics like Ayatollah Hossein Kazemeini Boroujerdi also rose to challenge hard-liners' aims over millenarian expectations. Although his political activities went back to the 1990s, Boroujerdi's call for the separation of religion and state appealed to both secular and religious sectors of Iranian society. With a large body of supporters who regarded him not only as a prominent cleric but also as a spiritual figure, Boroujerdi's "non-Khomeinist" millenarian views created a counterdiscourse to the official state conception of Mahdi.[56] His claim to titles such as "heir to Husayn's legacy" (*warith al-Husayn*) and "epitome of Haidar" (*bashir al-Haydariyya*), made Boroujerdi famous as a leader of a "crypto-messianic" movement, armed with a divine mission to reform the corrupt clerical establishment within the Islamic Republic.[57] While it remains unclear whether Boroujerdi claimed to be the awaited Mahdi, his movement represented a new undercurrent of millenarian movements in post-Khatami Iran that concurrently resembled the activities of various Shi'i movements in post-Baathist southern Iraq.[58] With distinct nationalistic agendas, Iranian and Iraqi Shi'i apocalyptic developments have challenged established concepts of authority and Shi'i traditions as represented by clerics based in Qom, Najaf, and Tehran.[59]

Since charismatic millenarianism in its politicized form ultimately seeks to undermine the status quo in preparation for a cosmic battle between the forces of good and evil, clerical figures like Boroujerdi came to be viewed by the state as a major threat. The Leader's 2006 condemnation of popular Mahdism as "un-Islamic" not only thwarted possible religious challenges to the ideology of the Islamic Republic as the only representative of the Mahdi, but also indirectly warned the newly elected president against apocalyptic zeal.[60] It was no surprise therefore that in October 2006 Boroujerdi and a number of his followers were arrested on charges of apostasy.[61] Although Mahdist fervor, in its diverse manifestations, appears to have subsided in the latter half of Ahmadinejad's first term as president, millenarian expectations, along with miracle cults of Imams, remain a strong feature of Iranian Shi'ism, with tremendous potential for the creation of effervescent sites of apocalyptic psyche and eschatological narratives of sacred protest through which new identities are formed.

The "Green Wave"

The protests that rocked the streets of Tehran and other major cities, triggered by accusations of fraud in the June 2009 presidential elections, marked a new development in antigovernment political activism, in which Shi'i activism played an integral role in the emerging social movement. The "Green Wave," a coalition of opposition groups and factions led by reformist candidates Mehdi Karroubi (a mid-level cleric) and Mir-Hossein Mousavi, as well as former president Mohammad Khatami, rose to challenge not merely the election results but also the lack of transparency and accountability under a theocratic state that has become increasingly dependent on the IRGC to maintain political power. The gradual extension of the IRGC has led to the progressive marginalization of old guard politicians like Rafsanjani, who see the politicization of the security-intelligence complex as a transgressive move, and a crisis of legitimacy over the parameters of theocratic governance. In many ways, however, in subsequent crackdowns on the antigovernment demonstrators, the issue in dispute has become the ideological rationale of the theocratic state, and the shadowy military-intelligence complex in the background.

Though the origins of the movement can be traced to the sporadic uprisings in the postrevolutionary period like the student unrest of the summer of 1999, the Green activists represented, in the words of Hamid Dabashi, a recovery of an "Iranian cosmopolitanism" with the aim to secure the civil liberties of citizens living under authoritarian rule.[62] In light of such cosmopolitanism, the Green Movement saw large factions within the clerical establishment emerge to play an integral role in this political culture of protest against a perceived tyrannical power (estebdad). Shortly after the elections, a number of senior clerical figures based in Qom publicly sided with the protesters and openly took issue with the hard-line clerics in power, including the Leader, for the way the elections and their aftermath were handled. What the events that followed the elections revealed was the extent to which Shi'i opposition reached beyond mid-ranking clerical circles, forming a de facto hierocratic coalition against the increasingly repressive state led by Khamenei. As the great bulk of the highest-ranking clergy articulated their opposition to the crackdowns and, especially, questioned Khamenei's ability to rule as a just leader, a fissure within the clerical establishment began to widen.

The Internet, in this sense, once again provided a powerful medium for the discontented grand ayatollahs to display their stance against what they perceived as excessive use of state-sponsored force in the name of Islam. While YouTube and Twitter were favored by antigovernment activists to post videos of demonstrations and police brutality, reformist ulama posted statements and correspondence on their official websites and Facebook, as a way to reach out to their followers and a disgruntled Iranian public. In many ways, the sudden popularity of social networking domains in the few months prior to the elections brought an added interest in sites such as Facebook and, to a lesser extent, Twitter. In February 2009, for example, the two ministries of Information and of Islamic Guidance, under the supervision of the Leader, unblocked Facebook (along with other social networking websites) with the aim of encouraging young voters to participate in the June elections.[63] The move, however, provided a new opportunity for dissident groups, especially students and women activists, to organize discussion groups and political meetings on unblocked sites, while taking advantage of the easing of cyber censorship to blog on human rights causes and the release of political prisoners.

In this respect, postelection unrest and the role of new technology in the process provided a new opportunity for reformist clerics and lay religious activists to redefine Islamic political authority. On the political level, the new belligerent Shiʻi opposition saw the Islamic Republic as no longer maintaining legitimacy (*mashruʻiyyat*) because of its harsh and unjust reaction to those who demanded a recount of the votes.[64] From the Shiʼi perspective, the ideal example of Shiʼi rule for many was that of Ali, the first Shiʼi Imam who is believed to have based his government on tolerance of opposing views. Yet, the Islamic Republic demonstrated in the aftermath of the elections how military repression could be justified in the name of the law and the defense of Islam.

Ayatollah Yusef Saneʻi, one of Qom's leading reformist clerics, emerged as one of the first ulama to express such critical theology in cyberspace. On his website, Saneʻi praised the street demonstrations and stated, "I hope that the path of the Iranian people to continue their legal protest could be open."[65] Following the elections and the ensuing state violence, Saneʻi issued a statement on his website, warning hard-liners against state repression and urging the regime to refrain from the "sin" of violating citizens' rights to peaceful demonstrations. In one of his famous remarks also issued on his website, Saneʻi described the public trial of protesters as an "oppressive" organ of a tyrannical state.[66]

Meanwhile, the late Ayatollah Montazeri posted the harshest critique of the regime on his website. On August 26, 2009, in a major statement, Montazeri argued that, in view of its behavior in the aftermath of the elections, the Islamic Republic was neither a republic nor a guardianship of Islamic jurists; it was rather a "government of a military guardianship."[67] Montazeri's accusation concerning the militarization of the theocratic regime resembled Grand Ayatollah Bayat-Zanjani's objection, also posted on his official website[68] that the Islamic Republic more closely resembled the political system of the Caliphate (known to Shiʻis for its brute military force) than the regime of "Imamate" based on accountability and justice, as exemplified by Imam Ali.[69]

Moreover, in a bold statement posted online and discussed on various Shiʻi blogs a month after the elections, the "Association of Researchers and Teachers of Qom," an influential clerical association, called the reelection of the incumbent president illegitimate and questioned the Guardian Council for its political factionalism in the electoral process.[70] The most devastating statement, however, appeared when an anonymous 11-page letter written by a group of clerics, posted on various reformist websites, including various sites on Facebook, demanded the leader's immediate removal.[71] The letter accused Ayatollah Khamenei of turning the Islamic Republic into a military state, run by the IRGC as his own private guard. The letter expressed views similar to that of a number of reformist clerics including Ayatollahs Seyyed Jalaledin Taheri and Abdolkarim Mousavi Ardebili, who went online to express their discontent with the postelection crackdown on protesters.[72]

While on one level, the increasing rift in the ranks of the clergy prompted the rise of new critical discourses of Shi'i political spirituality grounded in the ethos of accountability and justice, on another, behind these taboo-breaking oppositional outbreaks brewed a growing realization that the Islamic Republic was undergoing a major crisis of legitimacy. Such a crisis bespoke the absence of legitimacy of the political theology of Khomeini's "Mandate of the Jurist" and the problematic nature of authoritarian ways of preserving such a political order in light of growing unrest in a country known for its history of revolutionary movements. In many ways, new ways of communication like the Internet provided an alternative public sphere for oppositional clerics to carve out new spaces of dissent wherein critical discourses over the exclusive divine authority of the ruling clerical institutions continued to shape public opinion. Even though the Green Movement as a political force seems to have been suppressed, much of the symbolic religiosity and theological discourses that defy the Islamic Republic continue to be a source of inspiration to many Shi'i activists. Khomeini's transformation of Shi'i theology, which culminated in the institutionalization of the 1979 revolution, has now entered a new phase of refashioning that could produce new conceptions of political spirituality that defy both a secular and theocratic state.

Contesting Iranian Shi'ism: Between Officialdom and Discord

In this essay, I have argued that Shi'i Iran has undergone considerable change since the revolution, generating new dynamic discourses and practices in the context of state and society relations. In historic terms, the most critical phase in the fragmentation of clerical authority emerged with the drafting of the 1989 constitution. As the state attempted to consolidate power, it ironically engendered various unintended consequences that in many ways made the doctrine of *velayat-e faqih* a point of contestation. During the statist and reformist periods, Iran not only saw intellectual and social trends that challenged the conservative-dominated institutional barriers, including the extraconstitutional power of the Leader, but also witnessed a new conception of Shi'ism and a reinterpretation of authority in pluralistic terms.

The rise of a new hard-liner coalition ("neo-Khomeinists") in 2004–2005 as well as the subsequent advent of a Green Movement after the 2009 presidential elections added a new dynamic to the decentralization of Shiʻi Iranian identity. This new development has been less about competing groups of diverse religious or political backgrounds, and more about the formation of various Shiʻi identities, official and informal, with distinct claims over sacred authority. With the emergence of an agonistic politics, Iranian Shiʻism continues to be reshaped between the wavering space of officialdom and dissent.

In the context of such ongoing conflict, the clerical establishment has witnessed the formation of three distinct clerical groups since the revolution. The first group can be identified as clerical officialdom, a special status group with a distinct legal category, linked together through patronage, familial ties, and political alliances with the regime. The second clerical group comprises the dissidents: an oppositional clerical force that remains on the offside of hierocracy. With figures like Ayatollah Saneʻi, however, these oppositional clerics continue to wage a theological battle over the legitimacy of political and spiritual authority and how best to guide a just (Islamic) state without clerical involvement on the state level.

The third group consists of the "quietists." Although they share some of the theological views of many dissident clerics, particularly on the separation of clerical and state authority, the quietist clerics seek to preserve the Shiʻi seminary institution by keeping a relative distance from politics. However, the rise of Ayatollah Sistani as the most prominent democratic-minded cleric in the Shiʻi world, and his (indirect) influence on reformist politics in Iran, underlines the transnational dimension of a changing Shiʻi Iran. In the "Green Wave" period, the second and third clerical groups appear to have increasingly overlapped in terms of political and religious views. The state clerics, however, maintain a firm alliance with the military-security establishment.

On the societal level, Shiʻi religious culture has also witnessed major transformations, some of which include the formation of new sites of piety, ritual performance, and, especially, virtual interaction, wherein definitions of the common good are articulated and contested. In many ways, postrevolutionary religiosity remains more than a mere reconstruction of Shiʻi Iranian traditions, as it largely manifests itself in the shaping of new publics as seen in the case of Muharram rituals that involve complex experiential and interpretative domains as lived places of interaction in urbanite and rural Iran. New millenarian trends since 2003–2004, for example, point to new subjectivities of hope and redemption that ultimately have come to crystallize into new political movements, such as neo-Khomeinism. However, carnivalesque features in postrevolutionary Shiʻism, especially during the Muharram ceremonies, also underscore the formation of subversive publics that help accelerate the fragmentation of sacred authority in the context of everyday life. Likewise, the online appearance of Shiʻi culture has led to the construction of new decentralized sites of sacred knowledge that largely operate through virtual fields of interaction, wherein formal and counterpublics create alternative mediums of communication over definitions of identity and the sacred.

As the local, regional, and global political landscapes continue to undergo major transformations as a consequence of socioinstitutional and sociocultural changes, it remains to be seen how the emerging Iranian Shi'ism, with distinct discourses and practices in diverse, lived sites of interaction, will develop into new forms of religiosity, creating new political institutions and societal realities with distinct models of being (and becoming) modern. What remains certain, though, is that Shi'i Iran, 30 years after the revolution, remains a tension-ridden field of social imagination, endowed with diverse rationalities and modes of sacred expression.

Notes

1. I am most grateful for the very helpful comments I received from Ali Gheissari, Elham Gheytanchi, Jan-Peter Hartung, and Negin Nabavi on earlier versions of this article.
2. Sami Zubaida, "Is Iran an Islamic State?" in *Political Islam: Essays from Middle East Report*, ed. Joel Beinin and Joe Stork (Berkeley, CA: University of California, 1997), 104.
3. Janet Afary and Kevin B. Anderson, *Foucault and the Iranian Revolution: Gender and the Seductions of Islamism* (Chicago: University of Chicago Press, 2005), 255.
4. M. Foucault, "Questions of Method," in *The Foucault Effect: Studies in Governmentality*, ed. G. Burchell, C. Gordon, and P. Miller (London: Harvester Wheatsheaf, 1991), 82.
5. "Shi'i Iran" also implies how claims to Iranian Shi'ism are imagined and at times contested by other Shi'is on a transregional basis. See Roschanack Shaery-Eisenlohr, "Imagining Shi'ite Iran: Transnationalism and Religious Authenticity in the Muslim World," *Iranian Studies* 40, no. 1, (2007): 17–35.
6. Twelver Shi'ism is the largest branch of Shi'i Islam and has more adherents in Iran than other branches of Shi'i Islam. For a classic study on the subject, see Moojan Momen, *An Introduction to Shi'i Islam: The History and Doctrines of Twelver Shi'ism* (New Haven, CT: Yale University Press, 1987). Mysticism has also maintained strong mass appeal in Iran since pre-Islamic periods. The fusion of mysticism and Shi'ism has played a critical role in the formation of distinct political movements throughout medieval and (early) modern Iranian history. For a study of mysticism and the 1979 Iranian Revolution, see Daniel Brumberg, *Reinventing Khomeini: The Struggle for Reform in Iran* (Chicago: University of Chicago Press, 2001), especially 44–58.
7. Although some regions, especially near the Caspian Sea, maintained a Shi'i identity, orthodox Shi'i Islam was gradually introduced to Iran during the reign of Shah Tahmasp (1524–1576). The migration of Arab Shi'i clerics to Safavid Iran, under the auspices of the Shah, eventually led to the emergence of a body of Iranian clerics who "carried the legal discourses to wider circles of scholars and politically charged domains." Rula Jurdi Abisaab, *Converting Persia: Religion and Power in the Safavid Empire* (London: I. B. Tauris, 2004), 5.
8. Afary and Anderson, *Foucault and the Iranian Revolution,* 209.
9. Ervand Abrahamian, *Khomeinism: Essays on the Islamic Republic* (Berkeley, CA: University of California Press, 1993).
10. S. A. Arjomand, *The Turban for the Crown: The Islamic Revolution in Iran* (Oxford, UK: Oxford University Press, 1988), 98–99.
11. Ali Gheissari and Vali Nasr, *Democracy in Iran: History and the Quest for Liberty* (Oxford, UK: Oxford University Press, 2006), 90–91.
12. Time Magazine, September 24, 1979, http://www.time.com/time/magazine/article /0,9171,947428,00.html.

13. Such concerns grew when Khomeini chose Ayatollah Montazeri to be his successor in 1985 in what was seen by many clerics as a radical move to undermine the *hawzeh* in Qom and empower Tehran as the center of Shi'i authority. In a famous statement, Ayatollah Sadeq Rohani reacted to the news by commenting, "My duty is to say that I see Islam in danger, that *marja'iyyat* is in danger." (Arjomand, *Turban for the Crown,* 181).

14. Vali Nasr, *The Shia Revival: How Conflicts within Islam Will Shape the Future* (New York: Norton, 2006), 125. During his stay in Najaf (1964–1978), Khomeini and Khoei would avoid each other and engage in debates through their pupils.

15. Arjomand, *Turban for the Crown,* 140; Heinz Halm, *Shi'ism,* trans. Janet Watson and Marian Hill (New York: Columbia University Press, 2004), 120. Such instances of disqualification have continued, the most recent case being that of dissident Ayatollah Sane'i by the clerical establishment in Qom in January 2010.

16. Arjomand, *Turban for the Crown,* 156. After the Iran-Iraq war, Tehrani was able to return to Iran, with the help of his brother-in-law, Ali Khamenei, the future Leader, even though he was imprisoned at first.

17. Abbas Amanat, *Apocalyptic Islam and Iranian Shi'ism* (London: I. B. Tauris, 2009), 224–225.

18. Peter Chelkowski and Hamid Dabashi, *Staging a Revolution: The Art of Persuasion in the Islamic Republic of Iran* (New York: New York University Press, 1999), 272–279.

19. Said Amir Arjomand, *After Khomeini: Iran under His Successors* (Oxford, UK: Oxford University Press, 2009), 248–249. "Source of emulation" refers to the authority of the highest-ranking cleric, whose decisions and legal rulings over religious conduct and ideas are regarded as the model for others to follow.

20. By "secularization" here I refer to an enhanced bureaucratization of state power that entails the differentiation of authority in the formation of new institutions of governance.

21. Mehdi Khalaji, "The Last Marja: Sistani and the End of Traditional Religious Authority in Shi'ism," *Policy Focus,* no. 59 (September 2006): 22–23.

22. Mehdi Khalaji, "The Last Marja," 22.

23. Arjomand, *After Khomeini,* 174. The head of the judiciary, Ayatollah Mohammad Yazdi, advanced the notion that under the Islamic Republic, the institution of *marja',* with its multiple centers of authority, is unacceptable and therefore, should be abolished. It was the Association of Scholars of the Seminary of Qom (*Jame'eh-ye Moddaresin-e Hawzeh-ye 'Elmiyyeh-ye Qom*), however, that challenged the judiciary and later on the death of Ayatollah Mohammad Ali Araki in December 1994, issued a list of seven *marja',* hence, ensuring that the state would recognize a multiplicity of "sources of imitation."

24. For the list, see www.jameehmodarresin.com/bai/730911.htm.

25. Khalaji, "The Last Marja," 28.

26. Abdolkarim Soroush, *Ideolozhi-ye sheytani* (Satanic Ideology) (Tehran: Sarat, 1373/1994).

27. See Ziba Mir-Hosseini and Richard Tapper, *Islam and Democracy in Iran: Eshkevari and the Quest for Reform* (London: I. B. Tauris, 2006).

28. Ziba Mir-Hosseini, *Islam and Gender: The Religious Debate in Contemporary Iran* (Princeton, NJ: Princeton University Press, 1999).

29. Fieldwork observation, Bushehr, Isfahan, and Tehran 1999–2004.

30. Arjomand, *After Khomeini,* 93.

31. Baqer Moin, *Khomeini: Life of the Ayatollah* (New York: Thomas Dunne Books, 2000), 277. Several factors led to Khomeini's decision to denounce him as a successor. The most obvious was Montazeri's support for his son-in-law, Mehdi Hashemi, who had

embarrassed Akbar Hashemi Rafsanjani, the former first Speaker of Parliament (*majles*) of Iran, by exposing his secret dealings with the Reagan administration during the Iran-Contra affair. See Kaveh Basmenji, *Tehran Blues: Youth Culture in Iran* (London: Saqi Books, 2006), 180. Although Rafsanjani's resentment of Montazeri also helped drive a wedge between Khomeini and Montazeri, the execution of Mehdi Hashemi prompted Montazeri to be critical of Khomeini's excessive policy. Montazeri was also critical of the execution of thousands of Mojahedin members in 1988, which also caused friction between the two ayatollahs. Ultimately, the main impetus behind Khomeini's decision to remove Montazeri from the position of designated successor was ideological differences, underlined by the contentious definition of clerical authority in relation to the rights of citizens that Montazeri appeared to advocate in large part.

32. Mehran Kamrava, *Iran's Intellectual Revolution* (Cambridge, UK: Cambridge University Press, 2008), 163.

33. http://www.montazeri.com.

34. Montazeri's website has been rigorously filtered by the state, according to an article in the statement and opinion section of his website, "*Pasokh-e Ayatollah al-Ozma Montazeri beh chand porsesh.*" The site includes his biography, religious statements, scholarly texts, and opinions on various issues, which are exchanged and discussed online. Perhaps the most intriguing section of the website consists of photos dating from the early revolutionary period up to his house arrest in 1997.

35. Babak Rahimi, "The Politics of the Internet in Iran," in *Media, Culture and Society in Iran: Living With Globalization and the Islamic State*, ed. Mehdi Semati (New York: Routledge, 2008). For example, see http://www.kadivar.com.

36. http://www.webneveshteha.com/.

37. A. Sreberny and G. Khiabany, *Blogistan: The Internet and Politics in Iran* (I. B. Tauris, 2010), 204; Rahimi, "The Politics of the Internet in Iran," 48–51. For a selection of other reformist blogs, see http://www.ketabcheh.malakut.org. The new wave of clerical presence in the blogosphere also included major state figures, including the Leader. See Elizabeth M. Bucar and Roja Fazaeli, "Free Speech in Weblogistan? The Offline Consequences of Online Communication," *International Journal of Middle East Studies* 40, no. 3 (2008): 404.

38. Masserat Amir-Ebrahimi, "Blogging from Qom: Behind Walls and Veils," *Comparative Studies of South Asia, Africa and the Middle East* 28, no. 2 (2008): 235–249.

39. See Fereshteh Ahmadi, "Islamic Feminism in Iran: Feminism in a New Islamic Context," *Journal of Feminist Studies in Religion* 22, no. 2 (2006): 33–53.

40. By "quietist," I refer to a type of clerical authority that is oriented toward public guidance though not all democratic minded, in contrast to clerical involvement in state apparatus.

41. This revival echoes many of the principles advanced during the Iranian Constitutional Revolution of 1905–1911 by leading *marja`* such as Ayatollahs Mohammad Hossein Na'ini and Mohammad Kazem Khorasani who played an active role in the revolution.

42. Juan Cole, *The Ayatollahs and Democracy in Iraq* (Amsterdam: Amsterdam University Press, 2006).

43. Linda S. Walbridge, ed., *The Most Learned of the Shi`a: The Institution of the Marja` Taqlid* (Oxford, UK: Oxford University Press, 2001), 237–242.

44. Yitzhak Nakash, *Reaching for Power: The Shi'a in the Modern Arab World* (Princeton, NJ: Princeton University Press, 2006), 9.

45. Vali Nasr, *The Shia Revival*, 71 and 221. The financial infrastructure of the *hawzeh* (or seminary) consists of millions of dollars bequeathed to Sistani's foundation in the

form of religious taxes and pious endowments (*vaqf*), which are public- or privately-funded institutions to support the poor or needy. Religious taxes donated by believers (*zakat*) are intended to assist the poor, needy, orphans, travelers, and those in debt. Part of *zakat* is paid to cover the expenses of collecting taxes by religious administrators. *Khoms*, however, is a special annual tax that Shi'is pay as one-fifth the value of their land, silver, gold, jewelry, and profits made from goods found in the sea, which is spent mostly on the needy, orphans, travelers, and on the prophet and his family. However, one-tenth of *khoms* is paid to a high-ranking cleric or *marja'-e taqlid*, who is the most knowledgeable and pious among the clerics and whom the believers (*moqaleds*) are expected to emulate in everyday life and follow in religious matters. The role of *marja'-e taqild* is crucial to the institution of religious taxation since it is under his authority—as the definitive representative (*nayeb al-imam*) of the Hidden Imam, the twelfth male descendant of Mohammad who has been hiding since 874 C.E. and whose return is expected at the end of time—that the collected money is distributed to pious causes.

46. Interview, Tehran, August 16, 2008.
47. Fred Halliday, "Iran's Revolutionary Spasm," *Open Democracy*, June 30, 2005, http://www.opendemocracy.net/globalization-vision_reflections/iran_2642.jsp#.
48. Anoushiravan Ehteshami and Mahjoob Zweiri, *Iran and the Rise of Its Neoconservatives: The Politics of Tehran's Silent Revolution* (London: I. B. Tauris, 2007).
49. Kasra Naji, *Ahmadinejad: The Secret History of Iran's Radical Leader* (London and New York: I. B. Tauris, 2009), 79–49.
50. Said Arjomand, *After Khomeini*, 153.
51. Amanat, *Apocalyptic Islam and Iranian Shi'ism*, 227–232; Naji, *Ahmadinejad*, 95–98.
52. Naji, *Ahmadinejad*, 98–102.
53. Amanat, *Apocalyptic Islam and Iranian Shi'ism*, 225.
54. Kamrava, *Iran's Intellectual Revolution*, 94–108.
55. Amanat, *Apocalyptic Islam and Iranian Shi'ism*, 224–225.
56. See Sadeq Saba, "Iran Arrests Controversial Cleric," *BBC News*, October 8, 2006. http://news.bbc.co.uk/2/hi/middle_east/6032217.stm.
57. Amanat, *Apocalyptic Islam and Iranian Shi'ism*, 248–249.
58. It is important to note that most Iraqi Mahdist movements like "Ansar al-Mahdi" and to a certain extent the Sadrists maintain an anti-Iranian stance, and therefore, the crystallization of millenarianism in the two countries has been and remains far from a transnational phenomenon.
59. However, the Shi'i movements in Iran did not produce a military oppositional force, as in Iraq, and largely maintained a quietist character.
60. For Khamenei's criticism of unofficial apocalyptic currents, see Jean-Pierre Filiu and Mehdi Khalaji, "The Rise of Apocalyptic Islam," *Iranian.com* November 17, 2008, http://www.iranian.com/main/2008/rise-apocalyptic-islam.
61. At the time of writing, Boroujerdi remained in prison. It is likely that similar to his late father, Ayatollah Mohammad Ali Kazemeini Boroujerdi, a leading quietist cleric, he faces the prospect of death in prison. See D. W. Duke, "The Tragic Story of Ayatollah Boroujerdi," *Iranian.com* December 15, 2008, http://www.iranian.com/main/blog/dw-duke/tragic-story-ayatollah-boroujerdi.
62. H. Dabashi, *Iran, the Green Movement and the USA: The Fox and the Paradox* (New York: Zed Books, 2010), 144.
63. Elham Gheytanchi and Babak Rahimi, "The Politics of Facebook in Iran," *Open Democracy* June 1, 2009.

64. Field observation and interviews, Qom and Tehran, July–August, 2009.
65. Michael Theodoulou, "Cleric Join Chorus of Dissent," *The National,* July 5, 2009.
66. See http://saanei.org/?view=01,00,01,00,0.
67. See http://www.pbs.org/wgbh/pages/frontline/tehranbureau/2009/09/ayatollah -watch.html.
68. http://bayatzanjani.net/.
69. See http://www.pbs.org/wgbh/pages/frontline/tehranbureau/2009/09/ayatollah -watch.html.
70. Geneive Abdo, "Shark Attack: How Iran's Political Crisis Might Only Strengthen the Islamic Republic and Why Rafsanjani Could Be the Election's Real Winner," *Foreign Policy,* July 8, 2009.
71. Nazila Fathi and Robert F. Worth, "Clerics' Call for Removal Challenges Iran Leader," *The New York Times* August 17, 2009.
72. For Ardebili's statements, see the July 26, 2009 edition of http://www.norooznews.org.

Part II

National Ideology, the Economy, and the State

5

Matters of Authenticity: Nationalism, Islam, and Ethnic Diversity in Iran

Rasmus Christian Elling

During a ceremony in 2010, cameras caught Iran's president Mahmoud Ahmadinejad in a somewhat awkward situation: he was tiptoeing to place a *keffiyeh* around the neck of a tall man on a podium. The checkered *keffiyeh* scarf, recognized as a Palestinian national symbol in most of the world, is seen by Iranians as an insignia of the hard-line *Basij* militia. The absurdity of the scene lay in the fact that the man on the podium was dressed not as an Islamist storm trooper, but as a soldier of the ancient, pre-Islamic Achaemenid dynasty. The ceremony marked not only the return of an important antique relic to Iran—the so-called Cyrus Cylinder—but also an important shift in ideological discourse. Ahmadinejad's clumsiness in bestowing the *keffiyeh* seemed to suggest his unease not so much in the presence of the foreign guests attending the ceremony but rather with the potential reaction of the wider domestic audience—in particular those of his Islamist supporters who would be shocked by the scene. Yet, Ahmadinejad's *keffiyeh* bestowal did little to cover what was a blatant show of nationalist pride, unprecedented in Iran's 30 years as Islamic Republic.

Since its establishment in 1979, the Islamic Republic's relation to Iranian nationalism has been a sensitive topic. An underlying tension between national interests and ideological religious goals has not only made Iran's foreign policy seem arbitrary at times but has also caused ideological disputes on its domestic scene. As Ahmadinejad's show revealed, segments of the post-Khomeini ruling elite have embraced overt nationalism as part of their ideological discourse, despite the seeming theoretical contradictions between nationalism and Islamism. However, as Ahmadinejad's tiptoeing seemed to indicate, the decision to embrace nationalism in such a public position is not without its complexities. With international pressure over Iran's regional and nuclear ambitions, and with a protest movement that took shape in the aftermath of the 2009 presidential elections, the centrality of national identity and its contentious relations to nationalism, Islam, and democracy have become ever more pronounced in the discussion of Iran's future.

This is evident in Iranian public debate, in state rhetoric, and in opposition discourses. The secular and liberal nationalist opposition continuously challenge the regime's legitimacy by accusing it of sacrificing Iran's national interests on the Islamist altar. The regime responds with the argument that Islam is key to Iran's national identity. At the same time, the question of "Iranian-ness" has been further complicated since the late 1990s by growing ethnically framed mobilization and a budding movement for minority rights.[1] Roughly, half of Iran's population is made up of non-Persian–speaking minorities, with many co-ethnic populations living outside Iran.[2] The Islamic revolutionary promise of equality for all has not materialized, and minority activists today demand political and cultural rights from what is seen as a Shi`i Persian-dominated center without respect for minorities. The issue of minority rights is thus tied up with questions of both democracy and national identity—and by extension, Iranian nationalism.[3]

In the present chapter, these interrelated issues are analyzed with a focus on the representation of nationalism and ethnic diversity in the contemporary official literature of the regime. Through this analysis, a nuanced picture of the regime-sanctioned ideal for national identity and unity emerges, which complicates specific claims put forward by secular-nationalist opposition (that the Islamic Republic is unpatriotic and antinationalist in nature) and by ethnopolitical proponents (that the Islamic Republic is Persian chauvinist or racist). This more nuanced reflection on the rhetoric and ideals of Iran's current leaders is central to the understanding of where the Islamic Republic is heading, more than 30 years after the revolution.

The National Constant

The 1925–1979 Pahlavi regime partially adopted a European-inspired nationalist doctrine formulated by late nineteenth-century Iranian intellectuals. This secular state nationalism aimed to modernize Iran along Western lines and it idealized Indo-European–speaking Iranians as "Aryans" and pre-Islamic empires as symbols of superiority to be emulated in modern Iran.[4] In this worldview, the Persian language and culture was the primordial foundation of the Iranian nation and the quintessence of Iranian-ness. Non-Persian minorities and tribes were often seen as a potentially subversive and separatist element and an obstacle to modernization, which should be subdued and assimilated. Sometimes, the issue of ethnic diversity was distorted to fit a myth of homogeneity or conveniently "forgotten" in dominant narratives on national identity.

Despite the abolition of the monarchy, the Islamic Republic that Ayatollah Khomeini and his allies brought into existence after the revolution of 1978–1979 naturally inherited the Western-inspired nation-state framework of the Pahlavi regime. "Khomeinism" has been defined by Ervand Abrahamian as a "flexible political movement expressing socioeconomic grievances, not simply a religious crusade."[5] Yet, the state rhetoric that developed in the Islamic Republic would draw upon Shi`i mythology, Islamic notions of justice, support for anti-imperialist struggles, and expressions of solidarity with Third World countries. Instead of glorifying pre-Islamic times and looking to the "Aryan" brethren in the West, the new state would focus on the *Umma*, the world community of Muslim believers. In the idealist vision of Khomeini and his followers, the Islamic Revolution would not only encompass Iran, but also extend to the entire Muslim world.

However, this notion of exporting the revolution (*sodur-e enqelab*) met with obstacles already in the new regime's infancy. First, neighboring Iraq's 1980 attack on Iran reminded the ideologues that their revolution was first and foremost a national rather than an international project. The war was initially presented in Iran as a defense of Islam against blasphemy, and not a war of nationalisms.[6] However, many Iranians inevitably understood Iraq's attack in nationalistic terms, and as the war dragged on for eight years, the leaders of the Islamic Republic relied increasingly on appeals to the Iranian public duty to mobilize and defend the homeland. Furthermore, while the revolution had inspired many Muslims across the world and provided Iran with some allies such as the Lebanese Hezbollah, the differences between Iran and its neighbors prevented the revolution, as an Iranian, Shi`i phenomenon, from spreading into Arab, Sunni lands. The export of the revolution did not find many clients in Central Asia, Afghanistan, Caucasus, or Turkey either.

At least since the Constitutional Revolution of 1905–1911, the politically active Iranian clergy have expressed nationalistic sentiments. Indeed, nationalism in Iran has traditionally been intertwined with religion even though, historically, the focus of the ulama's rhetoric was on "freedom and independence" (*azadi va esteqlal*) rather than on "nationhood" itself.[7] Such was also the rhetorical focus of the revolutionary clergy at the time of the 1978–1979 revolution, and in order to distance the new revolutionary political order from its old secular rivals, explicitly nationalist symbolism was rarely utilized during the Islamic Republic's early years. Yet, the traumatic experience of the Iran-Iraq War and the need for national unity during testing times of regional and minority upheavals changed this. In the words of Suzanne Maloney, "Iran's experience... reveals that identity is not infinitely malleable, especially when survival of the nation itself is at stake."[8]

Thus, while Khomeini continued all his life to advocate a pan-Islamist utopia of a deterritorialized *Umma* united in brotherly love, he also had to rely—as the national leader of a nation-state with a nationalistic oriented population—on the cultural constant of (often Persian-centrist) Iranian nationalism.[9] Khomeini and his followers thus supplemented the articulated pan-Islamic idealism with more subtle tones of nationalism, and with nation-oriented policies that have been described as "realist" by several scholars.[10] This increased reliance on strong, entrenched nationalist sentiments in the Iranian public coincided with a gradual change in domestic and foreign policies. After Khomeini's death in 1989, Iran went through a period of economic reconstruction, international rehabilitation, and pragmatism under President Akbar Hashemi Rafsanjani, and then, from 1996 to 2005, a period of reformism, rapprochement with the West, and a relaxation of social and cultural politics under Mohammad Khatami. Ahmadinejad's election in 2005 marked a creeping militarization and the ascendancy of a new faction in the ruling elite.

Yet, despite the ideological and factional differences between Rafsanjani, Khatami, and Ahmadinejad, their presidencies have had one factor in common, namely the gradual emergence of overt nationalist symbolism in state discourse. For example, as Hooshang Amirahmadi observed of Hashemi Rafsanjani's presidency,

> In early 1995, no less august a figure than Rafsanjani ordered the Islamic Republic News Agency to establish a newspaper called "*Iran*." Not "Islamic Iran," just "*Iran*." Large advertisements for the newspaper—comprised of the three-color Iranian flag with no Islamic logos—adorned Tehran's walls and billboards. In keeping with its name, the newspaper itself displays a similar pattern. It is telling that the first issues of *Iran* reached the stands at the same time [that] the government banned *Jahan-e-Eslam* (the world of Islam), a leading pan-Islamist newspaper.[11]

During Khatami's presidency, Iran witnessed a blossoming of civil society movements, opposition activity, and cultural-artistic life. Among the currents that resurfaced were secular-nationalist (*melli gara*) and religious-nationalist (*melli-mazhabi*) groups such as the National Front, the Freedom Movement, and other small organizations. Although most such groups were officially outlawed, Khatami nonetheless tried to appeal to their sympathizers and to voters with similar nationalistic tendencies. As scholars have shown, *iraniyyat* (Iranian-ness) reemerged, in the reformist government's discourse, as a main pillar of national identity alongside *eslamiyyat* (Islamic-ness).[12] This "Islamist-Iranian" discourse did not aim to replace Islam but to enhance the national constant in order to strengthen a political order that was increasingly challenged by rival political and cultural trends.

The "Cyrus of Our Times"

During the Islamic Revolution, many observers feared that Islamist radicals would bulldoze the ruins of Achaemenid royal residences at Persepolis. Considering the latter as a symbol of *jaheliyyat* (pre-Islamic ignorance) and of centuries of monarchic despotism, some clerics allegedly called for the demolition of this 2,500 year-old World Heritage site. Yet today, the pre-Islamic legacy is once again openly utilized in state discourse. During a visit to the province of Fars in 2008, for instance, Ayatollah Seyyed Ali Khamenei—Khomeini's successor and current Leader—praised Persepolis as a source of pride for all Iranians.[13] In a similar vein, during Ahmadinejad's first term as president, the head of the Iranian Cultural Heritage Foundation suggested institutionalizing a National Kurosh Day as a way of co-opting the popularity of celebrations at the grave of the Achaemenid king, Cyrus.[14] When the so-called Cyrus Cylinder returned to Iran on loan from the British Museum in 2010—the ceremony referred to in the beginning of this chapter—Ahmadinejad gave an emotional speech hailing the ancient relic as a symbol of Iranian justice and human rights throughout the world.[15] After this event, the head of Iran's Cultural Heritage Foundation praised Ahmadinejad as "the Cyrus of our times."[16] As Iran scholar Ali Ansari had already noted in 2007, when Ahmadinejad appeared at a press conference in Tehran with his visiting Russian counterpart against a backdrop of Achaemenid symbols:

> [f]ew would have dared to exploit the symbolism as explicitly as Ahmadinejad—an unambiguous statement that Iranian nationalism, always a staple of the social consciousness, had returned to the political stage.[17]

Indeed, although he is known for his anti-imperialist, Islamist, and messianic statements on the international scene, Ahmadinejad is also an Iranian nationalist. Phrases like "the Great Nation of Iran," or describing Iran as "the dearest country in the world" are regular features in his speeches;[18] he has called Iranians the inheritors of pre-Islamic heroes "Rostam, Arash and Farhad"; his supporters have dubbed him a descendant of the *Shahnameh's* national savior "Kaveh the Blacksmith";[19] and, to the great consternation of his hard-line allies, Ahmadinejad has paid his respects to the widow of a secular-nationalist minister from Mohammad Mosaddeq's prerevolutionary cabinet.[20]

This increasing reliance on a nationalist rhetoric that is particularly aimed at the middle classes who have otherwise become disillusioned with the regime, peaked with statements by Ahmadinejad's controversial key adviser and confidant, Esfandiyar Rahim-Mashaei at a meeting for expatriate Iranians in August 2010. During the speech, Mashaei argued that in order to promote "the truth of Islam to the world, we should raise the Iranian flag," that "without Iran, Islam would be lost," and that "from now on, we must present to the world the School of Iran (*maktab-e Iran*)."[21] These words, which seemed to privilege Iran over Islam, unleashed a torrent of critique from prominent clerics, high-ranking military figures, and conservative intellectuals that otherwise supported Ahmadinejad.[22] The critics argued that Rahim-Mashaei's statements were blasphemous deviations from the revolutionary path and threats to national security. The president nonetheless defended his adviser.[23]

Despite ongoing contestations, it thus seems that the "Islamo-Nationalist synthesis" predicted by at least one scholar many years ago[24] has come full circle. As Haggai Ram has explained, the classic portrayal in Western scholarship of the Islamic Revolution as the "ultimate defeat of nationalism at the hands of radical Islam" is thus erroneous.[25] Simplistic dichotomies and the contraposition of "Islamic identity" and "national identity" (and, in some works, "radicalism"/"fanaticism" and "pragmatism"/"rationalism"), has served, in the words of Ram, to present nationalism in the Islamic Republic as a "deviation" rather than an "integral part" of official doctrine:

> [n]ationalism was transformed into a kind of false consciousness, an unnatural growth with which the Iranians had to come to terms, a pragmatic "compromise" they were compelled to strike in light of changing realities.[26]

As already indicated, this chapter is instead premised upon the view that nationalism has always been an inherent part of the ideology and politics of the Islamic Republic—just as in practically all other modern nation-states. What has changed is Ahmadinejad government's "rediscovery" and employment of overt, tangible nationalist imagery and rhetoric that at times even resembles prerevolutionary secular symbolism and the tendency to glorify pre-Islamic times (*bastan-gara'i*). This change allows a president such as Ahmadinejad to identify with both the pre-Islamic King Cyrus and with Khomeini's revolutionary Islamism at one and the same time. The question, of course, is whether this change in rhetoric also signals a potential future transition in the very structure of the Islamic Republic. To explore this question, we should consider how the establishment seeks to explain and justify the synthesis of Islamism and nationalism through the prism of Khomeinism.

Challenging and Reinventing a Patriot

A wide range of Iranian political forces contest the definition of nationalism. While nationalist symbolism is now a part of state discourse, it is certainly also a main staple of counterdiscourses. A standard approach of the secular-nationalist opposition is to present Khomeini, the founder and icon of the Islamic Republic, as unpatriotic and antinationalist. For example, quotes such as the following have been attributed to Khomeini:

> What is Iran? Iran is nothing but some mountains and some plains, some earth and some water. A true Muslim cannot love a country—any country. For his love is reserved only for his Creator. We do not worship Iran, we worship Allah. For patriotism is another name for paganism. I say let this land burn. I say let this land go up in smoke, provided Islam emerges triumphant in the rest of the world.[27]

While the source of this citation is dubious and the quote, itself, most probably fabricated,[28] it is noteworthy as an example of the claim typically forwarded by critics of the Islamic Republic: that Khomeini and the Islamists have never cared for Iran as a nation or a homeland, and that all that matters to them, instead, is the *Umma*. Such claims are not limited to polemical writing: they can also be discerned as an underlying idea in much scholarly and journalistic writing. In one example from a biography of Khomeini, we are told that the Ayatollah,

> leaving the airport in 1964, had asked his minder, a SAVAK colonel, whether he knew that he was being exiled because he had defended the honor of his homeland. Now, as he re-entered Iranian airspace, he was asked what emotions he felt after nearly fifteen years of exile. "None!" he replied bluntly. For a man who felt himself permanently imbued with the love of God, a homeland did not mean much. For mystics and puritanical Muslims, it is the *Dar al-Islam*, the House of Islam, not the *patria*, which is all-important.[29]

There are, indeed, several quotes in the official collection of Khomeini's speeches that support this antinationalist image. One was his slogan-like statement made in the 1980s: "[T]hose who say 'We want to revive nationhood' are standing in opposition to Islam…Islam is opposed to nationhood."[30] Khomeini repeatedly called nationalism a "source of misfortune" for Muslims and an imperialist tool to destroy the *Umma* from within.[31] He actively combated nationalists of all colors, and he dismissed pre-Islamic symbolism and ethnic/national chauvinism as forms of paganism. Taken together, these statements give the impression of Khomeini as someone utterly uninterested in and even opposed to nationhood and nationalism.

Khomeini is sometimes portrayed, in secular-nationalist discourses, as a traitor to Iran who preferred Arab to Iranian culture. Thus, some secular critics—in particular ultranationalists, pan-Iranists, and royalists—tend to describe the rulers of the Islamic Republic as *tazi-tabar* (being from Arab descent) or as *Zahhak* (a mythological "Arab" enemy of Iran from the *Shahnameh*). In this kind of popular political imagination, Khomeini is sometimes presented as being of British-Indian descent—and therefore, an agent of British colonial interests.[32] The legitimacy of the Islamic Republic as an authentic political system in the service of the nation, an image that the Islamic Republic has always been keen to project, is thus, challenged. This challenge is a key reason why the Islamic Republic's propaganda machine has been engaged in recent years in reintroducing Khomeini as a patriot in his own right.

In 2004 and 2006, two works appeared in Iran that serve as interesting examples of current official portrayals of Khomeini: one by Ali-Mohammad Baba'i-Zarech on the "The *Umma* and the nation in Imam Khomeini's thought," and the other by Yahya Fawzi-Toyserkani on "Imam Khomeini and national identity."[33] Published by the Center for Documents on the Islamic Revolution—a state-run press whose head is appointed by the Leader—the books arguably represent "the official line" of the regime. Generally, the Center publishes books that focus on the history of the revolution, commemorations of the Iran-Iraq War martyrs, and other Islamist and pan-Islamist themes. The two books by Baba'i-Zarech (henceforth BZ) and Fawzi-Toyserkani (henceforth YT) differed somewhat in topic, message, and audience as they dealt directly with issues of Iranian nationalism and nationhood. To understand why the Center would publish these books, we must consider the timing of their publications.

In this period, the US-led "War on Terror" raged in Iran's neighboring countries, Iraq and Afghanistan, and in response to a changed geopolitical reality, the Islamic Republic underwent domestic militarization and two dual (but not mutually exclusive) trends toward *osulgara'i* ("fundamentalism," referring to an ideological return to the Khomeinist tenets of the revolution), and nationalism. In the case of the latter, Iran's political leaders sought to muster support even among skeptical or disapproving segments of the population. One way to achieve this was to recast the image of Khomeini and his ideology in a more nationalistic light. These two books can thus be read as an attempt to bridge the gap between the ruling elite and Iranian citizens, especially the younger middle classes, many of whom have been born after the revolution, and arguably feel alienated from the pan-Islamist rhetoric. The embedded problematic in both books is how to legitimize nationalism without betraying the revolution's Islamist tenets. The writers are engaged in a tiptoeing balancing act: while on the one hand, they must stay true to Khomeini's religious message, on the other hand, they have to downplay radical pan-Islamist views that would contradict nationalist imperatives and offend patriotic readers.

The points that are of most interest and will be the focus of analysis here are those sites of apparent ambiguity, paradox, and contention in the ideological message conveyed in the books. The first is the authors' defense of the Iranian nation-state as a unique, continuous, and permanent territorial entity—despite Khomeini's vision of a global united *Umma*. The second is the authors' legitimization of patriotism or nationalism[34]—despite Khomeini's confessed rejection of nation-based ideology. The third is an essentialist notion of national identity very similar to those of secular nationalists—despite Khomeini's rejection of secular symbols as the basis for national identity.

Demarcating Authenticity

First, there is the discussion of territory. Both authors try to smooth over the inherent theoretical contradiction between the united global *Umma* and the demarcated nation-state by way of the concepts of *esalat* (authenticity) and *asil* (authentic). Baba'i-Zarech claims, on the one hand, that in Khomeini's view, national borders do not have *esalat*, that is, "authenticity" and "validity"; such borders are not *asil*, meaning that they are not "genuine" or "authentic" (BZ, 97–98). The only *asil* border is that of the *Umma*, which separates, through faith and belief, the *Dar-ol-eslam* (the Islamic realm) from the *Dar-ol-harb* (the rest of the world) (BZ, 100–101). However, on the other hand, Baba'i-Zarech claims that, according to Khomeini, borders are necessary to human life (*lazemeh-ye zendegi-ye bashari*), natural (*tabi'i*), and accepted by Islam (*beh rasmiyyat shenakhteh mi-shavad*) (BZ, 103).

Baba'i-Zarech assures his readers that Khomeini did not want to abolish borders, and that there is no reason for dissolving nationalities and races to achieve "Islam's united world government" (*hokumat-e vahed-e jahani-ye eslam*) (BZ, 94). Indeed, we are told that Khomeini never wanted to merge the Muslim nations into one (BZ, 169). The conclusion is that borders—geopolitical borders dividing states as well as ethnic and linguistic borders dividing people—are somehow natural and necessary facts of life that will exist forever, even if they are not authentic or essential—and even if an Islamic world government came into being. The demarcation between the acceptable and the unacceptable is thus an elusive concept of authenticity. According to the authors, Khomeini declared that since "the boundaries of the nation are the boundaries of Islam," the "defense of the Islamic countries is one of the [religious] prescripts (*vaje-bat*)" (BZ, 169). Thus, when Khomeini promised that he would not allow "one inch of Iran's soil" to fall into enemy hands, he was in fact defending Iran as an extension of Islam (BZ, 169).

The second point of ambiguity pertains to the discussion of *mihan* and *vatan* (homeland), as opposed to *mellat* (nation)[35] and *melliyyat* (nationhood or nationality)—and the interrelated question of nationalism and patriotism. Baba'i-Zarech argues that whereas *mellat/melliyyat* is a "new matter whose history does not extend beyond a couple of centuries," *mihan* and *vatan* are supposedly older concepts, and that "homeland" signifies something that is "as old as human kind" (BZ, 74).[36] He argues,

> [W]ith the appearance of Islam, and with the tendency towards this world-encompassing religion, the Iranian people did not let go of the sacred values of loving the homeland, nor did they equate propagating the Islamic values and promoting the religion with destroying this natural sentiment. (BZ, 40).

While Baba'i-Zarech refrains from using the actual term "nationalism," he does use the phrase *mehr-varzi beh vatan* or "love of the homeland," which he deems "natural" and even a "sacred value" (*arzesh-e moqaddas*), thus, lending a sacrosanct air to a patriotic sentiment that allegedly predates Islam. Such a statement seems to contradict Khomeini's rejections of national chauvinism and pre-Islamic ignorance mentioned earlier. However, Baba'i-Zarech explains the difference as follows:

> Interest in the country (*'alaqeh beh keshvar*) or love of the homeland (*hobb beh vatan*) is not incompatible with Islamic ideology (*ide'olozhi-ye eslami*); it is an idea nurtured in the womb of Islamic ideology, and it is something other than nationalism (*nasiyonalism*). In other words, one must recognize a difference between love of the homeland (*mihan-dusti*) and nationalism (*nasiyonalism*). [D]uring the Islamic Revolution, it was thus love of the homeland, and not nationalism (*nasiyonalism va melli-gara'i*) that supplemented Islamic ideology (BZ, 73).

This "love of the homeland" is not in itself an *ideology* but an *idea*, Baba'i-Zarech maintains, even though nationalism as an ideology *can* also be used for "homeland-loving" purposes (BZ, 74).

To detach and retrieve the idea of a "homeland" (*vatan*) from a potentially secular context, Fawzi-Toyserkani similarly refers to Khomeini's statements such as Islam "honors the homeland" and that "love for the homeland" and "defending the country" are "issues beyond doubt" (YT, 185). In fact, according to Fawzi-Toyserkani, what Khomeini rejected was Western nationalism: based on ignorance and employed by enemies, such nationalism will place Muslims in opposition to each other (YT, 178). This is why Khomeini declared that the concept of "nationhood" should not be confused with "paganism" (*gabriyyat*). Hence, even though Khomeini opposed using the concept of the nation as a "pretext for ideologies of ethno-nationalism, racism or nationalism," he nonetheless saw it as a potentially "constructive factor," and stated that "we will make any kind of self-sacrifice for the nation, but in the shadow of Islam" (YT, 177).

The authors' main point here seems to be that the meaning of *mellat/melliyyat* has changed from signifying "religious community" to "nation"/"nationhood." Caught in the destructive maelstrom of Western colonial modernity and deprived of its original religious meaning, it has become the basis for the "negative" nationalist ideology of imperialists, liberals, and secularists. "Love of the homeland," however, amounts to patriotism in its pure and positive sense since it can be defended as part of an Islamic context, the writers argue.[37] It appears that the only clear distinction between negative and positive nationalisms is in Khomeini's opposition to specific, domestic political currents and to Western ideologies more generally. Nonetheless, Khomeinism is presented in the official literature as a historically authentic, homegrown and ideologically/ religiously justifiable patriotism.

Identifying Authenticity

The third point of ambiguity and contention relates to national identity or spirit. Both authors explain that in Khomeini's view on identity, only Islam can be *asil* and *zati*, or authentic and constitute an intrinsic marker of identity—all other markers of identity, including national and ethnic ones, are *arzi*, or extrinsic and nonessential. Khomeini, they explain, argued that Islam is the "authentic basis and key to Iranian national identity," from which would rise "a national self-confidence" (YT, 186). In short, Khomeini did not view Iranian identity as something that could exist *sui generis* without being grounded in a deeper, authentic Muslim identity.

Yet, Baba'i-Zarech nonetheless suggests that *iraniyyat* (Iranian-ness)—the "secular" part of Iranian national identity, so to speak—*can* have *esalat* as long as it is confirmed through *eslamiyyat* (Islamic-ness). Indeed, despite their precarious geographical location, constant cultural exchanges, and numerous crises, the Iranian people, he argues, have always "risen to guard Iranian identity, and in this way, the Iranian spirit has protected its authenticity (*esalat*)" (BZ, 193). Hence, Iran as a nation—specifically, Iran as a spiritual rather than material concept (*mafhumi rowhani*)—has *esalat* (BZ, 168).

Fawzi-Toyserkani similarly argues that Islam was "flexible" when it came to nations, languages, races, and cultures, and that in the aftermath of the Muslim conquest, it actually facilitated rather than complicated the continuation of indigenous Iranian culture from pre-Islamic times (YT, 100). Furthermore, on its next level of refinement, the Iranian "spirit" found in Shi'ism "the best way to acknowledge and protect authentic/pure Iranian characteristics" and thus, guard local traditions, revive the Persian language, and create a national government in the Safavid period (YT, 101). The fusion of "genuine Iranian culture" (which originated in pre-Islamic times) and Islam, argues Fawzi-Toyserkani, created an "Iranian-Islamic culture" that brought out, rather than suppressed, the basic essence (*jan-mayeh*) of national identity (YT, 187).

The authors, thus, seem to circumvent Khomeini's fundamental premise that only Islam has *esalat*, and that Islamic identity, alone, is *asil*, with factors such as blood, race, color, politics, and geography playing no important role in shaping the true identity of a society (YT, 167, 196). The authors' arguments are not only markedly different from the radical Islamist perspective that deemed everything pre-Islamic as "ignorance" (*jaheliyyat*), but also in their praise for an Iranian national spirit, which is pure (*asil*) and possesses *esalat*, they even echo essentialist views similar to those of secular nationalists.

This tendency can also be seen in Fawzi-Toyserkani's statement that Khomeini not only "accepted nation and nationhood as grand, collective units," but that he also saw "some of the constituent elements of a nation, such as racial and linguistic differences, as natural facts and as necessary to the Order of Creation (*nezam-e afarinesh*)" (YT, 176). We are thus told explicitly, and in clear contradiction to the statement presented earlier, that Khomeini was *not* opposed to nationhood. Indeed, with the idea that the "nation" is part of "Creation," the authors provide justification for a state defined, clerically sanctified Iranian nationalism. This nationalism is embodied in Islam, Shi'ism, and Khomeini's vision of the Islamic Republic. The ideal to aspire to, of course, is Khomeini, the ultimate Islamist patriot: the authors point to the *vali-ye faqih*, the Islamic jurisprudent ruler, or Leader, as the "best defender of territorial integrity and national values" of Iran (BZ, 170).

Both authors argue that Khomeini operated with a combination of idealism and realism in his policies—even when it came to identity politics (YT, 131). Therefore, we could arguably conclude that Khomeini's view on national identity was instrumental or tactical: part of a shrewd balancing act between far-reaching idealist goals and utopian visions for humanity and the *Umma* on the one hand, and "pragmatic" short-term goals, national interest, and popular patriotic sentiments on the other. Yet, the balancing act is portrayed in the official ideological literature as the sign of a natural equilibrium, and not of cold calculations.

With these exclusivist territorial notions and nationalist essentialism, a critic cannot help wondering what became of revolutionary, internationalist statements such as "the Islamic Republic belongs to all Muslims" (BZ, 220). However, there appears to be an even more urgent and critical question: whether the Iranian state can even be said to belong to all Iranians?

A Chauvinist Republic?

Compared to its neighbors, Iranian society has historically been endowed with a relatively strong sense of unity despite (or because of) its ethnic diversity. Nonetheless, modern Iran has also experienced periods of regionalist and even sporadic separatist activity, often during times of political chaos and frequently spurred by foreign power meddling. Domestic political changes, developments in neighboring countries as well as transnational and global political and cultural trends are all factors that have stimulated a growing ethnic awareness and ethnopolitical activity since the late 1990s.[38]

From 2005 to 2007, Iran witnessed ethnically framed unrest in border provinces populated by Azeri, Kurdish, Arab, and Baluch minorities. In response to these emerging national security threats, Islamic Republic officials resorted to a two-pronged nationalist rhetoric.[39] On the one hand, this rhetoric glorified Iran as an ancient nation, praised patriotism, and vilified minority activists and organizations in terms very similar to the Pahlavi secular-nationalist discourse, namely as subversive "Internal Others" or as naive compatriots led astray by foreign plots to destabilize Iran. On the other hand, the rhetoric ostensibly aimed at national unity by means of officials praising the country's ethnic diversity and the role of minorities in national epics and particularly, in the defense of Iran's territorial integrity. While they condemned the violence, they also recognized socioeconomic problems in areas inhabited by minorities.

There is reason to assume that some radical ethnopolitical organizations have indeed been sponsored by foreign powers.[40] However, Tehran's allegations against discontented minorities have been disproportionate and used as a pretext for a violent clampdown on the opposition. The result has been an intensification of the crisis as discontented minority members find a voice in ethnically framed organizations and spokespersons who claim that minorities—for various historical, political, religious, social, and economic reasons—feel marginalized and discriminated against. When the state represses such organizations and spokespersons—including nonviolent human rights groups—and conflates their demands with anti-Iranian subversion, the result is radicalization.

There are indeed many examples of state policies and principles that discriminate against minorities. The political system is based on Shi`i Islamic authority, and therefore, partially exclusive of all other religious denominations in Iran (such as Christianity, Zoroastrianism, and Judaism) and all other sects of Islam (most importantly Sunnism, to which some 6 million Iranians adhere). Even though the Iranian constitution states that "[a]ll people of Iran, whatever the ethnic group or tribe to which they belong, enjoy equal rights; color, race, language, and the like, do not bestow any privilege,"[41] there are in fact several barriers in the political system for non-Persian, non-Shi`i Iranians. Accordingly, ethnopolitical proponents complain that minorities are not sufficiently represented in the political system, and that they suffer from socioeconomic marginalization.

The restrictions on minority languages arguably constitute the most visible legacy of discrimination against non-Persians in contemporary Iran. Article 15 of the constitution states that non-Persian languages are permitted in public education and mass media. Yet, they are still not taught in public schools, and most of them are either not studied at all, or dealt with only in a few small university departments.[42] Minority language media suffer from repression, censorship, and intimidation, and only at intervals are minority journalists and authors not affiliated with the state permitted to publish in their own languages. Furthermore, ethnic, religious, and linguistic diversity is seldom treated in school textbooks,[43] and in the academic literature, minority languages are often reduced to mere "dialects." All of these conditions are symptoms of a tendency to neglect or reject the existence or significance of non-Persian ethnic identities.[44]

It is beyond the scope of this chapter to discuss the juridical, political, social, cultural, and economic barriers that minority proponents describe, and it suffices to state that the scope and intensity of minority activism and unrest are signs of a growing political awareness and discontent. Rather than rejecting or defending the views of minority movements, this section of the chapter will focus on how the state discourse of "multiethnic harmony" seeks to counter the challenges of minority activism. This is clearly a question of great importance to the topic of nationalism and the discussion about what should constitute "Iranian-ness"— yet, it is also an understudied question that deserves more research attention.

The core argument put forward by radical ethnopolitical proponents is that despite all its assertions of multiethnic harmony and equality, the Islamic Republic is essentially Persiancentric.[45] One proponent, the Canada-based scholar and activist Alireza Asgharzadeh, claims that "under the Islamic rule, racism and xenophobia continued to flourish in Iran, just as they [did] under the previous Pahlavi regime."[46] To Asgharzadeh, even the late 1990s reformist discourse on pluralism and diversity was merely meant for "external consumption."[47] Indeed, it is a mainstay of the radical ethnopolitical discourse to designate the Islamic Republic as Persian chauvinist or "Farsist," claiming that the ruling elite seeks to assimilate or eradicate minorities, and force upon the population a vision of a uniform, ethnically homogeneous, and essentially Persian(-ized) Iranian-ness with no room for diversity.

Discourses of Unity, Perils of Diversity

The official ideological literature, however, actually *emphasizes* that Iran is a multiethnic society. In Fawzi-Toyserkani's work, for example, Iranians are described as a "heterogeneous conglomerate" that came into being through successive waves of migration, war and political-economic rivalries, and is characterized by "racial and ethnic diversity" (YT, 67). History, Fawzi-Toyserkani states, has endowed Iran with a mixed population of "Aryans and non-Aryans, Greeks and Macedonians, and other groups such as Black Africans" (YT, 68). Furthermore, he emphasizes that various ethnic groups, including Arabs and Turks, have ruled Iran throughout history, and that each of these groups contributed to Iranian national identity and culture (YT, 70–71). Fawzi-Toyserkani concludes that

> In the present circumstances, one cannot deem race, blood or ethnicity to be important and fundamental factors in Iran's national identity... [E]ven though Iran today is made up of different ethnic groups, there is no specific ethnic group that constitutes [Iranian] identity and basically, this [ethnic] factor does not enjoy an important standing in the national identity of Iran (YT, 71).

Khomeini's sparse statements on the topic of diversity play a crucial role in the official literature's message of multiethnic harmony. According to this message, Khomeini did not reject ethnicity but rather described it as "a starting point," an intermediate level on man's road to perfection (YT, 134). In the end, Islamic identity will override the significance of other identity markers such as ethnicity. In short, Khomeini's Islamism—and therefore, also ideal Iranian nationalism—is *not* opposed to ethnicity as a concept, but does not deem it important. Nonetheless, Fawzi-Toyserkani also accepts a potential contradiction between ethnic and national identity:

> If we acknowledge family, ethnicity, society, nation and the *Umma* as markers of collective identity, some will naturally be interpreted on the surface as homogeneous and others as heterogeneous... Since the emphasis on elements that make

up an ethnic identity stands in opposition to national identity, these differences conclude in a natural heterogeneity (*na-hamguni-ye tabi'i*) in identities. One of the markers of ethnic [identity] is an emphasis on the racial or lingual element, which is different from other ethnic groups; and on the other hand, in national identity, emphasis is on common, national features, and no attention is paid to ethnic elements (YT, 166).

The existence of such heterogeneity and of various ethnic and national identities is "necessary and essential," "natural facts" and part of "historical and social reality" (YT, 166, 175). Indeed, ethnic identities are "acceptable to Islam" as long as they are not turned into "radical sentiments" (*ta'assobat*) (YT, 131–132). Khomeini used Islam to iron out these differences so as to minimize the risk of radicalism. He stated that in "Islam, race is fundamentally not an issue"; that the coexistence of various ethnic identities "has never been an issue" (YT, 178); and that "in Islam…there is no separation between two Muslims who speak two [different] languages" (YT, 181). This view on diversity was, according to Fawzi-Toyserkani, based on Khomeini's understanding of the Quran and the Islamic philosophical notion of "unity within diversity, diversity within unity" (*vahdat dar 'eyn-e kesrat, kesrat dar 'eyn-e vahdat*) (YT, 166).

Another relevant Khomeini quote is from his historic "Speech to the People of Kurdistan" in which he attacked ethnicity-based ideologies as harmful to Islamic unity:

[T]o the inhabitants of Kurdistan[:] you…should not be fooled by these small groups. They have created an instrument against Islam! The instrument of racism[:] the project of separating Kurd, Lor, Persian and so on from each other, and of bestowing on each an independent entity for themselves. This is what Islam has come to put an end to[:] these walls; Islam has come to…place all of you and all of us and all Muslims under the banner of "There is No God But God," and in unity, to be together, breathing together and bringing forth Islam (Khomeini quoted in YT, 180).

Surely, the underlying message in this speech is a response to separatist guerilla organizations (what are referred to as "small groups") among the Kurds. However, apart from separatism, it is also addressed to the broader and deeper problem of racism, which is seen as the gravest threat brought about by ethnically framed ideology. Khomeini summed this up in the phrase *nezhad-bazi* ("the race game"), describing it in terms of a Turk wanting to pray in a "Turkish" fashion, an Arab demanding that "Arabism should govern," and an Iranian claiming that "the Aryan race should rule instead of Islam" (YT, 181). In Khomeini's view, Islam came to put an end to this "race game," and those who tried to revive this game in modern times by looking "2,500 years back in time" to Iran's so-called pre-Islamic splendor were little more than "reactionaries" (YT, 181). It is, thus, in an attempt to counter the latent Persian centrism of Iranian nationalism and the threat of ethnically framed minority mobilization, that the official ideological literature presents this notion of Islam as a progressive answer to regressive, racialized thinking.

According to some radical voices in the minority movement, the ideology of the Islamic Republic aims to promote cultural or even racial and ethnic homogeneity, if not an Aryan supremacy. However, the official literature of the regime analyzed above seems to suggest otherwise in that it puts forward a distinctly nonracial and nonethnic definition of national identity.[48] Referring to the sparse (and admittedly vague) passages in Khomeini's speeches, the literature depicts Khomeini's views on national identity as ethnically inclusive but ideologically exclusive. Islam is presented as the ultimate tool to combat discriminatory, reactionary ideologies that are by-products of "Western" modernity and imperialist schemes. The enemy, so to speak, has never been the non-Persian, the non-Shiʿi, or the non-Muslim minorities, but rather those who seek to abuse these communities for political and ideological goals contrary to those of the Islamic Republic. The threat is ideology, not ethnicity.

All this can of course be dismissed as deceitful propaganda; a smokescreen to cover the essentially intolerant nature of the current regime.[49] However, it is also possible to argue that even though discriminatory policies have persisted in the Islamic Republic and continue to harm Iran's minorities, Khomeini's vision—at least, in its professed idealistic core and on its articulated rhetorical surface—*can* accommodate ethnic diversity. The message of the official literature discussed in this chapter, regardless of whether we reject or accept it as truthful, is tolerant of minority rights. By reinterpreting Khomeini, the authors are formulating an Iranian-Islamist nationalism that can, at least nominally, include ethnic diversity while excluding ideological pluralism. The actual and increasingly evident problem, however, is that the line between minority awareness and that which can be labeled subversive activity is subtle and ambiguous; the state can brand, condemn, and repress any and all proponents of minority rights as traitors and political enemies. This is something of which some Kurdish, Bahaʿi, and Baluch communities—to mention a few—are painfully aware. Since the late nineteenth century, Iranian nationalism has favored and idealized Persian language and culture, and thus, the increased emphasis on nationalism in the current state discourse opens up the professed idealism of the regime to accusations of ethnic bias and discrimination.

At the ceremony marking the return of the "Cyrus Cylinder" in 2010, there was a group of people dressed in the traditional clothes of various ethnic groups of Iran. Indeed, ethnic groups are today very present in regime rhetoric, in election campaigns, in military parades, and so on. Yet, it remains to be seen if the Islamic Republic's leaders can successfully maintain the discourse of multicultural harmony while at the same time relying ever more on nationalist narratives. More importantly, it remains to be seen if the state can and will translate "Unity Within Diversity" into actual policy.

Conclusion and Perspectives

The discussion about the compatibility of two of the most important ideologies in the Muslim world, Islamism and nationalism, is far from over. The universalism of the concept of *Umma* as opposed to the particularism of that of the nation has been called "intensely contradictory" by scholars.[50] However, the official literature presents the contradiction as reconcilable: the particular interests of Iran can be defended as an extension of the universal goals of Islam; indeed, Khomeinism is an authentic, religiously sanctioned patriotism, and "love of the homeland" is a natural, essential ingredient in the symbolic material that legitimizes the regime. No matter how scholars and politicians scrutinize or question such claims, the analyzed literature squarely asserts that despite inherent contradictions, nationalism and Islamism have already entered a harmonious symbiosis. This, of course, does not mean that the implications of this fusion remain uncontested.

As this chapter goes into press, a conflict between Ahmadinejad and his supporters on the one hand, and Khamenei and the main body of conservatives on the other, is apparently escalating. A key point of contention is whether Ahmadinejad's adviser, Mashaei, has committed treason by resorting to such blatantly nationalistic rhetoric described above. The circle around Mashaei and, by extension, Ahmadinejad is now called the "deviant current" by high-ranking clerics, conservative politicians, and Revolutionary Guard commanders, many of whom used to support Ahmadinejad. Indeed, the Leader's representative in the Revolutionary Guards has threatened to intervene militarily to stop the "deviant current," which he has deemed to be the gravest danger in the history of Shi'i Islam.[51] However, despite the possible outcome of these interfactional battles, the issue of nationalism will continue to play an important role on the political scene and in any future government.

In the examined literature, the key underlying ideological clash is between particular secular-nationalist and Khomeinist ideas of the "nation" (*mellat*) and the "homeland" (*mihan*). However, this framework for discussing nationhood fails to take ethnic diversity into full account. Are the Kurds, Baluch, and Azeris, for example, to be seen as nations within the nation-state? And if so, what are their national rights? The authors argue that they represent an egalitarian philosophy in which religious and national identity subsumes the ethnic factor. However, one could also see this argument as a way to proscribe the topic of diversity and to deny minorities the right to define their own identities. The idealistic rejection of racism surely rings hollow when it is not followed up by real action. By accepting ethnicity as "reality," one must also face the political dimensions of the social construct we call ethnic identity. The attempt, in the official literature, rhetoric, and action, to separate "ideology" from "ethnicity" is problematic, if not self-contradictory.

In other words, while we cannot rule out that the ideal of the Islamic Republic could in theory be seen as a grand narrative of equality and unity, the Iranian state cannot have respect for cultural diversity without freedom for political pluralism. The inescapable fact is that though Khomeini rhetorically championed ethnic equality, he did not in effect grant the minorities the same rights as their Shi'i, Persian-speaking compatriots. Surely, the balancing act of accommodating ethnic diversity while securing national unity and territorial integrity is a truly formidable and complex task. Yet, unless the Islamic Republic supports and secures the cultural and political rights of minorities, and unless it pays attention to the underdeveloped areas of Iran's periphery, it will fail at attaining the standards on freedom, equality, and security professed during the revolution.

Indeed, there is good reason to fear that members of the minority communities will, as we have already seen, turn to violence and radical ideologies, even if regime ideologues can point to ethnic inclusion as allegedly inherent in Khomeini's vision. The emerging phenomenon of ethnically framed mobilization may force the Iranians, once again, to face the question of national identity.

Notes

1. This chapter was part of a PhD project on the politics of ethnic and national identity in postrevolutionary Iran at the University of Copenhagen. I would like to thank Drs. Claus Pedersen, Nikki Keddie, Don Watts, and Negin Nabavi for valuable input. In particular, I thank Dr. Frida Hastrup for her critical comments and suggestions.
2. For general information refer to Touraj Atabaki, "Ethnic diversity and territorial integrity of Iran," *Iranian Studies* 31, no. 1 (2005): 23–44; Nikki Keddie, "The Minorities Question in Iran," in *The Iran-Iraq War: New Weapons, Old Conflicts*, ed. Shireen Tahir-Kheli and Shaheen Ayubi (New York: Praeger, 1995), 85–108; Massoume Price, *Iran's Diverse Peoples: A Reference Sourcebook* (Santa Barbara, CA: ABC-Clio, 2005); and Nayereh Tohidi, "Ethnicity and Religious Minority Politics in Iran," in *Contemporary Iran: Economy, Society, Politics*, ed. Ali Gheissari (Oxford, UK: Oxford University Press, 2009), 299–322.
3. For an in-depth analysis of nationalism and the question of ethnic minorities in post-Khomeini Iran, and for the conceptual and political problems with using "Persian" to denote a particular ethnic group or type of nationalism, refer to Rasmus Christian Elling, *Minorities in Iran: Nationalism and Ethnicity after Khomeini* (New York: Palgrave Macmillan, December 2012 (forthcoming).
4. See for example Richard Cottam, *Nationalism in Iran: Updated through 1978*, rev. ed. (Pittsburgh, PA: University of Pittsburgh Press, 1979); and Firoozeh Kashani-Sabet, "Cultures of Iranian-ness: The Evolving Polemic of Iranian Nationalism," in *Iran and the Surrounding World: Interactions in Culture and Politics*, ed. Nikki Keddie and Rudi Matthee (Seattle, WA: University of Washington Press, 2002), 162–181.
5. Ervand Abrahamian, *Khomeinism: Essays on the Islamic Republic* (Berkeley, CA: University of California Press, 1993), 3.
6. Shahram Chubin, "Iran and the Persian Gulf States," in *The Iranian Revolution and the Muslim World*, ed. David Menashri (Boulder, CO: Westview Press, 1990), 73–84.
7. Cottam, *Nationalism in Iran*, 135, 145; David Menashri, "Khomeini's Vision: Nationalism or World Order?" in *The Iranian Revolution and the Muslim World*, ed. David Menashri (Boulder, CO: Westview Press, 1990), 40–57.
8. Suzanne Maloney, "Identity and Change in Iran's Foreign Policy," in *Identity and Foreign Policy in the Middle East*, ed. Shibley Telhami and Michael Barnett (Ithaca, NY: Cornell University Press, 2002), 90.
9. Shireen Hunter, *Iran after Khomeini* (New York: Praeger, 1992). Hunter notes that "strongly negative reactions to certain aspects of the [Islamist] cultural policy" made the regime "realize that excessive anti-Iranianism would damage its base of support among the Iranians." On Khomeini's vacillations between nationalist and pan-Islamist imagery, see Menashri, "Khomeini's Vision."

10. See notes 8 and 9; also see David Menashri, *Post-Revolutionary Politics in Iran: Religion, Society and Power* (London: Frank Cass, 2001); and Mehrdad Mashayekhi, "The Politics of Nationalism," in *Iran: Political Culture in the Islamic Republic*, ed. Samih K. Farsoun and Mehrdad Mashayekhi (London: Routledge, 1992), 56–79.

11. Hooshang Amirahmadi, "From Political Islam to Secular Nationalism," *The Iranian* January 11, 1996, http://www.iranian.com/Jan96/Opinion/SecularNationalism.html.

12. Shabnam Holliday, "The Politicization of Culture and Contestation of Iranian National Identity in Khatami's Iran," *Studies in Ethnicity and Nationalism* 7, no. 1 (2007): 27–45. An example of state nationalist politics during Khatami's presidency relates to the Persian Gulf as a symbol of Iranian pride. Capitalizing on and in response to the global Iranian outrage over the 2004 map published in the *National Geographic*, which referred to an "Arabian Gulf," Khatami's government instituted a National Persian Gulf Day, celebrated to this day. For an example of the nationalist rhetoric utilized to mark this day, see "Ruz-e melli-ye khalij-e fars," *IRNA* (website), accessed July 2, 2009, http://www2.irib.ir/occasions/khalijefars/khalijefars%20Day.html.

13. "Beh mafakher-e tarikhi-ye qabl az eslam niz beh 'onvan-e neshanehha-ye honar-e irani eftekhar mikonim" (We are also proud of the glorious pre-Islamic heritage as symbols of Persian art), *Fars* (news agency), May 7, 2008, http://www.farsnews.com.

14. "Mashaei: ijad-e ruz-e Kurosh dar taqvim-e rasmi-ye jomhuri-ye eslami" (Mashaei: the establishment of the Day of Cyrus in the official calendar of the Islamic Republic), *Shahab* (news agency), November 23, 2008, http://www.shahabnews.com.

15. "Ahmadinejad hails Cyrus Cylinder," *Press TV* (news website), September 12, 2010, http://www.presstv.ir.

16. "Hamid Baqa'i: Ahmadinezhad Kurosh-e zaman ast!" (Hamid Baqa'i: Ahmadinejad is the Cyrus of our times!), *Tabnak* (news agency), September 19, 2010, http://www.tabnak.ir.

17. Ali Ansari, "Iranian Nationalism Rediscovered," in *The Middle East Institute Viewpoints: The Iranian Revolution at 30* (Washington, DC: The Middle East Institute, 2009).

18. "Mosahebeh ba ra'is-jomhur hengam-e 'azimat beh New York"(An interview with the president upon his departure for New York), *Presidency of the Islamic Republic* (website), September 13, 2005, http://www.president.ir; "Artesh dezh-e mohkam-e defa' az 'ezzat-e mellat-e Iran ast" (The army is a strong bastion defending the honor of the Iranian nation), April 17, 2008, http://www.president.ir; "Ahmadinezhad: bar asas-e nazarsanji-ha mellat-e Iran 'aziz-tarin mellat dar jahan ast" (Ahmadinejad: Based on polls, Iran is the dearest nation in the world), *Shahab* (news agency), November 20, 2008, http://www.shahabnews.com. Despite these expressions of pride in Iran's ancient past, it should not be forgotten that historians and archaeologists around the world—including Abdollah Shahbazi, Kamyar Abdi, and others—have criticized Ahmadinejad's government for neglecting and mistreating Iran's cultural heritage.

19. See "Ahmadinezhad: az nasl-e Arash, Rostam va Farhadim" (Ahmadinejad: We are the descendants of Arash, Rostam and Farhad), *Entekhab* (news agency), May 10, 2009, http://www.entekhabnews.com; "Harandi: Ahmadinezhad az tabar-e kaveh-ye ahangar ast" (Harandi: Ahmadinejad is of the family of Kaveh the Blacksmith), *Iran* June 10, 2009, http://www.iran-newspaper.com. The *Shahnameh* is considered Iran's national epic and was composed by the poet Hakim Abolqasem Ferdowsi around 1000 A.D.

20. "Enteqad-e organ-e ayatollah Mesbah az didar-e Ahmadinezhad va hamsar-e doktor Fatemi: Mosaddeq va vazirash kha'en budand!" (Ayatollah Mesbah's newspaper's

critique of Ahmadinejad's visit with Dr. Fatemi's wife: Mosaddeq and his minister were both traitors!), `Asr-e Iran (news website), April 17, 2008, http://www.asriran .com. The widow, Parivash Fatemi (Sotuti), was among the first victims of the power struggle between Ahmadinejad and Khamenei when she was allegedly arrested together with other key supporters of Mashaei in May 2011—apparently accused of spying for Great Britain. See "Khorasan: Hamsar-e doctor Fatemi jasus-e britaniya ast" (Khorasan: Dr. Fatemi's wife is a British spy!), *Digarban* (news website), May 15, 2011, http://www.digarban.com.

21. "Matn-e kamel-e sokhanrani-ye Mashaei dar ekhtetamiyeh-ye hamayesh-e iraniyan" (The complete text of Mashaei's speech at the conclusion of the conference of Iranians), *Esteqamat* (news website), August 16, 2010, http://www.esteghamat.ir. Among Mashaei's many controversial statements, one that is of particular relevance to the present topic was when he proclaimed in 2004 that that "the age of Islamism is over." See "Mashaei: dawreh-ye eslamgara'i beh payan resideh ast" (Mashaei: the era of Islamism is over), *Jahan News* August 20, 2008, http://www.jahannews.com.

22. See, for example, "Pasokh-e daftar-e Ahmad Khatami beh Rahim-Mashaei" (The response of Ahmad Khatami's office to Rahim-Mashaei), *Parsine* (news website), August 7, 2010, http://www.parsine.com; "Firuzabadi: esharat-e Mashaei jorm 'aleyh-e amniyyat-e melli ast" (Firuzabadi: Mashaei's references constitute a crime against the national interest), `Asr-e Iran (news website), August 10, 2010, http://www.asriran.com.

23. "Emruz Iran yek maktab ast" (Today Iran is a school of thought), *Shafaf* (news website), August 7, 2010, http://www.shafaf.ir.

24. See Hunter, *Iran after Khomeini*, 92–100.

25. Haggai Ram, *Iranophobia: The Logic of an Israeli Obsession* (Stanford, CA: Stanford University Press, 2009), 46.

26. Ibid., 47.

27. Amir Taheri, *Nest of Spies: America's Journey to Disaster* (New York: Pantheon, 1989), 269.

28. Based on a private listserv discussion in the period between November 5 and December 3, 2008. Among those who refuted Taheri were Profs. Ervand Abrahamian, Shaul Bakhash, and Marsha Cohen.

29. Baqer Moin, *Khomeini: Life of the Ayatollah* (New York: Thomas Dunne Books, 2000).

30. Ruhollah Khomeini, *Sahifeh-ye emam: majmu`eh-ye asar, bayanat, mosahehbehha, ahkam, ejazat-e shar`i va namehha* (The Imam's book: the collection of works, speeches, interviews, decrees, legal certifications, and letters) (Tehran: Mo'aseseh-ye Tanzim va Nashr-e asar-e Emam Khomeini, 1382/ 2003), CD-ROM, 12: 274.

31. Khomeini, *Sahifeh-ye emam*, 13:78.

32. For examples of this kind of rhetoric, refer to websites of ultranationalist organizations including http://www.tondar.org, http://www.hambastegimelli.com, http://www.paniranist.org, and www.marzeporgohar.org.

33. Ali-Mohammad Baba'i-Zarech, *Ommat va mellat dar andisheh-ye Emam Khomeini* (The *Umma* and nation in Imam Khomeini's thought) (Tehran: Markaz-e asnad-e enqelab-e eslami, 1383/ 2004); Yahya Fawzi-Toyserkani, *Emam Khomeini va hoviyyat-e melli* (Imam Khomeini and national identity) (Tehran: Markaz-e asnad-e enqelab-e eslami, 1385/ 2006). The two writers are not introduced in the books, but from Internet searches, it appears that both are scholars. Fawzi-Toyserkani graduated with a PhD from Tehran University in 1998 and was, at least by 2008, Assistant Director of Research at The Imam and Revolution Institute and a faculty member at Imam Khomeini International University, Tehran. No specific information about Baba'i-Zarech could be found from Internet searches. All quotes are translated from Persian by me.

34. In this chapter, "nationalism" denotes particular political ideologies centered on the nation, and "patriotism" denotes more elusive popular sentiments of attachment to the *patria*. This choice is based on how the words *mihan* and *mellat* are used in the two works under discussion; in none of them is there a clearly defined role for the state.

35. For a discussion of nation (*mellat*), see Ludwig Paul, "'Iranian Nation' and Iranian-Islamic Revolutionary Ideology," *Die Welt des Islams* 39, no. 2 (1999): 183–217.

36. It may be that by *lafz-e qadimi*, Baba'i-Zarech meant "an old concept." However, *lafz* generally denotes "word," which makes it a problematic statement. *Vatan* probably entered Persian at the same time as *mellat*; both are Arabic words used in the Quran. Even if *mihan* and *vatan* are older words, it remains to be explained how their antiquity qualifies them over *mellat*. Indeed, one could interpret this statement as Baba'i-Zarech's defense of pre-Islamic authenticity, which would complicate the Islamic justification for "loving the homeland."

37. For other examples of "positive" and "negative nationalism," see Khamenei's quote in Menashri, "Khomeini's Vision," 51.

38. See notes 2 and 3; see also Hamid Ahmadi, *Qawmiyyat va qawm-gara'i dar Iran* (Ethnicity and ethnic nationalism in Iran) (Tehran: Nashr-e Ney, 1378/ 1999).

39. Rasmus Christian Elling, "State of Mind, State of Order: Reactions to Ethnic Unrest in the Islamic Republic of Iran," *Studies in Ethnicity and Nationalism* 8, no. 3 (2008): 481–501.

40. For two Western journalistic reports alleging US support for, among others, ethnic and sectarian-based militant groups in Iran, see Seymour Hersh, "The Iran Plans," *The New Yorker* April 17, 2006; and "The Secret War Against Iran," *ABC News Blog* April 3, 2007, http://blogs.abc.new.com.

41. *Constitution of the Islamic Republic of Iran*, Article 15.

42. Despite governmental promises and an unprecedented May 2009 ruling by the Supreme Council for Cultural Revolution, it does not seem that this has changed. See Rasmus Christian Elling, "A Step in the Right Direction for Iran's Forgotten Languages," *CUMNINet Blog* August 19, 2009, http://cuminet.blogs.ku.dk/2009/08/19/.

43. Golnar Mehran, "The Presentation of the 'Self' and the 'Other' in Postrevolutionary Iranian School Textbooks," in *Iran and the Surrounding World: Interactions in Culture and Politics*, ed. Nikki Keddie and Rudi Matthee, 232–253.

44. See Elling, *Minorities in Iran*.

45. See for example, Alireza Asgharzadeh, *Iran and the Challenge of Diversity: Islamic Fundamentalism, Aryanist Racism, and Democratic Struggles* (New York: Palgrave Macmillan, 2007); Ali Al-Taie, *Bohran-e hoviyyat-e qawmi dar Iran* (The crisis of ethnic identity in Iran) (Tehran: Shadegan, 1378/ 1999); and Zia Sadr-ol-Ashrafi, *Kesrat-e qawmi va hoviyyat-e melli-ye iraniyan* (Ethnic diversity and national identity of Iranians) (Tehran: Andisheh-ye Naw, 1377/ 1998).

46. Asgharzadeh, *Iran and the Challenge of Diversity*, 109.

47. Ibid., 112, 114.

48. In the words of Ahmadinejad, "Iran no longer signifies a geographical [entity], a nationality, an ethnic group or a tribe, but rather a *way* and a *school of thought*" (See "Emruz Iran yek maktab ast," *Shafaf* website).

49. Indeed, there are also examples of literature from state-run research institutes that contain views more similar to Persian-centrist secular nationalism. For a critique of this literature, see Elling, *Minorities in Iran*.

50. Maloney, "Identity and Change in Iran's Foreign Policy," 102.

51. "Zol-Nur: Sepah dar surat-e lozum bara-ye moqabeleh ba jariyan-e enherafi vared mi-shavad" (Zol-Nur: If necessary, the Revolutionary Guards, will enter the scene to counter the "Deviant Current"), *Journalist Club* (news website), June 6, 2011, http://www.yjc.ir; "Enheraf-e jadid az hameh-ye enherafha-ye tarikh-e shi`eh khatarnak-tar ast" (The new deviation is the most dangerous of all the deviations in the history of Shi`ism), *Mehr* (news website), June 6, 2011, http://www.mehrnews.com.

6

From "Enemies of the Revolution" to Unfulfilled Ideal: Private Industrial Entrepreneurs in the Islamic Republic of Iran

Kjetil Selvik

"Efforts to realize privatization policies are a kind of jihad."[1]

—*Seyyed Ali Khamenei*

Background

The 1979 Islamic Revolution dealt a heavy blow to Iran's private sector manufacturing industry. The leading entrepreneurs of the Pahlavi era fled the country, and a great number of factories were nationalized. Formerly thriving companies suffered mismanagement at the hands of young and inexperienced managers selected on political and ideological grounds. During the 1980s, the Islamic Republic entered a development course characterized by central planning and state-led growth. All major industries were to belong to the public sector, as required by the article 44 of the Constitution. The revolution also created an unfavorable ideological climate for industrial entrepreneurs. In the view of the leftists who dominated the revolutionary movement, private factories were a sign of "capitalism" and a remnant of the *ancien régime*. Entrepreneurs were perceived as opportunists who pursued their personal interest at a time when everybody ought to strive for the well-being of society. The ultimate goal, for the activists, was the establishment of a classless society. Judged by the standards of this Utopia, private entrepreneurs were counterrevolutionaries who undermined the movement's zeal.

Still, for all its obstacles, the Islamic Republic has given life to a new generation of private-industrial entrepreneurs. Benefiting for a long time from state subsidies and a protected home market, these antiheroes of the early revolution rhetoric have established businesses and made careers. They have overcome challenges of red tape, war, and instability, and persevered at the production lines. With time, their reputation has improved, and the entrepreneurs are increasingly recognized. Not much has been written about this brewing industrial class, but its story needs to be told. This article is based on in-depth interviews with more than 60 founders and owners of private manufacturing establishments in 1999–2009. It does not include managers in the religious foundations that Iran's Statistical Center classifies as belonging to the public sector.

The economic weight of private manufacturing industry in Iran is still very light. According to the Statistical Center of Iran, the manufacturing industry produced 14.9 percent of the country's GDP in 2003/2004.[2] Though this percentage is changing from one year to another, it has stayed between 14 and 17.5 since 1990/1991. Of the value produced by the manufacturing industry, the share of the public sector is estimated at 80 percent. The contribution of private manufacturing enterprises to Iran's GDP is, thus, approximately 3 percent. The number of private companies is, however, far greater than in the public sector. Out of 11,200 manufacturing units employing more than 10 workers in 2000/2001, more than 92 percent belonged to the private sector.

Filling the Void Left by Pahlavi Entrepreneurs

Owing to the setback of the 1979 revolution, private sector industrial entrepreneurs have gained a reputation as "victims" of the Islamic Republic. The single most important event in shaping this impression was the dispossession of the Pahlavi bourgeoisie by the Revolutionary Council in June 1979. In a symbolic and heavily politicized ruling, the Council expropriated the assets of 51 exiled industrialists, accused of collaboration with the Shah. One month later, a second revolutionary decree ordered the nationalization of the Pahlavi era's most heavily indebted companies. Thus, in the single year of 1979, a total of 580 companies were confiscated from the private sector.[3] Adding to the picture of victimization were populist attacks on private investors by clerics and political leaders. Many industrialists had to fight for their rights, in prison and in court, during the early years of the revolution. Those who were allowed to operate could, according to the Constitution's article 44, only be active in nonstrategic residual sectors of the economy. No wonder then that private entrepreneurs have been seen to be the "losers" in the revolution.

The problem with this perspective, however, is that it fails to consider the *opportunities* that were opened by the radical political changes. Though industrialists were clearly suffering from radicalism and political unrest, some knew how to deal with it and actually came out stronger of the process. The revolution also brought new actors into the field, with no previous experience in the manufacturing industry. To account for this recomposition, and avoid a static understanding of the origins of today's industrial class, it can be useful to distinguish the "*bourgeois*" from the "entrepreneur." For the former, the revolution represents a danger, by threatening private property rights and making investments unsure. He cannot capitalize on his advantages, like assets, contacts, and investment capital, when society is turned upside down and no one can foresee the future. For the entrepreneur, however, turmoil means openings and new spheres of venture. His hallmark is not wealth, but courage,[4] vigilance,[5] or innovation.[6] In the chaos of a postrevolutionary, war-ridden context, qualities like these are particularly valorized. Thus, while revolution paralyses the "owner of the means of production," it brings out the best in the "entrepreneur."

The revolution facilitated the rise of industrial entrepreneurs in several ways. First of all, it effectively removed the competition of the group of investors who had dominated the business sector since the 1960s. After years of industrial hegemony, the tycoons were dispossessed and exiled in 1979. Though their factories were taken over by the state and the religious foundations, the disintegration of the haute bourgeoisie created a void in the industrial sector that benefited smaller entrepreneurs. Newcomers with relatively little capital and experience could suddenly enter markets where only the "big ones" had been. Many young and unestablished Iranians seized the occasion, founding workshops and simple production lines. Sure, there was war and instability, but as some of the entrepreneurs put it later, they had nothing to lose. Second, the revolution also created opportunities by disrupting the market, and increasing demand for industrial goods. Production lines were cut off and factories left idle as strikes and upheavals continued after the fall of the Shah. In the nationalized companies, output decreased as a consequence of the "brain drain" and mismanagement. When, on top of this, the Iran-Iraq War broke out, and an international trade embargo was imposed on the country, the result was a constant lack of manufactured consumer goods. For private industrialists, this situation filled an important condition for growth and success. As long as they could provide raw materials and produce industrial goods, they didn't have to worry about being able to sell their goods.

A third source of opportunity was the protectionist economic policies of the 1980s that aimed at strengthening local industry and increased the entrepreneurs' access to state subsidies. Protectionism was not new in Iran in the sense that import-substituting industrialization was applied by the Pahlavi administration since the early 1960s. However, with the outbreak of the Iran-Iraq War and the dominance of the Islamic left under the premiership of Mir-Hossein Mousavi (1981–1989), the inward looking focus of Iran's development strategy increased. To break the pattern of dependency vis-à-vis the Western powers, the government's goal was self-sufficiency (*khodkafa'i*). This, in the revolutionaries' view, could only be achieved if the state took on a more active role in promoting agriculture and industry. As a consequence, in the early 1980s, the Islamic Republic introduced a wide range of direct and indirect subsidies to the manufacturing sector. Entrepreneurs who wanted to build or expand their factories were offered favorable loans, cheap land, and subsidized building materials. To compensate for the cost of rising inflation, they also obtained foreign currency at prices well below the market rate. In addition to this, the state protected their products from international competition through bans on import and high tariff rates. For entrepreneurs who knew how to deal with the system, the self-centered development policy of the Islamic Republic was a gold mine.

Patterns of Rentier Entrepreneurship

The combination of instability, protectionism, and state subsidies favored a particular kind of entrepreneurship in the Islamic Republic's formative years. Verily, in explaining the economic logic that underpinned the growth of Iran's private sector manufacturing industry, the classic entrepreneurial theory of Joseph Schumpeter is not very useful. Schumpeter describes the entrepreneur as an innovator whose modification of production factors alters the behavior of other economic actors, and disrupts a routine-like equilibrium called "the circular flow."[7] The entrepreneur's profit, according to this view, lies in the comparative advantage given by the innovation, which lasts until other actors have caught up with the superiority of his newfound methods or products. However, neither did the postrevolutionary Iranian economy resemble a routine-like circular flow, nor was innovation the only means by which an entrepreneur could gain a comparative advantage. The principal characteristic of the market was in fact its lack of stability and reliable information. A short cut to wealth could thus be the support of a leading decision maker, who would help the entrepreneur with previsions of markets, politics, and coming regulations. Another and related way to success could be the access to oil rents.

Iran is a rentier economy where revenues gained from oil sale to the international market are inserted into the domestic production system through various forms of redistribution. The entrepreneurs who engaged in manufacturing industry in the 1980s soon learned to conduct their business in a way that would maximize their benefits from such rents. The primary sources of rent seeking were credit and foreign exchange allocations, which were often transferred outside the framework of the official budget.[8] In keeping with the Islamic Republic's goal of strengthening productive sectors such as industry and agriculture, all entrepreneurs received quotas of subsidized dollars and credits. Subventions were meant to cover expenses for factory building and imports of necessities such as industrial machines and raw materials. The amount and actual distribution of oil rent, however, could be influenced through political contacts and economic cunning. An example of the many tricks in use was to overbill materials purchased abroad, in order to obtain a larger amount of subsidized foreign currency than what was actually needed for the transaction. The excess dollars would then be sold on the black market with a tremendous profit. Another way to exploit the system was to detract a part of the raw materials from production, and sell cheaply imported goods such as sugar or corn at the rates of the free market. At a time when Iran was subject to war and international trade embargo, and consequently, suffered shortages of vital commodities, these kinds of schemes could be very lucrative.

The predominant kind of entrepreneurship that has given rise to Iran's industrial class is close to the model described by Israel Kirzner.[9] Kirzner's starting point is a refusal of the neoclassical view of the "market as an equilibrium," and recognition of the fact that various forms of friction distort the relation between supply and demand. The source of an entrepreneur's profit, according to Kirzner, is a discrepancy between production costs and consumer expectations, which the entrepreneur discovers and acts upon. His primary qualities are thus not innovation, but *vigilance* and the capacity to evaluate the situation. In applying this, the distortions of the Iranian economy have given entrepreneurs ample room to maneuver. Production costs have been lowered, and public demand increased, by constant allocations of oil rent. Simultaneously, supply has been hampered by trade embargos and import restrictions. In fact, the absence of competition was the single most important cause for the growth of the manufacturing industry in the 1980s. Needless to say, this protectionism has created problems for the Iranian industry, which calls on structural reform today.

Social Origins

Whatever the problems of Iran's manufacturing industry, the opportunities that were opened by the 1979 revolution converged on the appearance of a new generation of industrial entrepreneurs. Where these people came from is of importance for our understanding of the Islamic Revolution, but unfortunately, the social origins of Iran's nascent industrial elite have not been subject to thorough research. This author tried to make a first step while conducting interviews with managers in Iran between 1999 and 2004. The social profiles of 83 industrial entrepreneurs were registered, 36 of which were obtained through personal meetings and 47 through a written survey. According to the material gathered, the typical industrial entrepreneur in Iran is a male, born in 1947, with a middle-class family background. The families have often long traditions of independent, nongovernmental work. Another typical feature is that entrepreneurs have received higher education. More than 80 percent of the respondents claim to hold a bachelor degree.

As to the degree of renewal of the industrial class since the 1979 revolution, the survey shows some interesting results. While the dispossession of the Pahlavi bourgeoisie is clearly a landmark in the history of Iranian manufacturing industry, the recomposition of the industrial class is far from complete. Fifty-seven percent of the entrepreneurs state that they had entered the manufacturing sector before the revolution, disallowing us from presenting the postrevolutionary field as a tabula rasa. Some of these veterans did not own their own companies during the Pahlavi era, but had acquired capital and knowledge that allowed for entrepreneurship when the industrial reshuffle set in. Others were already in possession of factories from the 1960s and 1970s, but were sufficiently well acquainted with the new political establishment, or economically insignificant, for the revolutionary organs to leave them in peace. Then, there are the 43 percent who had no experience in manufacturing industry before 1979. The present industrial class is thus a mixture of petty bourgeois from the Pahlavi era, and a new generation of entrepreneurs who saw a potential in the business sector under the new regime. For both groups, the revolution created opportunities, as indicated by the fact that 60 percent of the companies studied by the survey have been founded after 1979.

Another interesting aspect of the social profiles of the entrepreneurs in the survey concerns the frequency of links between the industrialists and *bazaar* families. According to a widely-held belief both inside and outside the industrialists' circles, the industrial and commercial "bourgeoisies" are strictly separated in terms of working culture, ethics, and family trees. This perception goes back to the reign of Mohammad Reza Shah, whose project for modernizing Iran included a dream of replacing the traditional *bazaari* bourgeoisie with a modern industrial bourgeoisie. The "old-fashioned" class of conservative religious traders in the bazaar did not fit his dreams of an industrial Iran that would become the region's superpower. He, therefore, undermined the structure of the bazaar economy, and concentrated the allocation of oil rents on a quickly-expanding industrial class. The dissatisfaction of the merchants, and their close historical ties to the clergy, made the bazaar a center for political opposition during the Islamic Revolution. Once Khomeini took power, the loyalty of the merchants paid off: members of *Mo'talefeh*[10] were put in charge of revolutionary foundations and state portfolios, and soon a group of well-connected traders came to dominate the economy.

Beyond the shifting favors of industry and commerce between the 1970s and the 1980s, the idea of "two bourgeoisies" also had a distinct ideological root. It was a variation on the Maoist theme of *national* versus *comprador* bourgeoisie that entered Iran in the 1960s, and was propagated by groups like *Sazman-e Enqelabi-ye Iran* (the Revolutionary Organization of Iran) and *Sazman-e Fada'iyan-e Khalq-e Iran-Aksariat* (Organization of Iranian People's Fada'ian—Majority). Whereas the Marxists of the Tudeh party favored a strictly noncapitalist development for the country, *Fada'iyan-e Khalq* and *Sazman-e Enqelabi-ye Iran* were prepared to accept the national bourgeoisie in the revolutionary line (*dar saff-e enqelab*). The national bourgeoisie was defined as those who had followed Prime Minister Mohammad Mosaddeq in the coup d'état of 1953, while the comprador bourgeoisie was an illegitimate child of the Shah and international capitalism. While the first group was thought to accelerate the coming of the revolution to Iran, the second was perceived as a reactionary power that served the cause of imperialism. This dichotomy created resentment toward the leading entrepreneurs during the Pahlavi era, and is crucial for understanding the dispossession of the upper-industrial class in 1979. However, the myth of "two bourgeoisies" has been reappropriated by the entrepreneurs of the Islamic Republic, and integrated into their legitimizing discourse. As we shall see, the managers I've interviewed make a distinction between "industrialists" and "traders," "speculators" and "producers," and between "capitalists" and "entrepreneurs."

The Fight for Recognition

The new generation of industrialists took shape in an ideological context that stigmatized "capitalistic" actors. With conspicuous proof of wealth in their easily detectable factories, private entrepreneurs were ready targets for attacks from populist politicians and workers' councils. Anticapitalist sentiment was a product of the radical leftist discourse that had galvanized the revolution. The primary contributor to this discourse was the activist philosopher Ali Shariati (1933–1977). Through his agitation for revolution against the Pahlavi monarchy, Shariati spread an image of capitalist society as the antithesis of an Islamic state. He distinguished between a "Shi'ism of the oppressors" (Safavid Shi'ism) and a "Shi'ism of the oppressed" (Ali's Shi'ism), where the first was portrayed as the "opium of the masses" while the second, considered an "authentic" Shi'ism, appeared like a progressive tool for action. The very essence of Shi'i religion, Shariati argued, was revolution: believers should fight the imperialists and capitalists until the victory of a classless society (*nezam-e tawhidi*). By using the traditional Islamic obligation of *tawhid* (unification/stating that God is one), and giving it a Marxist interpretation (classless society), Shariati gave a powerful religious aura to the theme of class struggle. Indeed, he depicted social differences as a form of polytheism (*shirk*) that should be erased to hasten the return of the *Mahdi*.[11]

Faced with the legacy of Shariati's radical discourse, the entrepreneurs were not at ease in postrevolutionary Iran. The radicals were the strongest political force of the Islamic Republic, and put the embryo of a new industrial bourgeoisie in a difficult light. Were not the entrepreneurs "profiteers" who enriched themselves at the expense of ordinary people? Would they not flee the country like their Pahlavi predecessors as soon as there came difficult times? To protect themselves from accusations like these, the entrepreneurs adopted a low public profile. They made sure to dress and speak with modesty, and shied away from polemical debates. Still, within the limits of their conformist image, the entrepreneurs also made attempts at promoting a more positive picture of manufacturing industry. Industry was not a sign of capitalism or counterrevolution, entrepreneurs argued, but a prerequisite of progress and national strength. If cultivated, it would actually help promote the revolution by strengthening its economic base. Moreover, insisted the entrepreneurs, by fabricating goods that had previously been imported to the country, they contributed to the revolutionary goal of self-sufficiency.

The industrialists' efforts to shape alternative representations can be illustrated by the history of the word *karafarin*. This translation of the English term "entrepreneur" first appeared before the revolution, but was not actively promoted before the creation of the Industrial Managers' Association in 1979.[12] The founders of the association saw *karafarin* as an alternative to the commonly used *karfarma* (employer), which belonged to the Marxist terminology. *Karfarma* literally means "commander of work/ labor" and evokes class conflict and workers' exploitation. As the word was steeped in the leftist discourse of the 1960s and 70s, the industrialists thought it had too many negative connotations. The word *karafarin*, however, put the entrepreneur in a more favorable light. Not only did it dissociate him from the ideological debate on capitalism, but it also portrayed the industrialists as promoters of development. *Karafarin* is composed of *kar* (work) and *afarin* (creator) and thus, literally means "a person who creates jobs." In a country with double-digit unemployment rates, the importance of such a renaming could hardly be overstated. The following quotation from an interview with a founding member of the Industrial Managers' Association illustrates the point:

> Do you consider yourself to be a capitalist (*sarmayeh- dar*)?
> We like the word "*karafarin*." We don't like the word capitalist. We consider the "*karafarin*" as a servant of society. "*Karafarin*" is a person who uses the Nation's wealth, the work force of the society and his own intellectual capacities to establish production.
> But what is your opinion of the capitalist system?
> Personally, I like the capitalist who...
> ...has been moderated
> ...favors the interests of society
> ...thinks of his world before thinking of himself
> ...loves the people
> ...loves his employees
> ...knows his mission; the role he is to play in this world
> ...refuses to use his capital against the interests of the people
> ...puts his capital in the service of the development of his fatherland
> ...strives to follow superior values
> ...has specific goals

Capitalism should not have authority (*hakemiyat*) over people's lives.[13]

The careful style of this entrepreneur's answer is typical of my interviews with private sector industrial managers in Iran. It also illustrates some central features of the industrialists' discourse and worldview. The entrepreneur in question belongs to the generation of managers that had entered the manufacturing industry at the time of the Shah. Running a factory of 2,100 workers at the time of the revolution, he was one of the biggest industrialists to escape the nationalization drive of 1979. Inevitably, though, for a company of this size, he still had his turn with the revolutionary authorities. For several years following the fall of the Shah, the "Committee for the Application of the Orders of the Imam" (*hey'at-e ejra-ye farman-e Emam*) imposed a parallel manager on the company who contested the rights of the owner and encroached on his power. Helped by his sheer persistence and political contacts, the entrepreneur managed to regain control of the company, but some 20 years after, the impact of the trauma can still be felt in his unease with a word like capitalism. More interesting, even, while rejecting the radical terminology of the 1980s, the entrepreneur's discourse is still very ideologized. His answer has nothing of a flatly stated free-market argument such as "investors have the right to gain money." Indeed, while defending private enterprise, he stresses the responsibilities and the moral obligations that come with wealth and investment. The entrepreneur will not allow anyone to accuse him of hedonism or speculation. On the contrary, he describes the work of industrialists to be like a "mission."

What does this entrepreneurial mission consist of? To summarize the industrial managers' discourse in two related words, the foremost issues are production (*tawlid*) and construction (*sazandegi*). Few are the interviews with Iranian industrialists where none of these words occur. Most often, they inspire lengthy reflections on the needs for the future of the country. The central point for the entrepreneurs is that the economy needs to produce, and not only recycle oil revenues. In light of this imperative, private industrialists find recognition and a *raison d'être*. The entrepreneurs define themselves in opposition to the speculator or the middleman (*dallal*). The archetype of a *dallal* is a relative of an influential political leader, who has large sums of money at his disposal, and exploits the fluctuations of the market. Typically, the middleman buys huge quantities of raw materials or vital commodities when prices are low, and resells them when shortages or seasonal fluctuations have changed the configurations of the market. This kind of speculation has been a constant problem under the Islamic Republic, and is very unpopular among the population. By contrasting industrial production with counterproductive middlemen activities, the entrepreneurs have managed to boost their own reputation.

The Adjustment

What has enhanced the industrial bourgeoisie's position the most, however, is a gradual reinterpretation of the revolutionary ideology. From the radical-socialist political climate where the entrepreneurs first made their appearance 30 years ago, the Islamic Republic has gone through some fundamental changes. A first landmark was passed with the death of Khomeini and the election of Akbar Hashemi Rafsanjani as president in 1989. Taking power at a time when eight years of war with Iraq had ruined the economy and exhausted the population, Rafsanjani announced that he would lead the country and the revolution through an adjustment (*ta'dil*). The main components of this reform process were a break from the command economy of the Mousavi government, and a less ideological approach to domestic and foreign policy. In order to reconstruct the country, the president argued, Iran should welcome private investments and normalize its ties with neighboring states. While the radicals saw this as abandoning the central goals of the revolution, Rafsanjani retorted that it was the only way of saving the revolution itself. The new watchword was *pragmatism,* as Rafsanjani demonstrated by favoring competence over religious credentials in the choice of his cabinet.[14] The president also entered an alliance with the Guardian Council to exclude the radicals from the political process. As a consequence, by 1992, the influence of the Islamic left was considerably reduced.

The "adjustment" made room for private investors in the canonized ranks of the revolution. Inasmuch as they contributed to the strengthening of the economy, they would henceforth be considered as pillars of the Islamic Republic. The president's focus on construction (*sazandegi*) was particularly beneficial to the entrepreneurs' public standing. If anyone questioned their revolutionary credentials, they could now refer to their efforts to "rebuild the country." The wartime experience gave additional credibility and prestige in this respect. Contrary to the Pahlavi bourgeoisie who had fled the country during the 1978/79 revolution, the new industrialists had stayed in Iran, and contributed to the war effort. Sure, there were accusations of rent seeking and speculation, but after all, the entrepreneurs had been supplying consumer goods at a time when Iran was facing shortages and an international embargo. They had, thereby, helped keep up the war machinery and make resistance possible. Moreover, years of odd repairs and technological improvisations had concretized the motto of self-sufficiency. By learning how to produce in the absence of Western technology and expertise, the entrepreneurs had gained a know-how that corresponded to Rafsanjani's calls for competence. Inevitably, the slogans of Rafsanjani, or the "Commander of Reconstruction" (sardar-e sazandegi) as he liked to be called, were appropriated by the industrialists. The following quotation from an interview with an entrepreneur in 2003 is clearly an echo of Rafsanjani's discourse, and shows how the themes of pragmatism and competence have been used to build legitimacy for the entrepreneurs:

> When I go to the doctor, I don't care about his political views. If he has the necessary knowledge to treat me, he can be a communist, a capitalist, a socialist or an Islamist; his convictions belong to himself. Similarly, whether a minister belongs to this or that party is not my preoccupation. I only demand that he have the ability to point out and solve the problems of our industry...Suppose that you would like to defend your country in a time of war. You don't go directly to the front with a rifle in your hands. First, you have to learn the art of warfare. If, by love for your nation, you get killed in action without having learned how to fight, the country will have lost a soldier. You could have been a good farmer for your country, a good university professor or a good salesman. Through incompetence, however, you inflict a loss on your country. Lack of knowledge is a kind of treason.[15]

For those who are familiar with the importance of martyrdom in the national myths of the Islamic Republic, the example of the "incompetent soldier" is very interesting. It shows the iconoclastic potential of the new pragmatism, and illustrates how much the ideological climate of the republic had changed by 2003. In the early years of the revolution, the notion of sacrifice was the key to public esteem. The marks of a hero were self-abnegation, and readiness to die for Khomeini. Here again, the ideals of the 1980s were unhelpful for the fame of private entrepreneurs. Like Schumpeter notes in Capitalism, Socialism and Democracy, the feats of the manufacturing industry are generally of an unheroic nature.[16] Indeed, while people were risking their lives to combat the Iraqi army, the entrepreneurs stood safe behind their industrial machines. Their "lack of courage" was used against them, and hampered their prestige. In the discourse of the entrepreneur above, however, the argument is turned on its head. The soldier is accused of wasting his talents because his devotion is blind. For the entrepreneur, the traitor is the martyr, and the hero, "he who masters his work." What matters is no longer the motive behind his actions, but the consequences of his deeds. This sort of pragmatism is fully in line with the discourse of ex-president Hashemi Rafsanjani, and the latter's call for the rationalization of the revolutionary dogma was an important gain for the industrial bourgeoisie. Furthermore, when the reformists came to power in 1997, the focus on pragmatism was not reversed. Rather, the rationalization process continued under President Khatami.

Reform

The reform movement that emerged within the Islamic system in the 1990s was a second ideological shift with important repercussions for the status of private industrial entrepreneurs. It sprang out from the ranks of the Islamic left, which during the lifetime of Khomeini had been the most ardent promoter of the doctrine of *velayat-e faqih*. By insisting that the will of the Leader was superior to the authority of republican institutions, they had asserted themselves in the country's political system at the expense of the more law-abiding and democratic currents. In the early 1990s, however, the radicals were themselves excluded from the electoral game as the then president Rafsanjani made a tactical alliance with the conservatives to marginalize opponents of liberal economic reforms. When seeking approval for participation in the elections for the Council of Experts in 1991 and the Parliament in 1992, the radicals were rejected for "lack of loyalty" to the Leader. As the argument the radicals had used to combat their political rivals in the beginning of the revolution was thus turned against themselves, their ideological posture began to change. Having felt the pain of exclusion by the conservative alliance of the early 1990s, activist-ideologues like Abbas Abdi, Alireza Alavi-Tabar, Majid Mohammadi, and Saeed Hajjarian found interest in civil liberties. Henceforth, the Islamic left would focus less on revolution, and more on the rule of law. Gradually, the radicals abandoned the theme of absolute obedience to the Leader, and refocused their agenda on "reform."

The reformists' swing from a radical revolutionary rhetoric to their new legalist discourse greatly enhanced the standing of Iran's industrialists. Judging by the standards of the pluralist ideal, the entrepreneurs were no longer counterrevolutionaries but qualified members of "civil society." The new approach was clear from the writings of Saeed Hajjarian, a leading ideologue of the reform movement and political adviser to President Khatami between 1997 and 2000. In an article published in the monthly *Ettela'at-e siyasi-eqtesadi* in 1997, he presents a history of the idea of progress (*taraqqi*) among religious intellectuals in Iran.[17] Hajjarian differentiates between three understandings of the concept associated with different historical paradigms: progress as elevation (*ta'ali*), perfection (*takamol*) and development (*tawse'eh*). The first, he says, was that of the Gnostics who saw progress as the elevation of human conscience. The second dominated the discourse of the religious intellectuals in the 1970s and the 1980s, who thought that history had a teleological goal and interpreted progress as a movement toward a perfect world. This was the view of Shariati who fought for a classless society through revolution, and which Hajjarian and most other reformists initially supported. During the 1990s, however, the religious intellectuals turned their back on absolutism and Manichean worldviews and embraced a third conception, where progress was seen as gradual development. According to Hajjarian, it can be summarized in five constituting principles: (i) denial of the teleological idea that history has a common destination for all societies; (ii) favoring prudent actions over Utopian projects, which carry too much risk; (iii) picking your means according to your object rather than following a predefined ideological doctrine; (iv) dissociating the role of the state from "saving human beings" and "creating heaven on earth"; and (v) focusing on internal rather than external reasons for the lack of development. In this new vision of progress of the reformists, private entrepreneurs could easily find their place as Hajjarian explicitly states: "the specialists (*fann-salaran*) and the national entrepreneurs (*karafarinan-i naw`-e vatani*) are the first bearers of this reading of progress."[18]

One should recall that the idea of production (*tawlid*) has always been central to the ideology of the Islamic left. Ali Shariati was an outspoken critic of the consumerist nature of the Iranian economy where neither products nor ideas were produced locally, and (instead) everything was imported from the West. The problem for the entrepreneurs of the 1980s, however, was that the radicals saw the manufacturing industry as the prerogative of the state. However, since the comeback of the Islamic left in 1997, their stress on the need for civil society has led reformists to look at the private sector with completely different eyes. The standard reformist diagnosis of Iran's economic and political ills is now in fact that the state is too big. The reformists blame oil revenues for having distorted the power balance between state and society, making political leaders financially independent of their social base.[19] In this new appreciation of the nation's problem, the crucial feature of a private businessman is no longer his class affiliation or ideology but that he represents a counterweight to the all-pervasive state. The Khatami government, therefore, saw no need to reverse Rafsanjani's economic liberalization and in fact, made several important steps to strengthen the private manufacturing sector.[20] Toward the end of ex-president Khatami's second term in office, I asked an entrepreneur whether the state and politicians were showing him "the respect that he deserved." The answer he gave was very telling:

> The situation is getting better. Some days ago, I was in a meeting with the governor of Mazandaran. He told me straight out that "after the revolution, we made a mistake: we regarded the capitalist as a cheat. Today, however, we understand that the government, the country and the regime depend on an active economy. And for the economy to function, we need to protect and encourage the capitalist."[21]

Populist Backlash

In the paradoxical world of Iranian politics, however, as the Islamic left made peace with capitalism, a new and state-oriented "right" emerged. What is often described as the Iranian neoconservative movement took shape through the process of fighting the reformists in the 1990s. Its members are predominantly young recruits of the conservative faction with background from hard-line militias and the Revolutionary Guards who defended the system against reformist "subversion." Having fought what they considered the "fifth column" of the Islamic Republic on the ground, these foot soldiers found their influence inside the conservative faction unequal to their effort. They criticized the old guard of leniency and demanded an ideological return to the original values of the Islamic revolution, meaning strict moral enforcement, social justice, and anti-imperialism. Mahmoud Ahmadinejad's victory in the 2005 presidential elections empowered the neoconservative faction. Under his leadership, Iran has experienced a reideologization of politics, strengthened populist rhetoric and increasing tensions with the West. The economic implications have been inflation, falling investor confidence, and flight of capital.

The neoconservative takeover confronted private industrialists with challenges of an ideological, political, and economic nature. The ideological threat was an extension of the rallying cry of "cultural invasion" (*tahajom-e farhangi*), as conceptualized by Mohammad Taqi Mesbah Yazdi and Seyyed Ali Khamenei in the early 1990s. According to the conservative ideologues, the enemy had lost hope in defeating Iran militarily and switched to the more subtle approach of undermining the Islamic Republic culturally. The outpouring of books, films, newspapers, and other cultural expressions following the liberalization policies of Khatami and Rafsanjani was in this perspective threatening to erode the foundation of the Islamic system from within. The radical right that emerged in the 1990s also saw economic liberalization as a source of "cultural invasion." In the eyes of the young and socially lower-class conservatives, market adjustment was increasing social differences and causing corruption. They particularly disapproved of the fact that a class of nouveaux riches was showing off its wealth by conspicuously consuming Western products.

The private sector's political problem was Ahmadinejad's intuitive distrust of entrepreneurs who had thrived under the Rafsanjani and Khatami governments. Suspecting that economic success spoke of hidden political allegiances, the neoconservative president would not go on strengthening what he saw as his predecessors' clients. Upon gaining power, Ahmadinejad signaled that his government would favor small and medium enterprises over "big business." He has since delivered on his promise through policies such as the rapid-return loans scheme, handing out some $70 billion to small businesses over the country in the form of heavily subsidized credit, and the justice share (*sahm-e 'adalat*) program, through which the government has been distributing shares in state-owned companies to the poor. President Ahmadinejad has at the same time effectively cut off the more established private industrial ventures from loans given out of the oil fund and frozen the implementation of regular privatization.

The government's preference for the petty bourgeoisie is in line with the antiestablishment discourse that brought Ahmadinejad to power in the first place. While running against the veteran Rafsanjani, Ahmadinejad focused his campaign on inefficiencies and corruption, and accused a self-serving elite of squandering the nation's wealth. He promised to deprive the insiders of their privileges, and to "put oil revenues on the people's table." Parts of this populist discourse added to the private sector's unease. The president's invocation of "economic mafias" in particular upset the business community. In the words of an articulate member of the Tehran Chamber of Commerce, "Ahmadinejad went on television saying the mafias were in the thousands and that he had their names in his pocket. The entrepreneurs reacted by freezing their investments, fearing that they would not be able to reap the fruits of their work in the future."[22] The pledge to restore the original values of the revolution was no less worrying for those who had experienced the anticapitalist propaganda of the 1980s.

His Master's Voice

Ahmadinejad's populist outbursts were however offset by a stronger commitment to private sector growth in the Islamic system as a whole. Within months of Ahmadinejad's ascendance to the presidency, the Leader increased the authority of the Expediency Council and its pragmatic conservative leadership, to comprise supervisory power of the government. The move aimed at counterbalancing the neoconservatives' growing influence and compel Ahmadinejad to stay within the economic framework spelled out in the Expediency Council's Five- and Twenty-Year plans. In 2005, the Expediency Council reinterpreted article 44 of the Constitution to allow private investments in most of all economic sectors, including banking, insurance, airlines, sea transports, and mining.[23] Moreover, in 2006, the Leader personally became engaged in the matter by ordering the privatization of 80 percent of public companies' shares.

The Leader's intervention in favor of privatization was both unprecedented and a landmark in the entrepreneurs' fight for recognition. As a rule, the Leader prefers not to interfere too much in economic affairs and rather focus on politics and spiritual concerns. This is partly out of the tradition set by his predecessor Ayatollah Khomeini—who famously stated that his followers had not had a revolution to "lower the price of melons"—but out of recognition that the economy, with its many problems, is an unpopular issue for which the government had better take the blame. The lack of engagement from the Leader has been an important reason for Iran's lackluster pace of economic reforms. One of the main obstacles in Mohammad Khatami's attempts at further privatization was notably the fact that he never had any explicit order from the Leader to refer to. With the far-less privatization-eager President Ahmadinejad in power, however, Khamenei suddenly spoke up and confirmed the regime's belief in the development benefits of the private sector. In a speech to state officials in charge of implementing economic reform, Khamenei even referred to privatization policies as a kind of *jihad*.[24] He thus sent a thinly veiled message to Ahmadinejad that he stay within the development path that has been laid out at the regime's highest levels:

> Certain people oppose implementation of the [privatization] policies because they are opposed to the economic prosperity and development of the Islamic Republic. These people, who are chiefly foreigners, are trying to hold back Iran's economy to pressure the Islamic Republic through economic means.[25]

Despite explicit support for private sector growth, however, what comes out of a discourse like this is not "the end of history."[26] The Leader's acknowledgment of the need for private investments is not a celebration of capitalism or democracy. In fact, while his message is one of economic rationalization, it is framed in a typical populist style. It draws on standard rhetorical devices such as demonizing foreigners, stressing threats against the Islamic Republic, and legitimizing national actors with reference to the enemies outside. The dilemma when applying the old rhetoric to defend these new actors is of course that tensions with the West are part of the problem the Iranian private sector has to grapple with in order to thrive. An ideological climate that undermines contact with the international economy and scares off investors is hardly compatible with private sector growth.

Unresolved Contradictions

There is indeed a point where the Islamic Republic's embrace of the private sector runs into contradictions with the central tenets of the revolution. Private industrialists may have come a long way from being considered a comprador bourgeoisie or "reactionary capitalists," but they still operate in a system that has not sorted out its ideological and economic orientation.

This ambiguity becomes clear in the above-mentioned "Twenty-Year Perspective" for the Iranian economy that was prepared by the Expediency Council and approved by the Leader. In the foreword, it marginalizes the old idea of import substitution and instead promotes a pledge to strive for export-led growth. Several ambitious goals are mentioned in this respect, such as becoming a leading exporter of various agricultural and industrial goods. At the same time, however, the "Twenty-Year Perspective" calls for "self-sufficiency," and to this end, the state is to grant subsidies and privileges to industry and agriculture. The question of how Iran can play the game of globalization without increasing its dependency on foreign countries is not discussed.[27]

Privatization has been pursued in an equally ambiguous manner. When Rafsanjani first introduced the idea of privatization and made it a central component of the First Development Plan, he did not proceed to change the Constitution. Instead, he referred to a "footnote" of article 44, which notes that the state-dominated ownership structure shall be protected "insofar as it ... contributes to the economic growth and progress of the country."[28] Claiming that public ownership over certain sectors had become a development restraint, he used this condition to justify privatization. This might have been reasonable as long as privatization only touched on certain sectors, and was set to happen on a small scale. However, as ambitions for privatization were heightened, and private actors were allowed in many more sectors of the economy, the question of the Constitution remained. Today, Iran has private companies in banking, insurance, transport (sea transport, buses, and airlines), all kinds of manufacturing industry (including petrochemicals, automobiles, and steel), and mining, all of which is in glaring contrast with the spirit of the above-mentioned article. From the regime's point of view, however, proceeding to change article 44 is a risky endeavor as it would remove the aura of "sacredness" from the Constitution and create precedence for constitutional changes in other areas, including the contentious issue of velayat-e faqih.

The ad hoc approach to economic liberalization produced results as long as the pro-business presidents Hashemi Rafsanjani and Mohammad Khatami were in charge of government. Under Ahmadinejad, however, the strategy's limits soon became clear. On the face of it, President Ahmadinejad has bowed to the pressures to abide with the country's development plans and has moderated his economic discourse. He pays regular tribute to the goal of private sector growth[29] and explicitly hails entrepreneurship.[30] However, at the same time he has exploited the ambiguities in the overall development framework to give privatization a populist twist. Instead of selling public company actions to investors who can gain a majority and effectively turn them into private corporations, the president has distributed shares to millions of the poor as government handouts in a way that does not improve the management of the companies.[31] Other aspects of his government's economic policies, such as dictating prices, increasing imports,[32] and awarding large-scale contracts to contractors from the Revolutionary Guard,[33] have also been detrimental to the private manufacturing sector.

Left in Limbo

For Iran's industrial entrepreneurs, the situation is paradoxical. On the one hand, their esteem has probably never been higher as the concept of entrepreneurship is now firmly entrenched in the corridors of power. Its attraction stems from awareness of the structural problems in the state-led development model and the urge to create employment for the huge youth cohorts. The Third Development Plan (2000–2005) made stimulating entrepreneurship an area of priority, providing funds for research and education, public awareness schemes, science and technology parks, and incubator facilities in universities. In 2004, the University of Tehran launched a Masters program in entrepreneurship—now the faculty of entrepreneurship—with financial support from the Ministry of Labor, the Ministry of Science, and the Tehran Municipality.[34]

Karafarini is no less of a buzzword for conservatives than for reformists. Minister of Labor in Ahmadinejad's first government, Mohammad Jahromi, has for instance been an ardent promoter of the virtues of entrepreneurship. As for Ahmadinejad himself, a 2008 article on the pro-government website *Rajanews* described him as an "entrepreneurial president" (*ra'is jomhur-e karafarin*). The reason, the author argued, was the president's personal courage and belief in radical change, which like Malaysia's Mahathir Muhammad and China's Deng Xiaoping, is destined to bring progress to the country.[35]

On the other hand, there is a sea of contradictions between the official idealization of entrepreneurship and the day-to-day realities the industrialists have to deal with. Industrialists complain of the constantly changing rules and regulations and the omnipresent red tape in their interaction with state institutions. In a document published by the World Bank, comparing business environments across 181 economies in 2009, Iran was ranked 142nd.[36] The Islamic Republic fared particularly badly on issues linked to obtaining authorizations from the state administration. A producer of car parts and entrepreneur of the IT sector summarized the paradox as follows: "When it comes to words, industrialists like us are treated with respect and heartily greeted by top officials in the government ministries. They realize they need us as the question of unemployment is worrying everybody in the country. But there is no far-reaching effort to strengthen productive activities in the country."[37]

As the leaders of the Islamic Republic struggle to resolve their internal and external predicaments, Iran's industrial entrepreneurs are left in limbo. President Ahmadinejad's economic populism and confrontational foreign policy have come at a high price for the economy and shrouded the future in a veil of uncertainty. Although private industrialists have gained legitimacy, the conditions that would further their growth and make manufacturing industry a mainstay of the Iranian economy are not in place. One fundamental problem is of course that the legitimacy of Iran's industrial entrepreneurs does not extend to their potential partners abroad. In today's global economy, private sector development is hard to conceive of without involving foreign investors who may be seen as undermining the national sovereignty, and that has been the Islamic revolution's most hard-fought goal.[38] The gap between the current prestige of entrepreneurs in Iran and the problems of the manufacturing industry is but one of several contradictions the Islamic Republic needs to resolve.

Notes

1. "Privatization will lead to prosperity," *Tehran Times* February 20, 2007 (Editorial).
2. Statistical Center of Iran (Management and Planning Organization), *Iran Statistical Yearbook 1383* (2004/2005), accessed March 7, 2012, http://amar.sci.org.ir/index_e.aspx.
3. Jahangir Amuzegar, *Iran's Economy under the Islamic Republic* (London and New York: I. B. Tauris, 1993), 197.
4. Richard Cantillon, *Essai sur la Nature du Commerce en Général* [1755], edited with an English translation and other material by Henry Higgs, C. B. Reissued for The Royal Economic Society by Frank Cass and Co., LTD., London, 1959, accessed from http://oll.libertyfund.org/title/285.
5. Israel M. Kirzner, *Discovery and the Capitalist Process* (Chicago: University of Chicago Press, 1985).
6. Joseph A. Schumpeter, *The Theory of Economic Development: An inquiry into Profits, Capital, Credit, Interest, and the Business Cycle* (New Brunswick, NJ: Transaction books, 1983).
7. Ibid.
8. See Hadi Salehi Esfahani and Farzad Taheripour, "Hidden Public Expenditures and the Economy in Iran," *International Journal of Middle East Studies* 34 (2002): 691–718.
9. Kirzner, *Discovery and the Capitalist Process*.
10. *Mo'talefeh*, or the Coalition of Islamic Associations (*hey'atha-ye mo'talefeh-ye eslami*), started as a cooperation between different trade associations and a group of clergymen following the expulsion of Khomeini in 1964.
11. *Mahdi* is a reference to the Twelfth and Hidden Imam. According to Shi'i belief, on the Day of Judgement, the Twelfth Imam shall return from his occultation and reinstall a just society.
12. The word *karafarin* has roots in the Persian language and is first known to have been used by the Twelfth-century Iranian poet Nezami Ganjavi to describe God's support for perpetual creation. It was, however, rarely used before the revolution and only figured in Persian dictionaries and encyclopedias in the sense of "God" before reemerging in its contemporary meaning of "entrepreneur" (See Mohammad Keyhani and Saeed Jafari Moghadam, "Language Barriers to Meme Contagion: The

Case of Entrepreneurship as a Concept in Iran," *Social Science Research Network* May 28, 2008, available at SSRN: http://ssrn.com/abstract=1145647).

13. Interview, May 10, 2002.
14. Of 22 Ministers in the Rafsanjani government of 1989, 7 held a PhD and 9 were engineers. Only 4 members of the cabinet were clerics. See Bahman Baktiari, *Parliamentary Politics in Revolutionary Iran: The Institutionalization of Factional Politics* (Gainesville, FL: University Press of Florida, 1996).
15. Interview, April 21, 2003.
16. J. Schumpeter, *Capitalism, Socialism and Democracy* (London: Unwin University Books, 1950).
17. Saeed Hajjarian, "Ta`ali, takamol, tawse'eh: tahavvol-e gofteman-e taraqqi dar andisheh-ye rawshanfekran-e dini" (Growth, fulfilment, development: the transformation of the discourse of progress in the thinking of religious intellectuals), in *Az shahed-e qodsi ta shahed-e bazaari: `urfi shodan-e din dar sepehr-e siyasat* (From the sacred witness to the profane witness: the secularization of religion in the sphere of politics) (Tehran: Tarh-e Naw, 1380/ 2001), 179–194.
18. Ibid., 193.
19. One of the most ardent proponents of this argument has been Abbas Abdi who supported Mehdi Karroubi during the 2009 presidential elections and repeatedly stressed the need to reduce reliance on oil revenues in the budget to make the government accountable to the people.
20. The single most important contribution to private sector growth was probably the Khatami government's decision to reserve 50 percent of the country's Oil Stabilization Fund for redistribution to private companies through subsidized loans.
21. Interview, April 21, 2003.
22. Author's interview with Pedram Soltanieh, January 27, 2009.
23. The only remaining sector where the state still claims an absolute monopoly on its activities is radio and television broadcasting.
24. "Privatization will lead to prosperity," *Tehran Times* February 20, 2007 (Editorial).
25. Ibid.
26. Francis Fukuyama, *The End of History and the Last Man* (New York: Free Press, 1992).
27. For the Persian text of the "Twenty-Year Perspective," see http://www.modir21.com/1388/08/.
28. Constitution of the Islamic Republic of Iran, article 44, http://www.iranonline.com/iran/iran-info/Government/constitution-4.html.
29. See, for instance, "President for Bigger Private Sector Role in Oil Sector," *Tehran Times* March 11, 2007; and "Ahmadinejad Pledges to Push Iran Privatisation," *IranMania News* February 25, 2007, www.iranmania.com.
30. See, for instance, "Karafarini moqaddameh-ye pishraft ast" (Entrepreneurship is the beginning of progress), *Jam-e Jam* 3 April 22, 2008, http://www.jamejamonline.ir/newstext.aspx?newsnum=100936533413.
31. See Jahangir Amuzegar, "Islamic Social Justice, Iranian Style," *Middle East Policy Journal* XIV, no. 3 (2007).
32. See "Roshd-e bist-o-haft darsadi-ye hajm-e varedat-e Iran dar dah mah-e emsal" (A 27 percent increase in the volume of imports in Iran in the first ten months of this year), *emruz.net*, February 14, 2009, http://emruz.biz/ShowItem.aspx?ID=20658&p=1.
33. See Frederic Wehrey et al., *The Rise of the Pasdaran: Assessing the Domestic Roles of Iran's Islamic Revolutionary Guards Corps* (Santa Monica, CA: RAND Corporation, 2009), http://www.rand.org/pubs/monographs/2008/RAND_MG821.pdf.

34. Keyhani and Jafari Moghadam, "Language Barriers to Meme Contagion."
35. Abdolreza Davari, "Ahmadinjead: ra'is jomhur-e karafarin" (Ahmadinejad: the entrepreneurial president), *Rajanews* November 25, 2008.
36. The World Bank Group: "Doing Business in Iran," http://www.doingbusiness.org /ExploreEconomies/?economyid=91.
37. Interview with Abbas Nasiri, January 27, 2009.
38. Mahmoud Sariolghalam, *The Evolution of the State in Iran: A Political Culture Perspective* (Kuwait: Center for Strategic and Future Studies, 2010).

Part III

Women, Youth, and Society

7

The Green Movement: A Struggle against Islamist Patriarchy?

Fatemeh Sadeghi

Many here and some in Iran are waiting for and hoping for the moment, when secularization will at least come back to the fore and reveal the good, old type of revolution we have always known. I wonder how far they will be taken along this strange, unique road, in which they seek, against the stubbornness of their destiny, against everything they have been for centuries, "something quite different."

(*Michel Foucault, 1988, p. 226*)[1]

Wearing a colorful handmade Turkmen scarf beneath her loose black chador, Zahra Rahnavard, a university professor of Arts and Political Science accompanied her husband, Mir-Hossein Mousavi, the main reformist candidate in his presidential campaign in summer 2009. Holding hands with her husband, she challenged the hegemonic gender ideology of the Islamic Republic based on the impenetrable public/private divide. Some days before the 2009 elections, Mousavi had published his agenda for women, which was remarkable in the postrevolutionary context. The agenda included a number of legal, economic, and sociopolitical rights and reforms women activists and ordinary women had demanded for many years.[2] Years before, at the juncture of the consolidation of the Islamist government, he had also maintained, "If women go back to kitchen, the revolution will fail."[3] Perhaps, Mousavi had also realized that women had to resist the factions determined to exclude them at this pivotal moment. This misogynistic tendency displayed by some revolutionary groups ran counter to the reality of massive participation of women in the 1979 revolutionary process, which made Ayatollah Khomeini confess that the revolution would have been impossible without women. Nevertheless, after the revolution, the Islamists made into law the public/private divide, requiring women to devote themselves to the domestic domain, because men were considered more competent at managing the sociopolitical and economic affairs. Although in postrevolutionary Iran, many women and men challenged this stereotype in different ways, the Green Movement represented the most defiant struggle against the gendered arrangements of the Islamic Republic. This was embodied not only in the actions, but also in the symbols and slogans that came to be associated with the Green Movement. The picture of the revolutionary couple hand in hand and adorned with the slogan "Mousavi, Rahnavard, Equality Between Men and Women," (*Mousavi, Rahnavard, tasavi-ye zan o mard*), for example, was distributed among the people in the days that preceded the elections, which seemingly promised a new era in which women, ethnic groups, and other marginalized parts of the society would be treated more equitably. In such a context, it was not by chance that the two conservative candidates, Mohsen Rezaie and Mahmoud Ahmadinejad, also appeared in public accompanied by their wives, even if the latter were thoroughly wrapped up in their black chadors. In contrast, Zahra Rahnavard was more than a silent company. Soon after the establishment of the Islamic Republic, she had criticized the compulsory *hejab* stipulated by Ayatollah Khomeini and other Islamists.[4] Years later, in May–June 2009, she took an active role in her husband's electoral campaign: she unequivocally condemned both political autocracy and gender discrimination including the compulsory *hejab* in her public speeches and interviews.[5] On many occasions after the elections, she also vehemently criticized the way the government treated women.

The Green Movement has been very much characterized by the novelty of its political actions as well as by its politically subversive symbolism propagated by means of the alternative nonstate social media. Apart from the aforementioned picture, speeches, and statements made by Rahnavard and Mousavi, another image that captured imaginations was that of the killing of Neda Agha Soltan, a 26-year-old woman and student of Art caught on camera-phone. She was reportedly shot to death by a plainclothes *Basiji* in Amir-Abad Street during one of the huge postelectoral street protests in Tehran. Whereas Zahra Rahnavard represented an older generation of religious women with little hope for a better and just society in the future, Neda represented women of the younger generation. Her death was, therefore, very challenging for the conservative establishment and it was for this very reason that the government did its best to manipulate it. Claiming the video to have been fabricated, the state media concertedly attributed it to foreign agents and oppositional groups. Despite these efforts, Neda became a strong icon of the Green Movement. Very much disenchanted with the false promises of the rulers of the country, Neda became the voice of many ordinary young Iranian women who had had no memory of the Islamic Revolution and had been apolitical and yet, had inevitably ended up taking action against their fate. Her death symbolized not only the suffocation of women's demands in the Islamic Republic but also unmasked the systematically intertwined autocratic and discriminatory rule of the country.

Yet, it was not just the Iranian government which had tried to manipulate her death. The monarchist opposition also tried to appropriate Neda's death. Calling Neda his daughter, the former Crown Prince of Iran Reza Pahlavi, son of the deposed Shah, broke down crying[6] at a press conference held on June 22, 2009.[7] A similar disingenuous gesture toward women was exhibited by Mahmoud Ahmadinejad after Neda's death, partly in order to calm the public anger and shock provoked by her death. He suggested that three women would be appointed as ministers in his cabinet. However, Ahmadinejad's claim was greeted with much skepticism by the reformists and feminists who viewed it as more of a trick than a genuine concern for the predicament of Iranian women.[8]

Apart from Neda and Rahnavard, thousands of women actively participated in the Green Movement. In doing so, they also challenged the principles intended to have been internalized by them. Nevertheless, massive participation of women in the political processes of the country was not particular to the Green Movement. Since the Constitutional Revolution of 1906, if not earlier, Iranian history had witnessed women from different strata of society taking part in the political processes.[9] Women of diverse backgrounds had, for example, demonstrated on the streets in support of the National movement of 1952 to have Mohammad Mosaddeq reinstated, the Iranian Revolution of 1979 led by Ayatollah Khomeini, and the Reform Movement of 1997 led by Mohammad Khatami. What is striking in the Green Movement, therefore, is not the fact that large numbers of women took to the streets, or even the diversity of their religious and secular backgrounds. In this chapter, I will argue that the active presence of women in the Green Movement has resulted in the breach of the public/private binary, and the male/female divide on which the gendered power relations of postrevolutionary Iranian society has been heavily grounded. In this way, among the achievements of the Green Movement, one can count not only the shaking up of the political order but also and more importantly for our purposes, defiance of the systematic gender discrimination of the postrevolutionary Islamic apparatus.

For instance, while the images and backgrounds of Zahra Rahnavard and Neda Agha Soltan are very different from each other in terms of the two types of Iranian women that they represent, with one being secular and the other religious/pious, they do share a common trait; the two women obfuscated the demarcations of religiosity and secularism, yet, both of them also embodied a contrast with the officially presented picture of Iranian womanhood. Looking at some of the initiatives embarked upon by women in the Green Movement, this chapter attempts to answer the following questions: in regard to the gender component of the political order, what role has women's social movement and civil society activism played in the Green Movement? How broadly have gender issues been addressed and included in the Green Movement and to what extent could these developments change the notion of womanhood, and gendered dichotomy of the male supremacy, which has been so central to the conservative rule in postrevolutionary Iran?

Based largely on eye-witness accounts, fieldwork, and sociopolitical research done both before and after the emergence of the Green Movement, as well as the news and analyses that appeared on various Iranian websites and Persian blogs (*Weblagestan*), this chapter will, further, trace back some of the reasons for the vast participation of women from diverse backgrounds in the Movement. It will also speculate on some of the challenges that the Movement faced in order to counter the government's repressive tactics effectively.

Against Humiliation

Perhaps more than any other factor, it was a common sense of humiliation among different strata of society that instigated the Green Movement. Apart from the inadequacy and incompetence of Ahmadinejad's government and policies, which included abuse of power and arbitrary rule, the acts, speeches, and conduct associated with his person and that of his allies generally ran counter to the social mores and customs prevalent in the Iranian way of life. Examples abound. Among them, was the case of an official parliamentary session in 2005, soon after Ahmadinejad's election to his first term as president. There, to the laughter of the conservative parliamentarians present, Ahmadinejad offended women by saying that men could not be expected to be monogamous and loyal to one wife.

Uniting around "Human Dignity" as the slogan of the oppositional candidates, many people were determined to stand against the systematic humiliation on the part of Ahmadinejad and his allies. Thus, the reformist factions, pro-civil rights groups, and different strata of society joined together on the one side, and the conservative camps including Ahmadinejad and his allies, the Leader, the majority of the members of the parliament, the judiciary, the Islamic Republic Guardian Corps, the *Basij* organizations, the governmental seminary, and the conservative ulama on the other. Once the election results were announced, the oppositional factions claimed them fraudulent and accused Ahmadinejad's administration of manipulation of votes. Soon after, the arrests began, of the leading members of the reformist parties, together with the violent suppression of the demonstrations of hundreds of thousands of people who peacefully demonstrated in major cities, especially in Tehran. While they began initially as protests against electoral fraud, with time, the demonstrations became increasingly radicalized, eventually targeting the Leader and the entire political establishment. Street protests were fiercely suppressed and finally, the leaders of the movement, Mir-Hossein Mousavi and Mehdi Karroubi, along with their wives were put under house arrest in January 2011.

Ahmadinejad's Discriminatory Policies toward Women

Although institutionalized discrimination against women has characterized the past 30 years of the Islamic Republic, the neoconservatives have shown strong determination to counter much of the progress that had been made by women and by 8 years of a reformist government (1997–2005). For the purpose of this chapter, I will focus mainly on some of Ahmadinejad's discriminatory gender policies and the responses to them on the part of ordinary women, as well as political and civil activists.

In the course of his first term as president (2005–2009), political freedom decreased dramatically. A range of independent newspapers and journals, as well as civil society organizations including women's associations were shut down and many civil and political activists intimidated and imprisoned. At the same time, these policies were followed by the consolidation of different economic and financial governmental organizations and paramilitary sectors like the *Basij*.[10] Ahmadinejad's inclination toward autocratic rule resulted in the cancellation or abolition of a number of administrative institutions like the "Management and Planning Organization," which had been responsible for the economic planning and management of the country. Such actions resulted in, among other things, the harsh criticisms by a range of conservative and reformist groups, accusing him of ignoring the law and the Constitution, thereby, further deepening the split among the political elite.

From the beginning of the conservatives' take over of power in 2005, they were suspicious of women's civil-right activism.[11] It was during Ahmadinejad's tenure that the gender quota system to limit the number of female students attending university was reintroduced. Moreover, the government's ideological machine was backed by institutions such as the "Center for Women and Family Affairs," which had proposed plans such as the "Family Bill" introduced in the summer of 2007, making it easier and more straightforward for men to take a second wife. This bill also imposed taxes on women's alimony.[12] Another program, called the "Mercy Plan" (*tarh e rahmat*), was introduced in 2006, with the goal of indoctrinating housewives to be more obedient to their husbands; yet another to ban women from work outside the home, and to promote polygamy. There was also an attempt by the government to enforce the "Plan to Promote Public Chastity," forcing all institutions to strictly enforce both women's dress codes as well as the rule against the mingling of men and women in workplaces, universities, and many other public spaces.[13] Similarly, in order to limit the participation of women in public life outside of the home, women's working hours were reduced to allow women to have more time for family chores. In short, all these programs aimed to confine women to the home and to compel them to take care of their husbands for fear that the husband would take another wife.

Perhaps Ahmadinejad's most aggressive policy was the "Social Security Plan" (*tarh e amniyat- e ejtema'i*). The plan mostly targeted "improperly-veiled" women, leading in turn to the harassment and police searches of thousands of young women on the streets of Tehran and other cities. It also included men, many of whom were arrested, accused of being "hooligans and saboteurs," and taken to places like Kahrizak camp, south of Tehran.[14]

As a result of these policies that were aimed at both the middle- and lower-middle-class women, many women became increasingly politicized. By the time of the 2009 presidential elections, many people from different strata of society became mobilized to vote for other candidates. The basis of the motivation for many was to stop Ahmadinejad from winning a second term.

In April 2009, almost two months before the presidential elections, 42 women's groups joined together to create a "Women's Coalition" in preparation for the elections. Without supporting any particular candidate, the Coalition raised two specific demands for the consideration of the candidates: the ratification of the "UN Convention on the Elimination of Discrimination Against Women" and the revision of Articles 19, 20, 21, and 115 of the Iranian Constitution enshrining gender discrimination. A number of women also chose to participate actively in the electoral campaigns of the reformist candidates. Among them was Jamileh

Kadivar, a well-known reformist political activist, and former parliamentarian, who came forward as the main supporter of Mehdi Karroubi's electoral campaign. As a reformist candidate, Karroubi not only promised the conditional ratification of the "UN Convention on the Elimination of Discrimination Against Women" that had been previously blocked by the Guardian Council after its ratification by the sixth reformist *majles* (1999–2003), but he also promised the loosening of the compulsory *hejab* regulations.

Politicization of Women

In addition to women activists, many students and ordinary women also joined the groups opposing Ahmadinejad, because of his damaging and discriminatory policies regarding women. Therefore, the presidential elections of 2009 were also a manifestation of the politicization of women from all sectors and backgrounds. During the presidential campaign, a number of students and civil rights activists, university professors, artists, intellectuals, and journalists published separate statements, in which they invited people to participate in the elections and vote for the reformist candidates. According to some personal observations, women voters outnumbered men, which was very similar to the presidential elections of 1997. Many women also participated in the mass demonstrations that followed the elections. They constituted not only the ranks of the prominent political civil activists, and journalists, but also have continued to pay a high price for their activism by being arrested, convicted, and sentenced to long prison terms. Compared to the previous events in the history of Iran, this time the number of women prisoners was quite significant.

As has been argued, the politicization of women is very much rooted in the Islamic Republic's gender discrimination and the four years of Ahmadinejad's presidency. The institutionalized discrimination affected middle-class women the hardest. With regard to lower-class women, while it is not yet clear what percentage from among them might have voted for the reformist candidates in the presidential elections of 2009, no definitive conclusion can be drawn either on whether the majority of men and women from the lower classes voted for the conservative candidates in the 2009 presidential elections. In fact, the findings of some research carried out regarding women and their political participation in different poor-suburban areas of Iranian cities including Mashhad, Tehran, Zahedan, Bam, and Kerman between 2006 and 2007, indicate that many women from the lower-class strata of society might have voted for Mousavi, since his economic agenda was based on social justice and he was known as an effective politician during the eight years of war with Iraq (1981–1989).[15]

According to my findings in a recently conducted research,[16] a large number of lower-class women[17] voted for Ahmadinejad in the 2005 presidential elections. However, many of them were not satisfied with the subsequent economic policies of his government when interviewed two years later. They maintained that the most important problems they suffered from consisted of unemployment (of both male and female members of their families including their husbands who were the heads of the households and the main breadwinners), high rates of inflation, increasing prices of basic needs including the cost of accommodation, drug addiction of many men, women, and youth, and the inability of families to financially help their children start their own families. In fact, Ahmadinejad's economic policies had impoverished many lower classes. Therefore, even if the Green Movement began first and foremost as a middle-class phenomenon especially with regard to its organization and social networks, there is ample evidence that its appeal broadened to comprise many people from the lower classes. Nevertheless, the political participation and mobilization of the lower classes seem to have been restricted to less costly actions like casting votes rather than taking part in mass demonstrations. Despite this, according to my personal observations at least in the early stages of the mass street demonstrations, large antigovernment protests also took place in the less affluent parts of south Tehran, where the lower classes traditionally live.

By and large, even though many members of the lower classes were not satisfied with the economic and political conditions they lived in,[18] in the long run they were unlikely to become involved in actions that were considered to have a high risk factor and political consequences that they could ill afford, unlike the middle classes who could take a chance. The level of participation of the lower classes in summer 2009 seems to have been very much similar to that of the Islamic Revolution of 1979, in which case, as indicated by Asef Bayat,[19] the majority of the lower classes were not only among the last strata of society to join the revolution but also among the first to leave it behind. As is well known, it was the young, educated middle classes that constituted the main agents of the Iranian Revolution.

Agonistic Practices in an Antagonistic Context

So far as women and gender relations are concerned, the Green Movement was characterized by sidestepping the public/private demarcation, a sociopolitically constructed boundary, which has nevertheless proved crucial for the gender ideology of the Islamic Republic. It was not only women, but also to some extent a large number of men including the reformist leaders, who bypassed the public/private divide. Merging the public/private roles, many women participants, at different levels, managed to embark on both domesticated roles such as being mothers, wives, daughters, and independent citizens at one and the same time. Therefore, the Green Movement, among other things, seems to have been tremendously empowering for those Iranian women, who were involved in it. One of the women's aims was to change the power relations in a more egalitarian and less discriminatory way. However, it would be more accurate to consider the movement as a process. That is why it would be safe to speculate that the Green Movement would most likely have a lasting impact on Iranian society, politics, and culture regardless of its degree of success in the near future.

It was not only ordinary women and women political activists that were involved in the movement, but there were also numerous civic activists, some of whom continue to be in prison at the time of writing this chapter. Although many women were not involved in the activities of women's organizations like the "One Million Signature Campaign," the Green Movement was able to surpass many civic activities including those particular to women's organizations. This was because the emergence of a new political situation necessitated different kinds of actions. The Green Movement was first and foremost nurtured by an antagonistic situation as indicated by the main characteristics of postelectoral politics. According to Chantal Mouffe,[20] a political situation is antagonistic if the confrontations between different groups reach such a point of hostility that society and politics get divided into adversarial camps. Such a situation seems to have been the case in the aftermath of the 2009 presidential elections. Whereas before the elections, many political and civil society activists, though with difficulty, could advance women's demands, as a result of the antagonistic situation that ensued the elections, many of these activities were suspended. In addition, many activists, either voluntarily or forcefully, left the country. By and large, the postelectoral atmosphere witnessed a decline in civil activities on the part of different sectors. A number of political and civil institutions and parties including *Jebheh-ye Mosharekat* (Islamic Iran Participation Front) along with its women's branch, human rights organizations, and NGOs including the "Center for the Defense of Human Rights" founded by Shirin Ebadi, the Nobel Laureate, were shut down, and some of their members, imprisoned. Furthermore, the "One Million Signatures Campaign," which had officially begun its activities in summer 2006, and which had received much recognition as the most effective campaign against the discriminatory policies of the Islamic Republic became much less active, with some of its members leaving the country. Thus, despite the strong conflict between state and society, the preelectoral circumstances seemed to have been more suitable for collective civic activities as compared to the postelectoral era.

Nonetheless, the suspension of the civil society activities and social movements does not necessarily entail their termination or dissociation from the political demands embodied in the Green Movement. Among the associations and groups whose activities were more political in nature, were the "Islamic Student Associations," which became incorporated in the Green Movement, and thereafter, had some of their most active members such as Bahareh Hedayat, the elected head of the Women's branch of "*Tahkim-e Vahdat*,"[21] jailed. Other civic organizations including those of women were marginalized with some of their members joining the "Greens." It seems that so long as the antagonistic situation endures, civic and political activities will remain suspended. Consequently, the postelectoral era has brought about at least two major changes with regard to civil society organizations in general and gender-specific groups in particular: First, there has been a profound transformation in the state-society relations resulting in the loss of trust and the emergence of an openly antagonistic situation, and second, the replacement of different kinds of civic activism with an overarching political movement, giving rise to an increasing policing of the society on the part of the authorities.

The Campaign of Veiled Men

Despite the repressive and very unpleasant situation of the aftermath of the election, so far as gender equality is concerned, the Green Movement signals a new era. If this era ends in a more democratic future, it is likely to be vested with a stronger level of gender equality. This would be primarily due to the struggles of women in postrevolutionary Iran in general, and the significant challenging role women played in the Green Movement more specifically.

The presence of women in the movement has not been limited to their standing alongside men and supporting them in their endeavors. Rather, the Green Movement provided an opportunity for many women to play a dual role: on the one hand, they became directly engaged in the political process in their capacity as independent civil and political activists, advocates, journalists, artists, and street protesters, and on the other, as wives, mothers, and daughters of men. While women managed to play these overlapping roles, they also succeeded to go beyond the well-established demarcations set by the postrevolutionary ideological apparatus. Men too, in effect, began to question the stereotypical roles embodied in the social norms and encouraged by the regime. The campaign in support of Majid Tavakoli represents a good example.[22] Majid Tavakoli, an activist student, was arrested and jailed on December 6, 2009, because of his outspoken public speech that he gave in the middle of the street confrontations. Soon after his arrest, the state-run media published pictures, in which he was most probably forced to wear a black chador and *maqne'eh* (a strict head cover). They allegedly claimed that by wearing a chador, he had planned to escape incognito. Regardless of what actually happened, the distribution of these pictures was apparently aimed at humiliating Majid by means of making him appear in women's clothing and, thus, taking away his manhood. The pictures and allegations provoked much anger among the "Greens." In response, many men, both inside and outside the country, wore chadors and headscarves in solidarity with Majid and disseminated their pictures on social media. Consequently, the act of the government that had initially been launched to humiliate Majid, inadvertently also targeted the compulsory *hejab*, since it contradicted the persistent message of the Islamic government that "*hejab* is immunity" (*hejab masouniyat ast*). Majid's pictures unwittingly communicated the idea that not only does compulsory *hejab* not serve as protection, but also that it actually can be used to humiliate both women and men. On the other hand, the campaign of the supporters of Majid bore the message that there was nothing humiliating and shameful in a woman's dress, even if a man were to wear it. Both the campaign in support of Majid and the action of the government contradicted the slogans and stereotypes of the Islamic Republic. This incident represented also a big difference with the events that took place in March 1979, when many women demonstrated against the compulsory *hejab* and were reportedly beaten in some cases, while many men were disinterestedly watching them. Furthermore, whereas in the Islamic Revolution, many unveiled women became veiled in solidarity with their veiled counterparts, in the Green Movement men became veiled in solidarity with another man. This signaled a dramatic change in the symbolic order of the society. Contrary to the propagated notion maintaining women as essentially "weak" (*za'ifeh*), both the action of the government in forcibly veiling Majid and the campaign of the "Greens" illuminated that femininity and masculinity are social constructs. Apart from challenging the fixed essentialist notions of femininity and masculinity, which were reinforced after the establishment of the Islamic Republic, the campaign also defied the underlying gender ideas of the Iranian Revolution of 1979, in which men and women kept apart as they demonstrated. It would be premature, however, to conclude that because of the episodes such as the one described above the society, as a whole, has realized the instability of gendered notions and roles. Nevertheless, it would be fair to say that as a result of some opportunities brought about by the Green Movement, many men and women have challenged these demarcations in an unprecedented way, and that it is likely that these actions will help shape the historical memory in some fashion.

Love as Politics

Above all, the actions and mediations initiated by women under the umbrella of the Green Movement clearly blurred the boundaries between the private and the public as illustrated in numerous examples, notably the cases of women's love letters and the "Mourning Mothers." Following the arrest and imprisonment of a large number of activists in the wake of the 2009 presidential elections, the publication of a series of love letters by the prisoners' wives on the Internet and social media, protesting against the unjust and brutal actions of the government toward their husbands while also expressing their own sentiments about their husbands was unprecedented. By referring to the violent atmosphere in the country, these letters represented not only a political testimonial and act of defiance but also an unparalleled action bypassing the public/private distinctions and hegemonic sociocultural stereotypes.

In Persian culture, love is treated in contradictory ways. While in the Sufi tradition (as in the poetry of Hafez and Rumi), worldly love is celebrated as a way toward spirituality, in the worldview of Islamists and orthodox conservative ulama, it is regarded by and large as shameful. Therefore, speaking of love in public is not only unusual but also highly defiant of social expectations, as in the case of the picture of Mousavi and Rahnavard holding hands, mentioned earlier. Furthermore, in a context where almost no male politician would appear publicly with his wife, it was antihegemonic. In a similar vein, by giving voice to personal feelings in public, the campaign of love letters rattled and upset the domestic (private)/public binary, which has been the center piece of not only Islamist gender attitudes, but also much of Persian culture. This campaign was initiated some time around January 2010, by the wives of political prisoners, whose husbands had been kept in jail for some months, illegally, without any charges. In response to these letters, some male political prisoners also wrote their own love letters. Notable among these letters was that of Fakhrosadat Mohtashamipour, the reformist political activist and wife of Mostafa Tajzadeh, the well-known reformist politician, and addressee of her letters.[23]

"In my opinion," Fakhrosadat wrote, "it is necessary to document all feelings, moods, thoughts and talk of these days as part of the history of our revolution and our times."[24] In publicizing love and transforming it into a political act as a way of making politics more humane, this women's initiative evoked much jubilation among the "Greens."

There are plenty such examples. In another similar instance, the wife of a well-known reformist politician was heard crying out to her husband, "I love you," as she stood outside the Revolutionary Court alongside the families of other political prisoners. Thus, it seemed that for the first time in the contemporary history of Iran, love was brought into the public not as something to be ashamed of, a view still held by conventional culture and politics, but as a human expression and a very effective political measure at the same time.

Other comparable initiatives also point to women adopting similar multiple roles. Among them was the founding of a group known as the "Mourning Mothers," whose purpose was to stand peacefully and protest the killings and acts of violence perpetrated against the Iranian youth and women. This initiative was in fact rooted in a previous campaign launched in 2007 by some women activists aimed at fighting against all acts of war and violence. Originally called "Mothers of Peace," it was set up to mobilize women against military attacks, nuclear proliferation, and armaments and any other actions that could instigate war. After the death of Neda Agha Soltan and Sohrab A'rabi, a 19-year-old young man reportedly murdered in prison, the campaign was reoriented toward actions against the violent suppression of the demonstrators and dissidents by the Iranian security police and plainclothesmen. This was very much influenced and inspired by the experiences of women in other countries like Argentina where the mothers of the "disappeared" and people murdered by the military Junta initiated the act of mourning as a means of protest and opposition. Just as the "Mothers of the disappeared" in Argentina, began a series of mourning ceremonies, which in effect added political meaning to the expressions of grief, turning an act of mourning into a means for protest and opposition, so did the "Mourning Mothers" in Iran initiate weekly gatherings in different public places.[25] Despite their peaceful protest, they were attacked by the police several times, leading to the arrest and imprisonment of a number of them in early January 2010. The "Mourning Mothers" represent another example of the diverse roles played by women in the Green Movement.

A third example consists of the cases of women's interventions to save the lives of both the protestors and the police in the course of street demonstrations. On many occasions when the police arrested the youth on the streets, women stepped forward and attempted to release them from the hands of the security police. On other occasions, women mediated between the angry protesters and the police in conflict situations, and when the security police fell into people's hands. As citizens with equal rights, these women saw no conflict between political involvement on the one hand, and "motherly" nonviolent actions on behalf of the whole nation on the other. Hence, the same women who chanted against the government, on other occasions initiated different campaigns and involvement to prevent violence against their own children. Again, these instances are manifestations of how deep women could break up the established notion of femininity as had been defined by the ideological apparatuses.

In addition to the numerous instances of women's involvement, it would be worth mentioning another unprecedented dimension of the Green Movement, namely, the publicizing of issues such as sexual harassment, which would have been considered too taboo to be discussed in public in the previous 30 years. The challenge against male supremacy as a fundamental aspect of Iranian politics, increasingly, gained a central role in the Green Movement. Therefore, although there were many women, who participated in the movement and played a major role in the whole process, the issue at stake went far beyond that. The sexual harassment and humiliation of the opposition, in fact, uncovered the aim of the phallocentric hegemony to humiliate its opponents as a way of discrediting and silencing them. In order to counter this, many "Greens" while disseminating information, gradually began publicizing reported violations. For instance, even though the news regarding Kahrizak detention camp as revealed mostly by Mehdi Karroubi was totally shocking and distressing, it also broke many taboos, and for the very first time, motivated public discussions against the harassment of the political opposition as a systematic action that had been resorted to by the Iranian regime over the past 30 years. While similar actions had been experienced by the members of the oppositional groups in the past, they had never managed to discuss it publicly either out of fear of becoming stigmatized or out of the internalization of the same principle that it is the victims of harassment, and not the agents of torture and persecution that are the guilty party.

Conclusion

Although the Green Movement has been suppressed in every way, the role of women in this symbolically subversive development was quite decisive in a number of ways. As has been argued, women took advantage of the Green Movement as an opportunity to cross the constructed sociopolitical divide between the public and the domestic/private, and the male and the female, and to claim equal citizenship through political action. Having become politicized as a result of discriminatory humiliating actions carried out by the conservatives, many women from different sectors of society and with various levels of political participation and experience became increasingly involved in the political process. Therefore, among other things, the Green Movement was proof of the failure of the conservative gender hegemony through the indoctrination of domesticity and discrimination, even though many women's civil activities of the previous years had been fragmented and suspended as a result of the antagonistic situation.

At the same time, the Green Movement provided an opportunity for men to revise many stereotypes that had been ruling their minds. The large protests, inadvertently, raised a number of issues that had been considered taboo in the past. Among them were the compulsory *hejab* and sexual harassment of the male and female prisoners that had always been a concern but had never been addressed in public before. Following the dissemination of the news about the torture and harassment of the detainees, it seemed more difficult to ignore and sweep it under the carpet, as had been the case in previous years.

One could argue that it was because of the Green Movement that women's demands regarding equality have been heard and recognized by more people. This is the case with the new family law, which has been ratified in March 2011.

Whereas before the 2009 presidential elections, it was mostly women activists who protested against the bill, now many more people, from different walks of life, are aware and talk about this. Despite this, many questions remain unanswered; among them, the extent to which women's claim to equality and full-fledged citizenship will be incorporated into the current and future politics of Iran, and whether their major role and rights will be recognized by any government in the future.

Perhaps Foucault's observations on the Iranian Revolution, quoted at the beginning of this article continue to have some validity. However, there is one exception: Similar to the 1978–1979 revolution, the Green Movement was neither secular nor religious; it could be considered beyond both secularism and religiosity. It was also a development in which many ordinary women and men from different backgrounds participated. In 2009 also, people rebelled "against the stubbornness of their destiny, against everything they have been for centuries." However, the one difference is the possibility that the Green Movement will come to be remembered as unique in that it was not only advanced by women, but also provided an opportunity for them, alongside men, to defy social attitudes toward gender, and patriarchal arbitrary rule over the country in unprecedented ways.

Notes

1. Michel Foucault, "Iran: The Spirit of a World without Spirit," in *Politics, Philosophy, Culture: Interviews and Other Writings, 1977–1984,* ed. Lawrence D Kritzman, trans. Alan Sheridan et al. (New York: Routledge, 1988), 211–226.
2. "Five Goals and Forty-five Strategies for Solving Women's Problems," *Kalameh-ye sabz* 1, no. 11 (May 30, 2009).
3. Mir-Hossein Mousavi's Interview, *Zan e Ruz* no. 1058, February 1985.
4. Parvin Paidar, *Women and the Political Process in Twentieth Century Iran* (Cambridge, UK: Cambridge University Press, 1995).
5. *Kalameh-ye sabz* 1, no. 1 (May 18, 2009).
6. http://www.youtube.com/watch?v=slFIQ2kLzyY
7. As indicated by Nicholas Mirzoeff, Neda Agha Soltan's death was used by the Crown Prince for making a renewed claim to be the "father" of Iran and of Iranian women. See Nicholas Mirzoeff, "What We Saw: Politics in the Mirror of Neda Agha-Soltan," *Social Text: Periscope* November 2009, http://www.socialtextjournal.org/periscope/2009/11/what-we-saw-politics-in-the-mirror-of-neda-agha-soltan.php#more
8. Nazanin Shahrokni, "All the President's Women," *Middle East Report* 39, no. 4 (Winter 2009): 2–6.
9. Eliz Sanasarian, *The Women's Rights Movement in Iran: Mutiny, Appeasement and Repression from 1900 to Khomeini* (New York: Praeger, 1982), 10–27.
10. Kaveh Ehsani, "Survival through Dispossession: Privatization of Public Goods in the Islamic Republic," *Middle East Report* 39, no. 250 (Spring 2009): 26–33.
11. Homa Hoodfar, "Activism under the Radar: Volunteer Health Workers in Iran," *Middle East Report* 39, no. 250 (Spring 2009): 56–60.
12. Many women activists at the time opposed some articles of this bill, which permitted polygamy, and, thus, requested the parliament to revise them. They also started campaigning against these articles through different means including sending letters to the

deputies, informing people about the consequences of this code, and finally gathering in the parliament building to negotiate with parliamentarians. Due to these efforts, the family code was temporarily suspended before its final ratification in March 2012. In the meantime, it also was criticized vehemently among others by Zahra Rahnavard and Ashraf Boroujerdi. See the following links: http://khabaronline.ir/news-34755.aspx; http://www.fardanews.com/fa/pages/?cid=99926; http://emruz.info/ShowItem.aspx?ID=27131&p=1.

13. Fatemeh Sadeghi, "The Foot Soldiers of the Islamic Republic's Culture of Modesty," *Middle East Report* 39, no. 250 (Spring 2009): 50–55.

14. At the time when the "Social Security Plan" was being carried out, some news came out confirming that Kahrizak was a detention camp, where people experienced the most severe mistreatment, without having any access to the law. The news, however, was not taken seriously until some time after the June 2009 elections when the camp turned out to be a horrible hidden detention center where a number of the young protesters were taken to. Some of them, not only, were tortured to death, but there were also allegations that others had been raped and intimidated. The abuse was so scandalous that a few months later, the *Majles* sought to investigate the case and indict Saeed Mortazavi as the perpetrator. However, the investigation was blocked. Finally, the court convicted not the main individuals responsible, but a number of soldiers, who reportedly were only carrying out orders. The case was finally closed without any clear result. Mortazavi was later appointed by Ahmadinejad as the head of another key organization in the administration.

15. Fatemeh Sadeghi, "Lower Class Women and Tradition in Iran," *Goft-o-gu* no. 56 (Summer 2010): 127–146.

16. Ibid.

17. By "lower class women," I mean women from low-income families, who have hardly had access to the formal education that middle-class women have enjoyed.

18. This is again based on the interviews and conversations that I had with a number of people in Tehran before the 2009 presidential elections.

19. Asef Bayat, *Street Politics: Poor People's Movement in Iran* (New York: Columbia University Press, 1997). See also, Ahmad Ashraf and Ali Banuazizi, "The State, Classes, and Modes of Mobilization in the Iranian Revolution," *State, Culture, and Society* 1, no. 3 (Spring 1985): 3–40.

20. Chantal Mouffe, *On the Political: Thinking in Action* (London and New York: Routledge, 2005).

21. *Tahkim-e Vahdat* was an Islamist student organization that was originally founded in 1979, but in the course of the years, changed its views and came to favor reform under Khatami.

22. Ziba Mir-Hosseini, "Broken Taboos in Post-Election Iran," *Middle East Report Online*, December 17, 2009, http://www.merip.org/mero/mero121709.html.

23. www.kaleme.com/1389/11/08/klm-45273/.

24. bayaniye02.blogspot.com/2011/01/blog-post_3176.html.

25. http://www.madaraneazadar.blogspot.com/; http://www.motherspeace.com/spip.php?article84.

8

Sociodemographic Changes in the Family and Their Impact on the Sociopolitical Behavior of the Youth in Postrevolutionary Iran

Marie Ladier-Fouladi

Introduction

Iran's sociopolitical environment has been dramatically transformed during the last three decades. The young age structure of Iranians, especially the significant percentage of the people under the age of 25 years, is often presented as the main factor behind these changes. No doubt, the youth constitute a major factor that can be held accountable for the recent transformations, but based on the existing statistics (more exactly since 1956), the youth have always constituted a large share of the Iranian population with those under the age of 25 years constituting almost 60 percent of the population. Besides, this feature is not exclusive to Iran. Until the early 1970s, as a result of the high rates of births and deaths, 58 to 65 percent of the population in the entire developing countries consisted of young individuals under the age of 25 years. Yet, none of these countries experienced revolutionary transformations in the 1970s in the way that Iran did in 1978–1979. Therefore, it is unlikely that the sheer number of the youth and the young age structure of population are the only factors accounting for the sociopolitical changes taking place in the country. It is, therefore, necessary to consider all historical, social, demographic, political, and cultural conditions that have influenced the youth at different times and have led them to take on the role of agents of change.

Indeed, the role of youth was decisive in the outbreak of the events that shook Iran in the 1970s. It was from the mid-1970s that the youth (generations born during the 1950s) expressed a desire for profound change and a more open sociopolitical arena. This culminated in the 1979 revolution in which the youth constituted the principal actors. Similar aspirations were also manifested in the shape of the broad participation of a new generation of youth in various elections that took place between 1997 and 2001, and later, in June 2009. Although these different generations of young people may have had similar objectives, namely a more open social and political environment, they acted in contrasting ways in fulfilling their aims. The youth of "yesterday" chose revolution, by definition a violent act, whereas, the generation of youth of "today" has opted for nonviolence and a civil rights movement. Thus, within less than 20 years, the political actions of the youth, belonging to two different generations, have resulted in two completely different sociopolitical configurations. What makes the previous generation of the youth so different from the present generation is most certainly the very different sociodemographic context of the 1970s in comparison to that of the 1990s, during which the youth have grown up and their social and political behavior is formed. The sharp decline in fertility, starting in the mid-1980s,[1] led to a rapid reduction in family size. These dramatic sociodemographic changes, which happened after the 1979 revolution and despite the Islamic Republic, have played an important role in the destabilization of the patriarchal system that at this time was still dominating the families. Moreover, the wide expansion of education from the 1980s onward has enabled a greater number of young people not only to attend school but also to prolong their schooling. Accordingly, the average age of young men and women at first marriage has continued to rise. Consequently, the new generations—born around the end of the 1970s—whose education level was higher than that of their parents, especially their fathers, continued to live for many more years with their parents. This situation is novel in Iran given the fact that for the first time, the hierarchy in the level of education has weakened the age hierarchy rooted in the patriarchal system. Fathers are no longer necessarily figures of authority, and parent-child relationships have increasingly become based on dialogue or conflict rather than on the traditional values of obedience and submission.[2] The argument here is that it is these significant changes that have resulted in the political transformation that occurred from the mid-1990s onward, with the mobilization of the youth and the emergence of a civil society.

This chapter will examine the substantial sociodemographic changes in the family in Iran and put this assertion to the test by analyzing the sociodemographic and the cultural characteristics of the youth as well as their aspirations for the democratization of the social and political arenas. This study is based on data provided by the 1976, 1986, 1996, and 2006 Iranian censuses and two sociodemographic surveys that were carried out in Iran in January 2002 and in January 2004.[3]

Demographic Changes and Social Transformations

Fall in Fertility

In 1966, the total fertility rate was very high and each woman was bearing on average 7.9 children (figure 8.1).[4] This fertility rate then fell very slowly to a level of 6.8 in 1979. Thus, during the 1960s and the 1970s, contrary to widespread

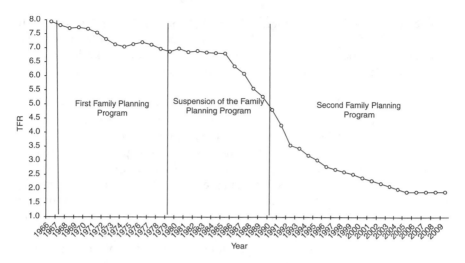

Figure 8.1   Total fertility rates (whole country).

Source: The author's own estimates based on adjusted birth data

opinion, demographic behaviors did not change rapidly.[5] The delayed socioeconomic development of the country had widely contributed to the preservation of
traditional values. In accordance with the patriarchal traditions, the high level of
fertility constituted a social norm, and women who had already been relegated to
an inferior position because of their gender and were at their spouses' service, had
to bear several children in order to raise big families. Fertility, then, was a guarantee allowing a woman to prolong her conjugal life, just as procreation and raising her children, by and large, constituted the entirety of the role of a woman and
the source of her identity, without which she would be marginalized. The influence of these traditions was so important that the first Family Planning Program,
implemented in 1967,[6] despite substantial financial support and the involvement
of several ministerial organizations, did not actually succeed. Within ten years,
the proportion of "family planning acceptors" among women aged 15–49 years
rose from 0.02 percent in 1967 to only 11 percent in 1977.[7]

After the 1979 revolution, the Islamic government put an end to the activities of family planning clinics for political reasons. In February 1980, however,
Ayatollah Khomeini issued a *fatwa* in which contraception was authorized on two
conditions: first, that the method employed did not impair the human organs,
and second, the spouse agreed to its use. Following this *fatwa*, the family planning clinics were reorganized under the auspices of the Ministry of Health, and
contraceptives were distributed free of charge, although in limited choices and
quantities owing to the war and the economic embargo against Iran; this time
round, however, no advertising campaigns in favor of birth control accompanied
the distributions. Nonetheless, the contraceptives were put on sale at affordable
prices in pharmacies.[8]

In spite of the fact that there were no birth control advertising campaigns,
the total fertility rate, after a short period of stability between 1979 and 1985,

took a very rapid downward course: dropping from 6.4 children per woman in 1986 to 5.3 in 1989 (a decline of 1.1 children in the space of only three years). However paradoxical this may seem, the fertility transition in Iran began under the Islamic Republic despite the political speeches and the *Sharia* laws, which were obviously gender biased.

It was following the end of the Iraq-Iran war (in August 1988) that the Islamic government finally adopted a population policy, which was overtly in favor of birth control.[9] The Ministry of Health was then invited to reorganize its Family Planning Department in order to steer the new population policy. Before putting its program in place, the Ministry conducted a KAP (Knowledge, Attitude, and Practice) survey on 9,000 married women aged 15–44 years, in 1989.[10] According to the results, 28 percent of women (33 percent in urban and 21 percent in rural areas) were then using a modern method of contraception (oral contraceptive, condom, or IUD) and 21 percent of them (31 percent in cities and 10 percent in villages) a traditional method of contraception (i.e., 50 percent of married women; 64 percent in urban and 31 percent in rural areas were using either modern or traditional methods of contraception). These percentages of contraceptive users among women together with the sharp decrease in fertility during a period when there was no active family planning program (1980–1989) reveal that the women were already motivated to control their fertility; indeed, the decline in fertility had started already in 1986, a full three years before the implementation of the Family Planning Program by the Islamic Republic in December 1989. In view of the motivation of women, the second birth control campaign, contrary to the first one, was received favorably. This new policy merely fell into step with a movement that was already under way and, by smoothing the route, accelerated the decline in fertility. Since then, fertility has continued to fall with a drop from 4.8 children per woman in 1990 to 1.9 in 2008.[11] In other words, fertility decreased by nearly 70 percent in only 15 years, between 1985 and 2000. This spectacular fall in fertility makes the Iranian demographic transition one of the fastest in history. The drop in fertility can largely be explained by the proportion of women contraceptive users, which continued to increase. In 1991, one year after an extremely active family planning policy had been implemented, a new KAP survey conducted by the Ministry of Health showed that 45 percent of married women aged 15–45 years were current users of a modern contraceptive method (pill, IUD, or condom) and 22 percent of them a traditional contraceptive method (i.e., two women out of three controlled their fertility).[12] In 2000, nearly 74 percent of married women aged 15–49 years were current users of contraceptive methods, of which 56 percent were using a modern contraceptive method and 18 percent a traditional one.[13]

Nevertheless, we should not make the mistake and assume that the fertility transition has its origin in the Family Planning Program of the Islamic Republic. It had already dropped by 1.6 children, between 1979 and 1989, and its considerable fall in the 1990s was first of all bound to the will of women to bear fewer children. The Family Planning programs have only facilitated the fulfillment of this aspiration.

The fertility transition was indeed the result of the transformation that occurred in the reproductive behavior of young women whose education level was higher than that of their elder sisters and who had for the most part participated in the revolution. It could even be claimed that young women continued *their own revolution* by taking control over their fertility. The 1979 revolution provided the opportunity to a great number of young women to participate for the first time in a collective sociopolitical action and fight alongside men against the monarchical regime. This experience influenced their aspirations and objectives profoundly. Henceforth, young women defined a new role for themselves in the family and society: they no longer submitted to the traditional values that confined their place to the domestic arena in which they were only supposed to carry out the role of subordinate spouse and mother of multiple children.[14] In this way, the fall in fertility constituted a very important event in the social history of Iran. It both pointed to and explained the beginnings of the transformation of the patriarchal structure of Iranian society, especially the significant change in the position of women in a political context that paradoxically was not favorable to women.

Women's Education and Labor Force Participation

The social keystone of this important transformation was unquestionably the progress in young women's schooling starting in the 1980s. As a result of the policy of the prerevolutionary governments that privileged the large cities at the expense of the rural and peripheral regions, an important part of the population, in particular women, could not gain access to education. Therefore, in 1966, among women of reproductive age (15 to 49 years) only 15 percent were literate (34 percent in urban and 2 percent in rural areas). These women had spent, on average, only 0.93 years in school (2.2 years in urban and 0.10 years in rural areas). Ten years later, by 1976, a large majority of women aged 15–49 years still remained illiterate. The literacy rate of women aged 15–49 years was 28 percent (50 percent in urban and 8 percent in rural areas) and they spent, on average, 1.9 years in school (3.6 years in urban and 0.4 years in rural areas).

After the revolution, the Islamic government embarked on a wide socioeconomic development program in order to meet the needs of men and women who had overthrown the monarchy and looked to the new regime to improve their living conditions, access to health, education, and housing.[15] One of the priorities in this program was to expand educational infrastructure rapidly in order to include all urban areas. Despite shortcomings in the organization of schooling and literacy, especially in the early 1980s, the expansion of education was particularly beneficial to women whose access to schools rose at an accelerated pace. Thus, female literacy rates rose constantly, from 49 percent of women aged 15–49 years (65 percent of them in urban and 27 percent in rural areas) in 1986, to 87.4 percent (92.1 percent in urban and 76.5 percent in rural areas) in 2006. More importantly, these women steadily increased the years of their schooling. They spent, on average, 3.4 years (4.9 years in urban and 1.3 years in rural areas) in school in 1986 and 7.4 years in 2006 (8.4 years in urban and 4.9 years in rural areas). No doubt, the educational level of rural women still seems fairly low but compared to what it was in the 1970s, its progress has been considerable. The implementation of a specific socioeconomic development program for rural areas, in particular, allowed rural communities to reduce the gap with urban communities and facilitate the propagation of new ideas and attitudes from the city on an increasingly large scale. The entry of new generations of women, increasingly literate in the 15–49 years age cohorts, constituted the decisive factor in the decline in the fertility rates.

Since the traditional patriarchal society preferred to maintain the schooling system exclusively for boys, a sizeable expansion of the school system was needed in order to admit girls at long last, particularly in small towns and villages. During the last three decades, rural women have progressed even more rapidly and the gender gap in education has continued to shrink.[16] The rise in women's schooling has allowed them to attain a level of education similar to that of men, so that by 2006, young men and women aged 15 years and over, had spent, on average, 7.4 and 6.3 years in school, respectively.

Despite the significant progress in the education of young women, however, the labor market has remained virtually closed to them. The proportion of Iranian women in the labor force is among the lowest in the world. In 2006, only 14.4 percent of women aged 15–64 years participated in the labor force (14.6 percent in urban and 13.9 percent in rural areas). It should be stressed that initially, patriarchal traditions, which confine women to the role of mother and homemaker, could be maintained thanks to the oil wealth, which helped alleviate household expenditures through state subsidies, and made it possible to live on one wage, namely that of the husband. However, the sharp drop in oil prices in the early 1980s, combined with runaway inflation, whittled down the share of state subsidies in the household budget. It, then, became increasingly necessary to have a second wage, namely that of the wife. Indeed, the Iranian economy, based essentially on the income from oil, could not create enough jobs because of its structural problems, and, thus, played a part in pushing women out of the labor market.[17] Hence, a large group of women, whose numbers are not included in the statistics, actually began to work in the informal booming market since the early 1980s.[18] Thus, the participation of the female labor force is probably higher than that presented by the censuses in 1986, 1996, and 2006. It is impossible, however, to verify the impact of the participation of the women's labor force on their fertility, since the lack of comprehensive statistics does not allow estimating the actual rate of their labor force participation. According to the Iranian decennial census results, the participation rates of the female labor force have remained practically unchanged between 1976 and 2006, whereas the total fertility rate varied widely between these two dates, from 7.2 to 1.9 births, respectively. While on the surface, such figures may imply that in Iran, contrary to the world at large, the participation of the female labor force has no impact on their fertility, this is actually not the case. In fact, the results of a survey on family and fertility in the city of Shiraz in 1996 show clearly that the fertility of working women is lower than that of nonworking women.[19] We can, therefore, assume that the recession and the continuous decline of the purchasing power of a majority of families since the 1980s, has pushed more and more women to contribute to the family income through employment in the informal market.

Family Composition

For a long time, the dominant model in Iran was the patriarchal extended family. Its members, linked by blood and by alliance, would include a married couple, their children, and the families of these children. This family model was characterized by the absolute power of the father as the head of the family, as well as by a strong solidarity between the sons, who had equal rights of succession and a high frequency of endogamy, usually between first cousins, the ideal being marriage between the children of two brothers. From the 1950s onward, however, the modernization of economic conditions in Iran linked to the development of a market economy and wage labor, urbanization, and a growing school enrolment particularly in towns and cities, started the process of the nuclearization of the family, although the family unit did not become independent.

Due to insufficient data, the composition of the family can be examined only from the statistics collected on the households during the last four censuses. According to the 1976 census, which provides information on the distribution of population according to sex, age, and relationship to the head of household, by this time, the nuclear family seems to have become the dominant model. However, the Iranian nuclear family differed from its Western counterpart in two ways: namely its size—the Iranian family was much larger with an average of seven children—and the very strong interdependence among kinship groups and obligatory reciprocity. Because of this relationship, the kinship group would intervene, among other things, in the choice of the spouse for its members as well as in the relations between the young and newly married couples. As far as the procreation pertaining to the familial group interest, the kinship group also exercised a strong pressure on women to bear a high number of children. This, in part, explains the high fertility level observed during this period.

Following the establishment of the Islamic Republic, which by and large reinforced patriarchal traditions, one would have expected a move back to the strengthening of this type of relationship between the family unit and the kinship group. Censuses taken in 1986, 1996, and 2006, describing the distribution of households according to type of family, however, confirm the opposite, namely the predominance of the nuclear family in both urban and rural areas. The proportions of nuclear families were 79 percent in 1986, 82 percent in 1996, and 88 percent in 2006.[20]

In recent times, in contrast to the earlier period, the dominance of the nuclear family is accompanied by an important reduction in its size, given the substantial decline in fertility between 1986 and 2006. In other words, it seems that the political context which had been rather favorable to the spread of the extended family has not succeeded to interrupt the growing nuclearization trend of the Iranian family between 1986 and 2006. Indeed, during the past decades, the Iranian nuclear family has begun to approach the Western model, at least with regard to size. The same could probably be said about relationships within families too. Women's control of their own fertility suggests not only the weakening of the kinship group's influence but also the establishment of families and individuals that are becoming increasingly independent. The primacy of the nuclear family and its shrinking size reveal a shock to the patriarchal system that is based on the subordination of women to men and the younger to the older. If women's control of fertility is a sign of their awareness regarding women's status in the family as well as the society, then the likelihood is that within couples, women have a greater chance of establishing themselves as full partners and having a say on the number of children that they desire to have. Indeed, by reappropriating their fertility, women can come out of "the male sphere of domination" and thus, attain dignity and equality.[21] Furthermore, inasmuch as a significant drop in fertility means a reduction in the number of siblings, then it considerably diminishes the chances of hierarchical relationships between brothers and sisters.[22]

Portrait of Iranian Youth

The Emergence of Youth as a Social Category

Even though the Iranian population has been very young for a long time, it was only in recent times that the young generations have been construed as a social group with its own social representation.[23] In the early 1950s, young people whose level of education was hardly different from that of their fathers seemed completely integrated into the patriarchal family system. In this family system, fathers not only imposed their authority but they also had the exclusive social representation of those that they were responsible for—forbidding any autonomous expression of the youth as such. Besides, due to the predilection for marriage at an early age, young adolescents, girls and boys, barely out of childhood, were immediately incorporated into the sphere of the adults by virtue of their newly gained status as the spouse.

This context changed gradually thanks to the expansion of schools in urban areas, particularly in big cities. The number of young urban girls and boys, born between 1952 and 1961, with access to the school system grew. The gender gap in education was reduced accordingly. It was in this new context that "youth" began to be recognized as a social category.[24] The emergence of the "youth" category in early 1970s, indeed, expressed a new form of individualization that extended to a broad social stratum in urban areas.[25] These young people, who were becoming aware of their common characteristics, began to consider themselves as a distinct social group and thus, sought to assert their points of difference. They were, in principle, opposed to the patriarchal system of the family, which rested on two pillars: young male subordination to the elders, and girl-women subordination to male members. At the same time, they tried to construct their own social identity and to invent their own social frameworks in the shape of gangs, gatherings, clubs, and associations.

However, political restrictions left no way out for the youth to gain auton-omy and fulfillment. One could argue that the absolute power of Mohammad Reza Shah was also inspired by the patriarchal system. He imposed his will from the top of the power-pyramid on the individuals in the nation and used vari-ous political tools to make the nation obey unconditionally. The young genera-tions were indeed obstructed by this absolute power, which for political reasons, prohibited any gathering or assembly of the youth that was beyond its control.[26] A feeling of frustration, anger, even revolt, developed among the Iranian youth, mainly from the urban middle classes. These young people, still dependent on their families, gradually transformed their conflicting relationships with their fathers' generation into an opposition to the system and a demand for politi-cal freedom—a symbol by which they sought, above all, the liberalization of the social arena allowing their individuality to blossom. It was under such circum-stances that the youth demanded the overthrow of the regime. In the late 1970s, young students fascinated by various political ideologies (Islamism, socialism, or communism), began to organize protests in the big cities. Other social classes gradually joined the street demonstrations, leading to the revolutionary days of 1978 and the overthrow of the monarchy in February 1979.[27]

The 1979 revolution in which the urban youth played a major part, not only awakened the young people in rural areas who until then had stayed away from the sociodemographic evolution observed in cities, but also encouraged greater interaction between the cities and the countryside. In this sense, one could argue that it was with the 1979 revolution that "youth" as a social category became rec-ognized not only in the cities but also in the rural areas. If the political context of the last weeks of the revolution divided the youth into two separate groups, of sup-porters and opponents, young Iranians shared, beyond their political differences, common ideals of self-affirmation and a strong desire to break free of parental financial care to gain their independence. There is no doubt that this youth was not homogeneous due to strong socioeconomic disparities. Nevertheless, in Iran, similar to other countries, the overall expansion of the school system allowing a great majority of the young men and women access to secondary education made the young generations aware of their common characteristics and the fact that they were distinct from the "adults' world."[28]

A New Context and a New Generation of Youth

The 1979 revolution inaugurated a new era. In the first decade of the revolu-tion, the youth, one of the main protagonists in the revolution, pursued their revolutionary aspirations by questioning the traditions that were stemmed in the patriarchal norms and still dominating the families and the society. These young individuals, a majority of whom were born between 1957 and 1961, and who were quite conscious of their role in the revolution, expressed themselves openly for the first time as the youth representing the new and distinctive social category. Neither of the two active groups of youths, namely the supporters or the oppo-nents of the Islamic Republic, hesitated to break up with their kinship groups, and to challenge the hegemony of the generation of their fathers. As the results of a sociological study conducted in 1978–1979 Iran confirm, "We are witnessing a true disintegration of the family, a revolt against parents, against both fathers and mothers."[29]

Although inherently patriarchal, the new revolutionary system paradoxically chose to trust these new social actors. The new leaders became aware of the importance of the youth movement and relied for the most part on these young people in order to establish their power throughout the country. A large number of these young people either joined the newly created social, political, and military organizations,[30] or played a part to further socioeconomic development plans designed particularly for rural areas and peripheral regions. At the outset of Iraq-Iran war (1980–1988), a vast majority of young supporters of the Islamic Republic volunteered for the *Basij* or joined the army of *Pasdaran*[31] and went to the war fronts.[32]

At the end of the Iraq-Iran war (in August 1988), the Islamic state, far from revolutionary management, opted for a planned management of the country. The Islamic government, now financially weakened due to a crucial economic crisis and at the same time strengthened by the war, intended to rely once again on the support of the "former youth," in order to exercise its authority in a new political framework. However, once it deferred the question of the formation of political parties and organizations, and closed the public arena to the young people, the new generation of youth was by no means inclined to be excluded from the social and political spheres. Besides, Iranians, from all social strata, tired of the eight-year war and disappointed at the political leaders breaking their promises of delivering a better life and greater social and political openness, expressed their disappointment and dissatisfaction, marking the beginnings of a state-society divide.

The new generation of youth, born between 1975 and 1985, emerged in this complicated and contradictory situation. This newly formed young generation shared neither the religious nor the traditional values that the Islamic Republic tried to propagate through the state media, otherwise known as the "Voice and Face of the Islamic Republic of Iran."[33] To circumvent this propaganda, young people resorted at first to foreign videocassettes that were banned although available on the black market, then, to prohibited satellite dishes, and finally, to the Internet to learn about, and stay in touch with the outside world. The Iranian Diaspora consisting of several hundred thousands of people living in North America and Western Europe, also played an important role in the transmission of lifestyle, culture, and values of Western democracies. This conversion of the young generations to the Western cultural model was on such a scale that at the end of the Iraq-Iran war in August 1988, the Islamic Republic began denouncing "Western cultural aggression" (*tahajom-e farhangi-ye gharbi*) as the new "enemy" of the Islamic homeland.[34] In fact, the state was caught in an impenetrable dilemma. The Islamic state was forced to open the country to the outside markets and to international exchanges for its economic needs, among others, and therefore, could not close all the borders. Thus, all it could do was to attack the symbols of Western culture without proposing any attractive or alternative model for that matter.

From then on, new forms of expression in the artistic and cultural domains emerged, which also included new manners of dress, revealing the extent to which Western values had penetrated Iranian society and were giving substance to its own shape of modernity. These social upheavals show the process of the changing of Iranian society and the transformation of its traditional family model, the result of one of the fastest fertility declines in history.

These important events, taking place within a short span of time have profoundly influenced Iran's social, demographic, and political environment since the mid-1990s. The new generations of young people who constructed their social representations in this context, also adopted new principles in their sociopolitical protests distinguishing them fundamentally from the youth of "yesterday." Contrary to their predecessors, they did not try to overthrow the Islamic Republic but to establish a dialogue in order to reform it. The wide participation of young people in elections between 1997 and 2001 (presidential in 1997 and 2001, municipal in 1999, and parliamentary in 2000), leading to victories of reformist candidates, as well as the presidential elections of 2009, constitutes a very significant indicator of this fundamental change in youth behavior.

The Sociodemographic and Economic Characteristics of "Youth"

Although definitions of "youth" are based on societal, political, cultural, and individual factors, an age range is also frequently used to define the contours of "youth." The United Nations treats the age group of 15–24 years as the core of "youth." It goes without saying that the age range varies from one period to another, according to socioeconomic changes of each country. In Iran, during the 1960s, 1970s, and 1980s, individuals between the ages of 15 and 24 years were considered "young persons." Being unmarried also constituted another of the main criteria of "youth." According to these definitions, in 1966, 15 percent of the total Iranian population was composed of young men and women aged between 15 and 24 years.[35] These young people belonged to the generations born between 1942 and 1952. As mentioned above, during this period, many women were getting married at a young age: only 36 percent of women (40 percent in urban and 31 percent in rural areas) against 83 percent of men (87 percent in urban and 79 percent in rural areas) were unmarried in 1996. In other words, almost two women out of three had got married before their twenty-fifth birthday and were probably mothers of one or two children given that the average age of women at their first marriage was 18 years. In view of the fact that a segment, particularly a majority of women, had entered married family life, they were not recognized as "youth." Since a great number of them, especially young women, for the most part, had had no access to schooling, the literacy rate among these women aged 15–24 years was only 24 percent (50 percent in urban and 4 percent in rural areas) and that of the young men in the same age bracket was 52 percent (74 percent in urban and 32 percent in rural areas). Besides, the young women had spent, on an average, only 1.6 year in school (1.4 year in urban and 0.2 year in rural areas) while the average years of schooling of young men was slightly higher, namely

2.9 years (2.4 years in urban and 1.4 year in rural areas). Finally, the ratio of young women in the labor force compared to that of young men, for the reasons explained above, was quite low: 14.9 percent of women (10.8 percent in urban and 17.9 percent in rural areas) against 77.8 percent of men (65.5 percent in urban and 89.3 percent in rural areas). These important gender gaps in education and the labor force indicate that the socialization of most young Iranian women differed very clearly from that of young men in the 1960s.

This situation of young women, in particular those living in the cities, had improved slightly by 1976,[36] when 19 percent of the total population was composed of young men and women aged 15–24 years, belonging to the generations born between 1952 and 1961. By 1976, the proportion of singles among young women rose, compared to 1966, while those among young men fell. Furthermore, 46 percent of young women aged 15–24 years (50 percent in urban and 42 percent in rural areas) and 80 percent of young men (85 percent in urban and 72 percent in rural areas) were still unmarried in 1976. So, by 1976, practically three years before the revolution, half of the urban women aged 15–24 years, and more importantly still, 69.5 percent of women aged 15–19 years (belonging to the generation born between 1957 and 1961) were single. As a result, the average age of women at first marriage had risen to 19.7 years. Like the men of the same age bracket, these young women had, thus, the same socialization experiences as men starting with school. Indeed, the literacy rate of urban women aged 15–24 years was 68 percent and that of women aged 15–19 years was 75 percent. Besides, these young women had spent, on an average, 5.4 years and 6.1 years, respectively, in school. Since the literacy rates of the young men of the same age group were 85 percent and 86.8 percent, respectively, and their average years of schooling were 5.3 years and 7.7 years, the gender gap in education among urban young people had reduced in this period.

In regard to young women living in villages, their situation was quite different. Despite their progress, the rural female literacy rates continued to remain low. Only 15.5 percent of young women aged 15–24 years and 19.8 percent among them aged 15–19 years were literate while the literacy rates of young rural men of the same age were 51.2 and 55.4 percent, respectively.[37] The average years of schooling of these women were not high either: 0.7 years while those of young men were 2.8 years. It should be stressed that in the rural areas, despite being dominated by traditional values, young men could take greater advantage of schooling, and consequently, the gap between young men and young women in education had widened.

By contrast, both in urban and in rural areas, inequality between young women and young men in accessing the labor market was very important. In 1976, the ratio of young urban women in the labor force was 11.5 percent compared to 56 percent of men and that of young rural women was 22 percent against 83 percent of men. The women's participation rate in rural areas seemed rather higher than that of women in urban areas. In fact, in rural areas, the main part of the female labor force was made up of "family workers." Conversely, in urban areas the majority of the female labor force consisted of employees in private or public sectors. However, in spite of considerable progress in the educational levels among young urban women, the labor market continued to be practically closed to them. It was under such circumstances that young urban men and women, especially the generations born between 1957 and 1961, began to see themselves as belonging to a social category with social representations, distinct from that of "adults."

In 1986, the young men and young women aged 15–24 years, belonging to the generations born between 1962 and 1971, constituted 19 percent of the total population.[38] Although, after the revolution, the legal minimum age of marriage was reduced to the age of puberty (generally 9 years for girls and 15 years for boys), to comply with the Sharia, the ratio of singles among women aged 15–24 years remained practically unchanged, compared to those in urban areas in 1976. However, this percentage rose in the rural areas, to 46.5 percent and 46.8 percent for women and men, respectively. Accordingly, the average age at first marriage of urban women in 1986 was almost the same as that of urban women in 1976, namely 20 years, whereas the average age at first marriage of rural women rose slightly: 19.7 years in 1986 as opposed to 19.1 years in 1976. Thus, the return to the *Sharia*—regarding the legal minimum age at marriage—affected neither the upward trend in proportion to the unmarried nor that of average age of women at first marriage. As for young men aged 15–24 years, the proportion of the unmarried women in 1986 as compared to 1976 fell slightly in urban areas and rose in rural areas to an overall of 75 percent (78 percent in urban and 72 percent in rural areas).

In view of these figures, it seems that by 1986, in both urban and rural areas, three out of every four young men and almost one out of every two young women, could have had the same socialization experience by attending school. This compares to similar ratios among the majority of the population of young urban men and women aged 15–19 years in 1976. Furthermore, since after the revolution, the authorities built many more schools, education expanded vastly in both urban and rural areas during the 1980s, even though the number of schools remained insufficient, and the staff inadequate. As a result, the total literacy rates of young men and women aged 15–24 years increased considerably: 85 percent for young men (91 percent in urban and 76 percent in rural areas) and 66 percent for young women (81 percent in urban and 46 percent in rural areas). What is especially interesting to note, is the sharp rise of rural female literacy rate, compared to previous periods. Almost half of young rural women were already literate in 1986. Even more significant is the schooling of young women in both urban and rural areas, which rose notably. They spent, on an average, 4.5 years in school (6.3 years in urban and 2.2 years in rural areas), while the average years of schooling of young men was 6.2 years (7.4 years in urban and 4.7 years in rural areas). However paradoxical it may appear, in spite of the discriminatory laws and policies of the Islamic Republic toward women in particular, the gender gap in education shrank both in urban and rural areas by 1986.

Conversely, in 1986, the gender gap concerning access to the labor market remained unchanged, compared to that of 1976. The rate of economic activity among young men was 66 percent (61 percent in urban and 73 percent in rural areas) whereas it was 10.6 percent for women (10.5 percent in urban and 10.8

percent in rural areas). However, it is important to note that compared to 1976, the rate of unemployed young women who were seeking jobs increased considerably in 1986 to 42 percent of young female labor force (55 percent in urban and 27 percent in rural areas). No doubt, the economic crisis exacerbated by the embargo against Iran as well as the Iraq-Iran war affected the private sector, causing severe cutbacks, which became an economic concern for the active population particularly women.[39] Furthermore, because of the Iraq-Iran war, many young men, in addition to the draftees were sent to the front through *Pasdaran* and *Basij* organizations.[40]

What differentiates the young people of the 1980s from those of the previous periods, in particular, was their massive participation in the political and civil activities through various and newly created organizations soon after the 1979 revolution. As the result of their full and active participation in all aspects of life of the city, the youth became a full-fledged social group. Certainly, the youth differ according to the social class to which they belong, the young people are aware of it and oscillate *"perpetually between solidarity and social class gap."*[41]

Taking into account the socioeconomic changes over the past two decades, and especially the increase in the average age at the first marriage of young people, it would seem necessary to stretch the upper limit age to 29 years. In other words, in the 1990s and the 2000s, individuals between the ages 15 to 29 were considered "young persons." Thus, by 1996, the young men and women aged 15–29 years, belonging to the generations born between 1967 and 1981, constituted 28.4 percent of the total population.[42] Due to the sharp decline in fertility, the segment of the population composed of 15 to 29 year olds, increased considerably. In 2006, these young people, belonging to the generation born between 1977 and 1991, constituted 35.4 percent of the total population.[43] Almost three out of every four young men and one out of every two young women were unmarried in 1996 and in 2006. In 1996, the proportions of male and female singles were, respectively, 70 percent of men aged 15–29 years (72 percent in urban area and 67 percent in rural areas) and 50 percent of women of the same age (49.4 percent in urban and 50.1 percent in rural areas). Ten years later, in 2006, these proportions remained practically the same: 73 percent of young men (74 percent in urban and 71 percent in rural areas) and 53.5 percent of young women (53.6 percent in urban and 52.9 percent in rural areas) were single, respectively. The interesting point to note is the situation of young women in rural areas; their age at first marriage has continued to increase. More importantly, among those between the ages of 25 and 29, almost one out of four was still single in 2006. This situation is very new and reveals the great sociocultural changes that have occurred during these last two decades, radically breaking down the ancestral traditions in rural areas.

These changes were confirmed by the progress of the young rural women's schooling. Not only did the number of young women gaining access to the school system grow, but also their educational level approached that of young rural men. Furthermore, during the last two decades, the increase in the number of young rural population attending school has shrunk the gap between young rural and urban population in the domain of education. By 1996, the literacy rates of the young men and women in urban areas, aged 15–29 years, were, respectively, 96.7 percent and 94 percent while those of young men and women in rural areas were 91 percent and 78.4 percent, respectively.[44] These rates have continued to rise. By 2006, 98 percent of young urban men and 97.5 percent of young women were literate while in rural areas 95 percent of young men and 90 percent of young women were literate.[45] In the same way, the average number of years of schooling of young men and women both in urban and rural areas has risen constantly. Between 1996 and 2006, the average number of years of schooling of the young urban and rural men increased by 1.2 year, whereas that of young urban and rural women increased by 2 years. In 1996, the young men spent, on an average, 8.4 years in school in urban and 6.2 years in rural areas, whereas the young women spent 7.9 years in urban and 4 years in rural areas. Ten years later, this figure had changed to 9.6 years for urban men and 7.5 years for rural ones. In case of women, it had risen to 9.9 years in urban and to 6.4 years in rural areas.[46] Thus, the gender gap in education has continued its downward trend both in urban and rural areas. Indeed, the increase in women's schooling has allowed them to approach the men's educational level or even surpass it slightly in the cities: in 2006, the urban young women aged 20–24 years spent, on an average, 10.4 years in school, whereas the urban young men of the same age spent 9.9 years. It is also very important to note that during the first decade of the twenty-first century, in particular, women's education took an important turn. Since the academic year 2003–2004, the number of female university students has exceeded that of male university students. In 2006–2007, from among 2.8 million university students, 52.4 percent were female.[47] This new configuration clearly shows the determination of young women in Iran to break with patriarchal traditions and follow the paths that allow them to take greater control of their lives.

As with the previous decades, the gender gap in accessing the labor market remained constant, although the rate of economic activity among young men began to fall, due to a severe economic crisis as well as an increase in the number of years at school. In 1996, the economic activity rate among young men was 62 percent (57 percent in urban and 70 percent in rural areas) whereas that of young women was 11.6 percent (9.5 percent in urban and 14.9 in rural areas). In 2006, these figures had changed to 64 percent for young men (61 percent in urban and 72 percent in rural areas), and 15.3 percent for young women (14.8 percent in urban and 16.4 percent in rural areas).[48]

Apart from the gender gap in accessing the labor market, the new generation of "youth" appears more homogenous in its socioeconomic characteristics than the "youth" of previous periods especially that of the 1970s. Today, due to the sharp decline in fertility, a great number from among the new generation of young men and women, whose level of education is almost equal to each other, live in restricted nuclear families both in urban and rural areas. In addition, the increase in their age at first marriage[49] has led them to live much longer with their parents. Since their educational level is higher than that of their parents, particularly their fathers, these young people have managed to establish a new relationship with their parents based, for the most part, on dialogue and mutual respect. These new conditions, which we qualify as "modern," have transformed the social representation of the youth. This important social transformation will be illustrated by means of two sociodemographic surveys that were conducted in Iran in 2002 and 2004.

From Modernization of Family Relationships to Aspiration for Democracy

Characteristics of Nuclear Families and Unmarried New Youths in 2002

The relative small size of nuclear families indicates clearly that the fertility rate has dropped extensively to low levels in both urban and rural areas. Within our sample, consisting of almost 7,000 households, 89 percent in urban and 85 percent in rural areas constituted nuclear families (table 8.1). The average number of the members of the nuclear family (parents with their unmarried children) was 4.6 in urban and 4.9 in rural areas. The average age of fathers and mothers in urban nuclear families was 44 and 38 years (belonging to the generations born in 1958 and 1963), and in rural nuclear families 43 and 38 years (belonging to the generations born in 1959 and 1964), respectively. So, in each of these cases, parents were of the generation of former young revolutionaries.

These couples were married probably in the two or three years that followed the revolution, between 1981 and 1982. Their average ages at first marriage were, respectively, 24 years for men and 19 years for women in urban areas;

Table 8.1   Distribution of households by family type (2002)

Household composition	Number of households	Proportion of the household (in %)	Average family size
		Urban	
Single individual	201	4.8	1.0
Head of household (HH) and his wife	440	10.6	2.0
HH, his wife, and their unmarried children	2689	64.5	4.6
HH, his wife, and their ever married children	149	3.6	5.4
HH and children	186	4.5	3.3
Total nuclear families	**3665**	**87.9**	**4.0**
Extended families	505	12.1	5.7
Total	4170	100	4.2
		Rural	
Single individual	101	3.6	1.0
Head of household (HH) and his wife	280	10	2.0
HH, his wife, and their unmarried children	1730	62	4.9
HH, his wife, and their ever married children	120	4.3	5.7
HH and children	135	4.8	3.7
Total nuclear families	**2366**	**84.8**	**4.4**
Extended families	424	15.2	6.3
Total	2790	100	4.7

Sources: Socio-economic Characteristics Survey of Iranian Households 2002
Statistical Center of Iran, CNRS "Monde iranien."

and 22.4 for men and 18 years for women in rural areas. Among the generation of their children, in urban nuclear families, the average age of the unmarried 15- to 29-year-old youth was 20.3 years for boys and 19.4 years for girls. More importantly, 10 percent of this population consisted of 25- to 29-year-old young men and 7 percent of young women of the same age. In rural areas, among nuclear families, the average age of the 15- to 29-year-old youth was very close to that of the urban households: 19.5 years for young men and 19.8 years for young women. In rural areas, the percentage of unmarried 25- to 29-year-old young women was slightly above that of unmarried 25- to 29-year-old young men: 9 percent for women against 8 percent for men. Thus by 2002, significant changes had occurred within nuclear families in both urban and rural areas.

Besides, in urban areas, the educational level among young females was higher than that of young males: 65 percent of young girls and 56.4 percent of young boys had received a high school diploma with 16.5% of young women and 13.2% of young men having gained access to university education. This novel situation highlights the very distinctive characteristic of today's young generations in Iran. The trend seems to follow a pattern of a narrowing gap between men and women, similar to that of Western countries. In regard to the rural areas, due to delayed socioeconomic development, the educational level among young males was still higher than that of young females: 39.4 percent of young men against 21.8 percent of young women have received a high school diploma,with 8.7 percent of young men and 5 percent of young women having had access to university education. However, it is important to note that the gap in education between young girls and young boys aged 15–19 years has been reduced considerably.

The educational level of the youth in both urban and rural areas was higher than that of adults aged 30 years and over, especially among women. In other words, the hierarchy of generations has been reversed through education, and this generation gap in education has certainly affected the intergenerational relationships.

Although benefiting from a higher level of education, young people face great difficulties to fit into the labor market. According to the estimation of unmarried 15- to 29-year-old young individuals of our sample, in urban areas, 52 percent of men and only 14 percent of women were employed. Almost 31 percent of the former and 43 percent of the latter were seeking jobs. Consequently, a significant proportion of urban youth was dependent on their parents. In rural areas, the proportion of young men and women in the labor force was higher: 61 percent of young men and 29 percent of young women were employed. Still, 25 percent of these young men and 12 percent of young women were seeking jobs. However, it should be emphasized that these rates are misleading. More than half of these young men and the majority of young women were indeed "family workers."[50] Because of difficult living conditions in rural areas and the need to financially assist their families, these young men and women could not pursue their studies for a longer period. Nearly a third of the rural youth were students as opposed to 40 percent of urban young men and just over half of urban young women who pursued their studies.

According to the results of our survey, for the first time in the social history of Iran, young people, in the cities as well as in the villages, continue to live at home with their parents for a longer period. Indeed, young people tend to delay marriage in part because of the changes in their family aspirations but more importantly, because of the chronic economic crisis that has increased the difficulties they have to face in order to find a stable employment.

Father-Child Relationship

One of the questions asked from unmarried 15- to 29-year-old young individuals concerned the behavior of their parents, the father and mother separately:

In most cases, which of the following defines your parents' behavior towards you?
1. Violence with physical punishment (if necessary)
2. Extreme strictness
3. Persuasion through dialogue
4. Open-mindedness while expecting to be consulted when making decisions.

Given our assumption that the patriarchal system in the family was weakened since the 1979 revolution, our analysis is here restricted to the response of youths regarding their fathers' attitude.

In urban areas, only 6.4 percent of young men and 5.3 percent of young women chose option 2, "Extreme strictness" (table 8.2). Nearly half of both young men and young women reported that their fathers had an attitude based on dialogue and persuasion; and about 40 percent of them marked option 4 as the description that matched the behavior of their fathers. It should be noted that the proportion of young men aged 25–29 years who expressed that their fathers let them make decisions independently, stands a little above that of the young women of the same age: 51.5 percent as opposed to 47.5 percent, respectively. Anyhow, what must be taken into account here is that the behavior of the fathers of almost 90 percent of the single young men and women in urban nuclear families was not in conformity with the rules and beliefs advocated by the patriarchal system. This spectacular transformation, to a large extent, may be explained by the gap between the level of education attained by the children and their fathers. It is important to emphasize that in urban nuclear families, the fathers' average years of schooling were 6.4 years whereas that of their children was 10.4 years (figure 8.2). As demonstrated in table 8.2, there is a direct correlation: the higher the educational level of the children, the higher is the percentage of fathers who allow their children to make decisions independently.

In rural areas, 48 percent of young men and 53 percent of young women characterized the relationship with their fathers as based on dialogue and persuasion; 34 percent of young men and nearly 30 percent of young women expressed that their fathers let them make decisions independently (table 8.3). The fathers of 3.9 percent of young men and 1.8 percent of young women were described as aggressive (option 1) and those of 12.5 percent of young men and 12 percent of young women were strict (option 2). Compared with urban youth, those in

Table 8.2 Percentage of unmarried 15- to 29-year-old young individuals still living with their parents—Urban Areas, 2002 (by sex, level of education, and habitual behavior of fathers)

Youth education level	Habitual behavior of fathers					
	Violence with physical punishment (%)	Extreme Strictness (%)	Persuasion through Dialogue (%)	Open-mindedness while expecting to be consulted when making decisions (%)	Not Mentioned (%)	Total (%)
Men						
Primary	2.1	7.7	53.5	32.4	4.2	100
Highschool junior level	0.9	7.2	53.7	34.6	3.6	100
Highschool senior level	1.3	6.1	51.5	39.3	1.8	100
Preparation year for university	0.0	8.1	44.1	46.3	1.5	100
Highschool diploma+2yrs	0.0	7.2	33.3	58.0	1.4	100
Other university graduates	0.0	4.3	41.2	54.0	0.5	100
Others	0.0	0.0	100.0	0.0	0.0	100
Total	1.0	6.4	50.1	40.3	2.2	100
Women						
Primary	2.4	6.1	64.6	23.2	3.7	100
Highschool junior level	1.3	12.6	58.5	25.8	1.9	100
Highschool senior level	0.4	4.7	49.3	43.3	2.3	100
Preparation year for university	0.9	4.7	43.9	48.1	2.3	100
Highschool diploma+2yrs	0.0	4.0	46.0	50.0	0.0	100
Other university graduates	0.0	2.6	42.3	51.5	3.6	100
Others	0.0	11.1	66.7	22.2	0.0	100
Total	0.6	5.3	49.5	42.2	2.4	100

Sources: Socio-economic Characteristics Survey of Iranian Households 2002
Statistical Center of Iran, CNRS "Monde iranien."

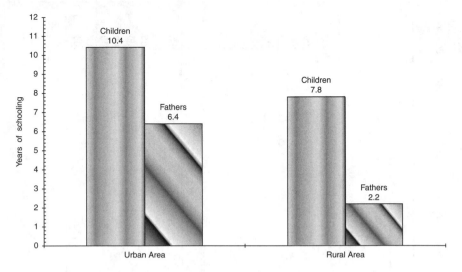

Figure 8.2   Fathers' and children's average age of schooling (2002).

Source: Socio-economic Characteristics Survey of Iranian Households 2002; Statistical Center of Iran, CNRS "Monde iranien."

villages expressed a higher percentage of severe treatment and violent behavior by their fathers. This suggests that the resistance of fathers to independent mindedness among the youth in rural settings was higher than their peers in urban areas. Indeed, it is important to note that in rural nuclear families, the fathers' average years of schooling were only 2.2 years whereas those of their children were 7.8 years (i.e., a gap of 5.6 years) (figure 8.2). Based on these figures, it is clear that by 2002, the youth had started questioning the dominating age hierarchy, demanding instead a more equal relationship with their fathers. As a result, instances of confrontation between children and their fathers, especially between sons and fathers, seems to be more prevalent in rural settings where tradition appears to be more entrenched. What this implies is that unlike the urban areas, as demonstrated in table 8.3, the behavior of rural fathers was not necessarily impacted by the higher educational achievement of their children. On the contrary, it seems that the higher the educational level of the offspring, the more hostile the attitude of the fathers.

Despite this, 82.5 percent of young men and 83 percent of young women in rural areas characterized their fathers as being inclined toward persuasion through dialogue or open-mindedness and nonintervention.[51] That is to say, among a majority of nuclear families in rural areas, constituting our sample, the dominating age hierarchy stemming from a patriarchal system has been undermined, and replaced by a new type of relationship between fathers and children, which can be viewed as more egalitarian. This development is very important because it demonstrates a fundamental change that has taken place in the rural areas. These areas, which for several decades had remained intact and not subject to any significant social and demographic change, have now undergone

Table 8.3 Percentage of unmarried 15- to 29-year-old young individuals still living with their parents—Rural Areas, 2002 (by sex, level of education, and habitual behavior of fathers)

Youth education level	Habitual behavior of fathers					
	Violence with physical punishment (%)	Extreme Strictness (%)	Persuasion through Dialogue (%)	Open-mindedness while expecting to be consulted when making decisions (%)	Not mentioned (%)	Total (%)
Men						
Primary	8.2	20.4	41.3	26.0	4.1	100
Highschool junior level	4.6	11.6	47.6	35.8	0.5	100
Highschool senior level	2.3	9.7	51.7	35.9	0.4	100
Preparation year for university	0.0	16.9	44.1	37.3	1.7	100
Highschool diploma+2yrs	0.0	12.5	62.5	25.0	0.0	100
Other university graduates	0.0	8.3	37.5	54.2	0.0	100
Others	0.0	0.0	33.3	66.7	0.0	100
Total	3.9	12.5	47.9	34.6	1.1	100
Women						
Primary	3.8	13.9	53.5	25.0	3.8	100
Highschool junior level	1.4	13.7	53.6	27.0	4.3	100
Highschool senior level	1.0	9.6	54.0	33.2	2.2	100
Preparation year for university	0.0	8.5	50.7	39.4	1.4	100
Highschool diploma+2yrs	0.0	0.0	66.7	33.3	0.0	100
Other university graduates	0.0	11.1	48.1	37.0	3.7	100
Others	0.0	16.7	52.8	30.6	0.0	100
Total	1.8	12.0	53.5	29.7	3.0	100

Sources: Socio-economic Characteristics Survey of Iranian Households 2002
Statistical Center of Iran, CNRS "Monde iranien."

transformations in attitudes and patterns of behavior as a result of the development and widespread expansion of communication tools and facilities in the entire country. Therefore, the rural community, without reaching the same level of urban socioeconomic development, is demonstrating a similar level of competence and capacity in understanding and accepting novel attitudes and values.

These results confirm our hypothesis that the patriarchal system, thus traditional values, which not so long ago dominated the relations between men and women, and younger and older generations, has been undermined. Nowadays, new values constitute the foundation of relationships, which we consider more egalitarian, within families. Our surveys also demonstrate that these newly established relationships are not restricted to a specific geographic area, but encompass all segments of the population, extending to all geographic areas of the country, both urban and rural. The sociodemographic developments that took place in the postrevolutionary era have generated fundamental transformations in the structure and composition of nuclear families, resulting in turn in a new structure of relationship among family members. In short, it would be accurate to say that today, dialogue and a tendency to convince and inspire, has gained dominance within families.

The Youth's Disapproval of the Moral Order and Absolutism of the Islamic State

This new sociodemographic situation, which we consider modern, has transformed the social representation of the youth as an entire social group. In Iran today, similar to Western societies, "youth" constitutes a "transition age," a stage at which both young women and men prepare their entry to adulthood. However, a combination of factors such as continuing with higher education together with the relatively late access of a majority of young people to a stable employment, contributes to the perpetuation of a status of dependency, further lengthening this "transition age." The young generations, today, similar to the generation of their parents, are also in search of their own social frameworks, to experience their "youth" collectively. However, they have come up against the moral order of Islamic Republic, which has significantly reduced individual liberties by imposing restrictions on dress for both men and women and restrictions regarding interaction between unmarried men and women, single-sex clubs, censorship of books and films, and control of public spaces.[52] These young people, who, for the most part, have got accustomed to enjoying conditions that allow their individuality to blossom in the family context, cannot accept the ideology of the Islamic state.

Already in the 1990s, they began to transgress such proscriptions, especially in big cities. The main demand of this new generation, who enthused by Western democracy, had followed with interest the activities of the civil society in these countries, was the "rule of law." This was the necessary condition that would allow them to construct their own social identity and assert themselves as "young people" distinct from the "adults' world." So, their demands were not so different from that of the previous young generation, with the one difference that whereas the latter chose to achieve their objective by means of a revolution, the new young generations adopted a dialectic approach based on mutual respect within the existing legal framework and without questioning the legitimacy of the Islamic Republic.

Inasmuch as these young people had grown up under the Islamic Republic, they were its children. The Islamic state, therefore, could not criticize their behavior insofar as it was implicitly an admission of the failure of its own cultural project. It could neither adopt an aggressive policy in response to the youths' demands made in this manner, because it would risk losing connection with the young generations. Thus, by conceding some of the freedoms in the second half of the 1990s, a more open social and cultural environment came about, marked by an increase in the number of daily, weekly, and monthly publications that reflected various social, political, and cultural views. New political groups and organizations emerged as the existing ones became more active. This led to a new sort of enthusiasm. Dialogue, which was the demand of the young generations, was progressively established and the political conditions underwent profound changes in the late 1990s.

The large participation of the youth in a number of elections between 1997 and 2001 not only proves this transformation, but also the fact that a new balance of power between the government and the youth was established. The youth, by electing the candidates who promised the promotion of dialogue, tried to improve and stabilize the new political conditions. This time, without resorting to a revolution, young generations, both men and women, urban and rural, succeeded in asserting their right to public expression, thus, challenging state absolutism. This major change heralded the beginning of a process toward democratization. As a result of the new generation's strong thirst for freedom of expression, one imagined that this process would gain further momentum. However, events did not turn out as expected and the democratization process of Iranian political life was set back until some point in the future.

Move toward Questioning the Legitimacy of the Islamic State?

The "Iranian spring" was short-lived. The attempt at the modernization of the political sphere, threatening the privileges of the leaders of the Islamic state, was not tolerated for long. The nonelective state institutions[53] made use of their powers to put an end to attempts at political reform. At the same time, a number of different means that included intimidation, arrests and detentions, and even murders of intellectuals and political personalities, were used by various bodies under the control of the same nonelective state institutions in order "to punish" the reformists in particular. Furthermore, in order to counter the strong reformist aspirations of the youth that were in keeping with global trends, the "principlists" (osulgarayan), supported by the establishment, began to make a comeback to the political scene as early as 1999, thus thwarting any chances of effective reform."[54]

Paradoxically, one of the key factors allowing the principlists success was the boycott of the elections by the reformist electorate. Deeply disappointed by broken promises of reformists, young generations and women, in particular, who had strongly supported the reformists during several years began to shun the polls. The record rate of nonparticipation, officially declared by the Ministry of the Interior, was around 51 percent at the municipal elections of 2003,[55] indicating the measure of disappointment among reformists' electorate. Their electorate participated neither in the legislative elections of 2004 nor in the presidential elections in 2005. Consequently, both the legislative and presidential elections led to the fundamentalists' electoral success and particularly to the election of Mahmoud Ahmadinejad as the president of the Islamic Republic in June 2005.

Following his election, the sociopolitical situation became tense. In a short period of time the new president, supported by the Leader, ended the dialogue with the youth and imposed a strict moral order. This repressive policy immediately provoked the hostility of the youth, especially those from urban middle classes, toward the government of Ahmadinejad. This hardening of the moral order, primarily designed to prevent any interaction between young men and women, led the young people of the cities to invent a new use of public and private spaces in order to gather and live their lives of young people. Thus, in large cities, young men and women turned coffee shops into private spaces to get together and do what was considered forbidden by the authorities. They converted the basement or the gardens of big houses to concert halls, where local musicians belonging to the new generation of the "Iranian Underground Music," performed. Great enthusiasts of the Internet and blogs, these young people made of this virtual sphere a new public arena in which they expressed themselves freely, compensating for the limitations they faced in everyday life.

However, young women's rights activists and students, who had established diverse associations and labor unions during the reformist years, did not delay reacting actively to this shift in the policy of the Islamic state. These activists mobilized, at first, around specific claims: by 2006, young women rights activists demanded change in the discriminatory laws against women, whereas young students demonstrated on a number of university campuses, demanding their right to freely elect their representatives. The government severely repressed these protests and imprisoned a large number of them. The violent repression and the severity with which the Islamic state responded to these peaceful demonstrations only strengthened the movements whose claims became increasingly political. Although not always sharing the same political views, student associations decided nonetheless to support each other, and moreover, to join their forces with women rights activists as well as workers and teachers who had been arrested and sentenced to prison terms. For the first time since the Cultural Revolution of 1980, students declared their solidarity with the unions and associations and demanded the release of all the imprisoned activists.[56] The relationship between the Islamic state and its youth remained tense due to the increasingly brutal repression of young activists who continued demanding freedom, democracy, and the establishment of the rule of law. Risking jail, these young people held regular protests, condemning the absolutism of the Islamic state and openly criticizing the government of Ahmadinejad. By the end of Ahmadinejad's first term as president, young people appeared to have broken away from the Islamic Republic. The deployment of the military and paramilitary groups in the capital in the summer and fall 2008, under the pretext of ensuring the safety of citizens, shows that the government feared these movements of protest becoming more radical and subversive at any time.[57]

On the eve of the presidential elections of 2009, dissatisfaction was at its peak. Both "moderate" and "reformist" candidates had sought to use this discontent to mobilize voters, especially among the reformist constituency. The latter who during almost six years had not participated in elections let itself again be won over by the pledges made by Mir-Hossein Mousavi and Mehdi Karroubi, the two reformist candidates. The seemingly competitive atmosphere together with the forceful campaigns of the candidates made it appear that the outcome of the elections was undetermined and for the taking. The turnout, therefore, was substantial. It was no surprise then that following the hasty announcement of the results, the voters, in particular, young men and women, spontaneously came out into the streets. "*Where is my vote?*" was the question/slogan chanted by hundreds of thousands of Iranians protesting the results, in the streets of Tehran, expressing above all their dissatisfaction at this implicit closure of the space of dialogue with the state. An unprecedented violent crackdown that included arrests, long prison sentences, and even executions, while putting an end ostensibly to the protests in the short term, contributed to the beginning of a contestation of the system of the Islamic Republic.

This protest movement, however, which brought many social categories together, has encountered much difficulty in determining the path ahead, because of the varied nature of its composition. The point of contention among the many factions seems to be over their different visions of government. At the time of writing, the majority had not yet questioned the legitimacy of the Islamic Republic. There is, however, no guarantee that this outlook will last, especially if the state persists in suppressing and blocking all peaceful solutions.

Conclusion

Youth does not constitute a fixed, specific, and predefined social group. The definition of what comprises "youth" constantly changes according to changing conditions. No matter the time period or the geographic location, the young generations always want to establish their own identity as the "youth" in order to distinguish themselves from the "adults." In Iran, it was only under the social and cultural conditions of the 1970s that the question of "youth" arose as a social issue for the first time. The young generations in these years who were pioneers of the later generations encountered numerous obstacles in establishing their social identity. The unquestionable power of the fathers in the family together with the authoritarian approach of the political leaders, both based on a patriarchal system, had led to a complete denial of the existence of these people as "young individuals." Consequently, the young generations did not have either the space or the occasion to let their voices be heard and their demands, articulated.

In the situation where the political authorities resorted to force and violence to assert their power, the youth had no choice but to respond with force to establish their social identity and independence over the "adults." The frustration, even the anger, of the young people due to the political circumstances of the country resulted in confrontation with the monarchical regime in the second half of the 1970s, eventually ending up in the revolutionary movement. After the 1979 revolution, the young generations who had earned a valuable position in society, sped up the process of the destabilization of the values and traditions of the patriarchal system.

Today's young men and women, thanks to the relatively equal access to education and training, are more homogeneous and egalitarian compared to the previous young generations. In addition, they have obviously benefited from the social and cultural transformations that were the result of the struggle of the "former young generations." Today's young generations whose social identity is now recognized, have managed to forge a new relationship with their parents within the family which has grown smaller in size due to a fall in the rate of fertility. This relationship, which is based on dialogue and mutual respect, has its roots in the profound transformations in the position of women in the family and society as well as the change in the composition and structure of the family. These changes could be considered as providing the basis for the recent political transformations, as large segments of the new young generations can no longer accept that a different type of relationship, other than what they have experienced within the family, dominate the social and political scene. In the late 1990s, this manifested itself in terms of a dialectic approach based on demands for reform and greater tolerance for opposing views within the existing legal framework without questioning the legitimacy of the Islamic Republic. Since the fraudulent reelection of Mahmoud Ahmadinejad in June 2009, the state seems to have implemented a policy of repression and intimidation aimed primarily at the youth and women's rights activists, who have constituted the main protagonists of the new protest movement. This is unlikely to succeed; the Islamic Republic may temporarily curb the spread of this new movement for freedom but won't be able to eradicate it, given that the aspiration for democracy and modernization of social arena has its origin in the profound changes that have occurred within the Iranian family, and the relationships among its members.

Notes

1. Marie Ladier-Fouladi, "The Fertility Transition in Iran," *Population: An English Selection* 9 (1997): 191–214.
2. Marie Ladier-Fouladi, *Population et politique en Iran: De la monarchie à la République islamique.* Les Cahiers de l'INED, no. 150 (Paris: INED-PUF, 2003).
3. I was one of the supervisors of these two scientific surveys that were conducted in close collaboration between France's "National Center for Scientific Research" (CNRS), l'UMR 7528 "Monde iranien," and the Statistical Center of Iran (SCI). The first survey had a sample of 7,000 households spread over 28 Iranian provinces in both urban and rural areas. At the time of this survey, young singles aged 15–29 years

who continued to live with their parents were specifically questioned about their spare time, relationship with their parents, main obstacles toward marriage, and so on. The second was a qualitative survey I carried out in four provinces—Tehran, Hormozgan, Golestan, and Sistan & Baluchistan. I personally interviewed 35 young male and female singles between the ages of 18 and 29, selected from the quantitative survey sample.

4. For further information on the fertility trend in Iran, see Ladier-Fouladi, "The Fertility Transition in Iran."

5. Ladier-Fouladi, *Population et politique en Iran,* 21–40.

6. An ad hoc department was created within the Ministry of Health in order to manage this program. The government measures stipulated that several ministerial organizations, as well as a division of conscripts constituting the *Sepah-e behdasht* (the Health Corps), help this department achieve its principal goal, namely to reduce the number of births.

7. Data taken from D. Nortman, "Reports on Population/Family Planning" (New York: The Population Council, 1969–1976); D. Nortman and E. Hofstatter, "Population and Family Planning Program" (New York: The Population Council, 1978–1980); Akbar Aghajanian, "Population Policy, Fertility and Family Planning in Iran," in *Fertility Policies of Asian Countries,* ed. K. Mahadevan (New Delhi: Sage Publications, 1989), 228–247.

8. Ladier-Fouladi, *Population et politique en Iran ,* 247.

9. The first seminar on population and development was held barely a month after the cease-fire with Iraq, on September 10, 1988. In his "Charter of Fraternity" (*manshur-e baradari*) dated November 7, 1988, Ayatollah Khomeini spoke for the first time of the need to discuss the "stance to be taken in relation to family planning: should there be encouragement in regard to limiting family size or to spacing between pregnancies alone?" *Keyhan* November 7, 1988, 1–2.

10. Hossein Malek Afzali, "Jam`iyat va tanzim khanevadeh dar jomhouri-e eslami-ye Iran" (Population and family planning in the Islamic Republic of Iran), *Nabze* (Pulse), no. 2 (1371/ 1992): 3–7. Also Anonymous, *An Analysis of the Population Situation in the Islamic Republic of Iran* (Tehran: UNFPA, 1993).

11. M. Ladier-Fouladi, *Iran: un monde de paradoxes* (Nantes: Atalante, 2009), 57. Since his reelection in June 2009, Ahmadinejad has tried to reverse this trend by encouraging women to have more children, offering them 10 million riyals for every new baby born.

12. *An Analysis of the Population Situation in the Islamic Republic of Iran*, 63.

13. Population and Health in the Islamic Republic of Iran: Demographic and Health Survey (DHS) (Tehran: Iranian Ministry of Health and Medical Education and UNICEF, 2000), 64–65.

14. Ladier-Fouladi, *Population et politique en Iran,* 39.

15. Ibid., 159–162.

16. Ladier-Fouladi, *Iran: un monde de Paradoxes,* 62–63.

17. Ladier-Fouladi, *Population et politique en Iran,* 213–216; Thierry Coville, ed., *L'économie de l'Iran islamique: Entre l'état et le marché* (Tehran: IFRI, 1994), 17–25.

18. Firouzeh Khalatbari, "L'Inégalité des sexes sur le marché du travail: une analyse des potentiels économiques de croissance," in *Les femmes en Iran: pression sociales et stratégies identitaires,* ed. N. Yavari d'Hellencourt (Paris: L'Harmattan, 1998), 159–188.

19. Marie Ladier-Fouladi et al., *Famille et fécondité à Shiraz.* Dossiers et Recherches 60 (Paris: INED, 1996), 26–30.

20. These ratios were 80 percent in 1986, 83.5 percent in 1996, and 88 percent in 2006 in urban areas, and 78 percent in 1986, 80 percent in 1996, and 88 percent in 2006 in rural areas, respectively.

21. Françoise Héritier, "Vers un nouveau rapport des catégories du masculin et du féminin," in *Contraception: Contrainte ou Liberté ?* ed. E. E. Beaulieu, Françoise Héritier, and Henri Leridon (Paris: Odile Jacob, 1999), 37–52.

22. Philippe Fargues, "La femme dans les pays arabes: vers une remise en cause du système patriarcal?" *Population & Sociétés* no. 387 (2003): 1–4.

23. "Social representation" is a commonly used concept by social scientists, and denotes a system of values, ideas, and practices that are shared by the members of a group or community. For a classic definition, see Serge Moscovici, "Foreword," in *Health and Illness: A Social Psychological Analysis*, ed. C. Herzlich (London: Academic Press, 1973), xiii.

24. Ladier-Fouladi, *Population et politique en Iran*, 86–92.

25. Farhad Khosrokhavar, "Le nouvel individu en Iran," *Cahiers d'études sur la Méditerranée orientale et le monde turco-iranien*, 26 (1998): 125–155.

26. Ladier-Fouladi, *Population et politique en Iran*, 280–283.

27. The studies on the origins of the revolution of 1979 are as varied as they are contradictory. Since they are beyond the scope of this paper, they are not discussed here. However, the point that is important to recognize for the purposes of this chapter, is that in its genesis, the revolutionary movement was neither Islamist nor Khomeinist.

28. Georges Balandier, *Antrhopo-logiques* (Paris: Librairie générale française, 1985), 87–88.

29. Paul Vieille and Farhad Khosrokhavar, *Le Discours populaire de la révolution iranienne*. 2 vols. (Paris: Éditions Contemporanéité, 1990), 138.

30. Among these organizations were the Islamic Revolutionary Committees (*Komitehha-ye Enqelab-e Eslami*), the Revolutionary Guards (*Sepah-e Pasdaran-e Enqelab-e Eslami*), the Mobilization of the Oppressed (*Basij-e Mostaz'afin*) or the Mobilization of Resistance Force (*Basije-e Nirouyeh Moqavemat*), the Organization for Combating Illiteracy (*Sazman-e Melli-ye Mobarezeh Ba Bisavadi*), and the Organization of the Crusade for Reconstruction (*Sazman-e Jahad-e Sazandegi)* based mainly in rural areas. The mission of both the last two organizations was to contribute to the socioeconomic development of these regions. For further information see Ladier-Fouladi, *Population et politique en Iran* , 139–141 and 181–189)

31. The military and paramilitary organizations of the Islamic Republic were created for the most part in the year of the revolution, namely 1979, although the *Basij* was established a little later in the context of the Iraq-Iran war.

32. In the absence of official statistics, for a long time, the Iraq-Iran war fatalities were thought to approximate those of the two world wars. For example, the number of deaths on the Iranian side alone was considered to range from 1 to 1.5 million. However, our estimation as well as later estimates by the official statement of the Islamic Republic Martyrs Foundation (on September 23, 2000), put forth a more moderate figure, namely around 200,000 killed, among both military and civilians, of whom a majority were young people between the ages of 18 to 25 years. For further information see Ladier-Fouladi, *Population et politique en Iran*, 123–128.

33. Masserat Amir-Ebrahimi, "Une révolution et deux jeunesses," *Les cahiers de l'Orient*, no. 60 (2000) : 111–123.

34. Ladier-Fouladi, *Iran: un monde de paradoxes*, 100–101.

35. According to the 1966 Iranian census, the resident population was 25,788,723. Only 38 percent of the total population lived in urban areas.

36. According to the 1976 Iranian census, the resident population was 33,708,744, and the urbanization rate was about 47 percent.
37. This is why the total literacy rate of young women compared to that of young men was quite low in 1976, namely 42 percent of women aged 15–24 years versus 70.2 percent of men.
38. According to the 1986 Iranian census, the resident population was 49,455,010, and the urbanization rate rose to 54 percent.
39. It is important to note that the war between Iraq and Iran, unlike the two world wars, did not contribute to bringing more women into the labor force. It was a frontier war and combatants were either conscripts or to a large extent, young volunteers; the overwhelming majority had not previously entered the labor force. In addition, the embargo against Iran had completely paralyzed the country's economy and swollen the numbers of the unemployed.
40. It is important to mention that in the population censuses, the conscripts are counted as economically active. This is why, despite the economic crisis, the proportion of young men in the labor force had not decreased.
41. Anne-Marie Sohn, *Age tendre et tête de bois: Histoire des jeunes des années 1960* (Paris: Hachette Littérature, 2001), 11.
42. According to the 1996 Iranian census, the resident population was 60,055,488, and the urbanization rate rose to 61 percent.
43. According to the 2006 Iranian census, the resident population was 70,495,782, and 68 percent of the total population lived in urban areas.
44. The total literacy rates among young men and women were 94.4 percent and 87.7 percent, respectively.
45. In 2006, the total literacy rates among young men and women were 97 percent and 95 percent, respectively.
46. In 1996, the total average years of schooling for young men and women were 7.5 years and 6.4 years, respectively, whereas in 2006, the total average years of schooling for young men and women had risen to 8.9 years and 8.8 years, respectively.
47. While this ratio concerns the students at the BA level, it is expected that in the next few years, in the event of this trend continuing, it will also apply to those studying for a Master's degree.
48. It is important to note that the rise in the rates of economic activity for both young men and women is due to the change in the definition of the economically active in the 2006 Iranian census.
49. According to the 2006 Iranian census, the average age at the first marriage of men was 26.5 years, and that of women, 24 years.
50. "Family workers" are defined as workers who work for their families without being paid.
51. Almost 48 percent had chosen option 3 (persuasion through dialogue), and 34 percent chose option 4 (open-mindedness while expecting to be consulted when making decisions.)
52. Farhad Khosrokhavar and Olivier Roy, *Iran: comment sortir d'une révolution religieuse* (Paris: Seuil, 1999), 162–163.
53. Among the nonelective state institutions, are the "Leadership Council," the "Guardian Council," and the "Nation's Exigency Council."
54. Ladier-Fouladi, *Iran: un monde de paradoxes*, 264–299.
55. Ibid., 262, 272, and 285.
56. See student organizations' statements, posted on their websites, namely Amirkabir University Student Website and Advarnews, in 2006 and 2007.
57. Ladier-Fouladi, *Iran: un monde de paradoxes*, 111–112.

Selected Bibliography

Books and Articles in English and European Languages

Abisaab, Rula Jurdi. *Converting Persia: Religion and Power in the Safavid Empire*. London: I. B. Tauris, 2004.

Abrahamian, Ervand. *A History of Modern Iran*. Cambridge, UK: Cambridge University Press, 2008.

———. *Iran between Two Revolutions*. Princeton, NJ: Princeton University Press, 1982.

———. *Khomeinism: Essays on the Islamic Republic*. Berkeley, CA: University of California Press, 1993.

Afary, Janet and Kevin B. Anderson. *Foucault and the Iranian Revolution: Gender and the Seductions of Islamism*. Chicago: Chicago University Press, 2005.

Aghajanian, Akbar. "Population Policy, Fertility and Family Planning in Iran." In *Fertility Policies of Asian Countries*, edited by K. Mahadevan, 228–247. New Delhi: Sage Publications, 1989.

Ahmadi, Fereshteh. "Islamic Feminism in Iran: Feminism in a New Islamic Context," *Journal of Feminist Studies in Religion* 22, no. 2 (2006): 33–53.

Ahmadi Khorasani, Noushin. *Iranian Women's One Million Signatures: Campaign for Equality, the Inside Story*. Washington, DC: Women's Learning Partnership, 2009.

Amanat, Abbas. *Apocalyptic Islam and Iranian Shi'ism*. London and New York: I. B. Tauris, 2009.

Amir-Ebrahimi, Masserat. "Blogging from Qom: Behind Walls and Veils," *Comparative Studies of South Asia, Africa and the Middle East* 28, no. 2 (2008): 235–249.

———. "Une Révolution et deux jeunesses," *Les Cahiers de l'Orient* no. 60 (2000): 111–123.

Amuzegar, Jahangir. *Iran's Economy under the Islamic Republic*. London and New York: I. B. Tauris, 1993.

———. "Islamic Social Justice, Iranian Style," *Middle East Policy Journal* XIV, no. 3 (2007): 60–78.

Anonymous. *An Analysis of the Population Situation in the Islamic Republic of Iran*. Tehran: UNFPA, 1993.

Ansari, Ali. "Iranian Nationalism Rediscover ed." In *The Middle East Institute Viewpoints Special Edition: The Iranian Revolution at 30*. Washington, DC: The Middle East Institute, 2009.

Arjomand, Said Amir. *After Khomeini: Iran under His Successors*. Oxford, UK: Oxford University Press, 2009.

———. "The Law, Agency, and Policy in Medieval Islamic Society: Development of the Institutions of Learning from Tenth to the Fifteenth Century," *Comparative Studies in Society and History* 41, no. 2 (April 1999): 263–293.

———. *The Turban for the Crown: The Islamic Revolution in Iran*. Oxford, UK: Oxford University Press, 1988.

Asgharzadeh, Alireza. *Iran and the Challenge of Diversity: Islamic Fundamentalism, Aryanist Racism, and Democratic Struggles*. New York: Palgrave Macmillan, 2007.

Ashraf, Ahmad and Ali Banuazizi. "The State, Classes, and Modes of Mobilization in the Iranian Revolution," *State, Culture, and Society* 1, no. 3 (Spring 1985): 3–40.

Atabaki, Touraj. "Ethnic Diversity and Territorial Integrity of Iran," *Iranian Studies* 31, no. 1 (2005): 23–44.

Bakhash, Shaul. *The Reign of the Ayatollahs: Iran and the Islamic Revolution*. London and New York: I. B. Tauris, 1985.

Baktiari, Bahman. *Parliamentary Politics in Revolutionary Iran: The Institutionalization of Factional Politics*. Gainesville, FL: University Press of Florida, 1996.

Balandier, Georges. *Anthropo-logique*. Paris: Librairie générale française, 1985.

Basmenji, Kaveh. *Tehran Blues: Youth Culture in Iran*. London: Saqi Books, 2006.

Bayart, Jean-François. "Jeux de pouvoir à Teheran," *Politique internationale* 82 (Winter 1998–1999): 107–122.

Bayat, Asef. *Street Politics: Poor People's Movements in Iran*. New York: Columbia University Press, 1997.

Behdad, Sohrab. "From Populism to Economic Liberalism: The Iranian Predicament." In *The Economy of Iran: Dilemmas of an Islamic State*, edited by Parvin Alizadeh, 100–149. London and New York: I. B. Tauris, 2000.

Behnam, Djamshid. "Familles nucléaires et groupement de parenté en Iran," *Extrait de Diogène* 76 (1971): 124–141.

Behrooz, Maziar. *Rebels with a Cause: The Failure of the Left in Iran*. London and New York: I. B. Tauris, 1999.

Bennani-Chraibi, Mounia and Olivier Fillieule, eds., *Résistances et protestations dans les sociétés musulmanes*. Paris: Presses de Sciences Po, 2003.

Bessis, Sophie. *Les Arabes, les femmes, la liberté*. Paris: Albain Michel, 2007.

Bromberger, Christian. "Islam et révolution en Iran : quelques pistes pour une lecture," *Revue de l'Occident musulman et de la Méditerranée* 29 (1980): 109–130.

Brumberg, Daniel. *Reinventing Khomeini: The Struggle for Reform in Iran*. Chicago: Chicago University Press, 2001.

Bucar, Elizabeth M. and Roja Fazaeli. "Free Speech in Weblogistan? The Offline Consequences of Online Communication," *International Journal of Middle East Studies* 40, no. 3 (2008): 403–419.

Chelkowski, Peter and Hamid Dabashi. *Staging a Revolution: The Art of Persuasion in the Islamic Republic of Iran*. New York: New York University Press, 1999.

Chubin, Shahram. "Iran and the Persian Gulf States." In *The Iranian Revolution and the Muslim World*, edited by David Menashri, 73–84. Boulder, CO: Westview Press, 1990.

Cole, Juan. *The Ayatollahs and Democracy in Iraq*. Amsterdam: Amsterdam University Press, 2006.

Connor, Walker. "Beyond Reason: The Nature of the Ethno-national Bond." In *Ethnicity*, edited by J. Hutchinson and A. D. Smith, 69–74. Oxford, UK: Oxford University Press, 1996.

Cottam, Richard. *Nationalism in Iran: Updated through 1978*, rev. ed., Pittsburgh, PA: University of Pittsburgh Press, 1979.

Coville, Thierry, ed., *L'économie de l'Iran islamique: Entre l'état et le marché*. Tehran: Institut français de recherche en Iran, 1994.

Dabashi, Hamid. *Iran, the Green Movement and the USA: The Fox and the Paradox*. New York: Zed Books, 2010.

Ehsani, Kaveh. "Survival through Dispossession: Privatization of Public Goods in the Islamic Republic," *Middle East Report* 39, no. 250 (Spring 2009): 26–33.

Ehteshami, Anoushiravan and Mahjoob Zweiri. *Iran and the Rise of Its Neoconservatives: The Politics of Tehran's Silent Revolution*. London and New York: I. B. Tauris, 2007.

Elling, Rasmus C. "State of Mind, State of Order: Reactions to Ethnic Unrest in the Islamic Republic of Iran," *Studies in Ethnicity and Nationalism* 8, no. 3 (2008): 481–501.

Fargues, Philippe. "Changing Hierarchies of Gender and Generation in the Arab World." In *Family, Gender, and Population in the Middle East: Policies in Context*, edited by Carla Makhlouf-Obermeyer, 179–198. Cairo: The American University of Cairo Press, 1995.

———. "La femme dans les pays arabes: vers une remise en cause du système patriarcal?" *Population & Sociétés* no. 387 (2003): 1–4.

Farhi, Farideh. "Crafting a National Identity Amidst Contentious Politics in Contemporary Iran," *Iranian Studies* 38, no. 1 (2005): 7–22.

———. "Iran's 2008 Majlis Elections: The Game of Elite Competition," *Middle East Brief* May 29, 2008.

———. "Religious Intellectuals, the 'Woman Question,' and the Struggle for the Creation of a Democratic Public Sphere in Iran." In *Intellectuals in Post-Revolutionary Iran*, edited by Ahmad Ashraf and Ali Banuazizi, special issue, *International Journal of Politics, Culture and Society* 15, no. 2 (Winter 2001): 315–339.

Farzin, Y. Hossein. "Foreign Exchange Reform in Iran: Badly Designed, Badly Managed," *World Development* 23, no. 6 (1995): 987–1001.

Fathi, Nazila and Robert F. Worth. "Clerics' Call for Removal Challenges Iran Leader," *New York Times* August 17, 2009.

Foucault, Michel. "Questions of Method." In *The Foucault Effect: Studies in Governmentality*, edited by Graham Burchill, Colin Gordon, and Peter Miller, 73–86. London: Harverster Wheatsheaf, 1991.

Gauthier, Madeleine. "L'âge des jeunes: un fait social instable," *Lien social et politique* 43 (2000): 23–32.

Ghamari-Tabrizi, Behrooz, Mansour Bonakdarian, Nasrin Rahimieh, Ahmad Sadri, and Ervand Abrahamian. " Editors' Introduction." In "The Iranian Revolution Turns Thirty," special issue, *Radical History Review* 2009, no. 105 (Fall 2009): 1–12.

Gheissari, Ali and Vali Nasr. *Democracy in Iran: History and the Quest for Liberty*. Oxford, UK: Oxford University Press, 2006.

Gheytanchi, Elham and Babak Rahimi. "The Politics of Facebook in Iran," *Open Democracy* June 1, 2009.

Halm, Heinz. *Shi'ism*. Translated by Janet Watson and Marian Hill. New York: Columbia University Press, 2004.

Hashemi, Nader and Danny Postel, eds., *The People Reloaded: The Green Movement and the Struggle for Iran's Future*. New York: Melville House Publishing, 2010.

Héritier, Françoise. "Vers un nouveau rapport des catégories du masculin et du féminin." In *Contraception: Contrainte ou Liberté?* edited by E. E. Beaulieu, F. Héritier, and H. Leridon, 37–52. Paris: Odile Jacob, 1999.

Holliday, Shabnam. "The Politicization of Culture and Contestation of Iranian National Identity in Khatami's Iran," *Studies in Ethnicity and Nationalism* 7, no. 1 (2007): 27–45.

Hoodfar, Homa. "Activism under the Radar: Volunteer Health Workers in Iran," *Middle East Report* 39, no. 250 (Spring 2009): 56–60.

Hourcade, Bernard. "Iran: Revolution islamiste ou tiers-mondiste?" *Hérodote* 36 (1985): 138–158.

———. "Vaqf et modernité en Iran: Les agro-business de l'Astan-e qods de Mashhad." In *Entre l'Iran et l'Occident: Adaptation et assimilation des idées occidentales en Iran*, edited by Yann Richard, 117–141. Paris: Editions de la Maison des Sciences de l'Homme, 1989.

Hourcade, Bernard and Farhad Khosrokhavar. "La bourgeoisie iranienne ou le contrôle de l'appareil de spéculation," *Revue Tiers Monde* 31, no. 124 (1990): 877–898.

Hunter, Shireen. *Iran after Khomeini*. New York: Praeger, 1992.

Kamrava, Mehran. "The Civil Society Discourse in Iran," *British Journal of Middle Eastern Studies* 28, no. 2 (2001): 165–185.

———. *Iran's Intellectual Revolution*. Cambridge, UK: Cambridge University Press, 2008.

Kashani-Sabet, Firoozeh. "Cultures of Iranian-ness: The Evolving Polemic of Iranian Nationalism." In *Iran and the Surrounding World: Interactions in Culture and Politics*, edited by Nikki Keddie and Rudi Mathhee, 162–181. Seattle, WA: University of Washington Press, 2002.

Katouzian, Homa. *Iranian History and Politics: The Dialectic of State and Society*. London and New York: Routledge, 2003.

Keddie, Nikki. "The Minorities Question in Iran." In *The Iran-Iraq War: New Weapons, Old Conflicts*, edited by Shireen Tahir-Kheli and Shaheen Ayubi, 85–108. New York: Praeger, 1995.

Keyhani, Mohammad and Saeed Jafari Moghadam. "Language Barriers to Meme Contagion: The Case of Entrepreneurship as a Concept in Iran," *Social Science Research Network* May 28, 2008, http://ssrn.com/abstract=1145647.

Khalaji, Mehdi. "The Last Marja: Sistani and the End of Traditional Religious Authority in Shi'ism." *Policy Focus* no. 59 (September 2006), Washington, DC: Washington Institute for Near East Policy.

Khosrokhavar, Farhad. "Le nouvel individu en Iran." *Cahiers d'études sur la Méditerranée orientale et le monde turco-iranien* 26 (1998): 125–155.

Khosrokhavar, Farhad and Amir Nikpey. *Avoir vingt ans au pays des ayatollahs: vivre dans la ville sainte de Qom*. Paris: Robert Laffont, 2009.

Khosrokhavar, Farhad and Olivier Roy. *Iran: comment sortir d'une révolution religieuse*. Paris: Seuil, 1999.

Ladier-Fouladi, Marie. "The Fertility Transition in Iran," *Population: An English Selection* 9 (1997): 191–214.

———. *Iran: un monde de paradoxes*. Nantes: Atalante, 2009.

———. *Population et politique en Iran: De la monarchie à la République islamique*. Les Cahiers de l'INED, no. 150. Paris: INED-PUF, 2003.

Ladier-Fouladi, Marie, Jean-Claude Chasteland, and Youssef Courbage. *Famille et fécondité à Shiraz*. Dossiers et Recherches, no. 60. Paris: INED, 1996.

Levitsky, Steven and Lucan Way. "The Rise of Competitive Authoritarianism," *Journal of Democracy* 13, no. 2 (April 2002): 51–65.

Lust, Ellen. "Competitive Clientelism in the Middle East," *Journal of Democracy* 20, no. 3 (July 2009): 122–135.

Mahdavi, Pardis. *Passionate Uprisings: Iran's Sexual Revolution*. Stanford, CA: Stanford University Press, 2009.

Maloney, Suzanne. "Identity and Change in Iran's Foreign Policy." In *Identity and Foreign Policy in the Middle East*, edited by Shibley Telhami and Michael Barnett, 88–116. Ithaca, NY: Cornell University Press, 2002.

Mashayekhi, Mehrdad. "The Politics of Nationalism." In *Iran: Political Culture in the Islamic Republic*, edited by Samih Farsoun and Mehrdad Mashayekhi, 56–79. London and New York: Routledge, 1992.

Al Massawi, Zein. "Spéculation et marché noir: L'état au quotidien," *Peuples méditerranéens* 29 (1984): 85–90.

Mehran, Golnar. "The Presentation of the 'Self' and the 'Other' in Postrevolutionary Iranian School Textbooks." In *Iran and the Surrounding World: Interactions in*

Culture and Politics, edited by Nikki Keddie and Rudi Mathee, 232–253. Seattle, WA: University of Washington Press, 2002.

Menashri, David, ed., *The Iranian Revolution and the Muslim World*. Boulder, CO: Westview Press, 1990.

———. *Post-Revolutionary Politics in Iran: Religion, Society and Power*. London: Frank Cass, 2001.

Mir-Hosseini, Ziba. "Broken Taboos in Post-Election Iran," *Middle East Report Online* December 17, 2009, http://www.merip.org/mero/mero121709.html.

———. *Islam and Gender: The Religious Debate in Contemporary Iran*. Princeton, NJ: Princeton University Press, 1999.

Mir-Hosseini, Ziba and Richard Tapper. *Islam and Democracy in Iran: Eshkevari and the Quest for Reform*. London and New York: I. B. Tauris, 2006.

Mirsepassi, Ali. *Democracy in Modern Iran: Islam, Culture and Political Change*. New York: New York University Press, 2010.

Moin, Baqer. *Khomeini: Life of the Ayatollah*. New York: Thomas Dunne Books, 2000.

Momen, Moojan. *An Introduction to Shi'i Islam: The History and Doctrines of Twelver Shi'ism*. New Haven, CT: Yale University Press, 1987.

Moslem, Mehdi. *Factional Politics in Post-Revolutionary Iran*. Syracuse, NY: Syracuse University Press, 2002.

Naji, Kasra. *Ahmadinejad: The Secret History of Iran's Radical Leader*. London and New York: I. B. Tauris, 2009.

Nakash, Yitzhak. *Reaching for Power: The Shi`a in the Modern Arab World*. Princeton, NJ: Princeton University Press, 2006.

Nasr, Vali. *The Shia Revival: How Conflicts within Islam Will Shape the Future*. New York: Norton, 2006.

Paidar, Parvin. *Women and the Political Process in Twentieth Century Iran*. Cambridge, UK: Cambridge University Press, 1995.

Paul, Ludwig. "'Iranian Nation' and Iranian-Islamic Revolutionary Ideology," *Die Welt des Islams*, n.s., 39, no. 2 (1999): 183–217.

Pesaran, M. Hashem. "The Iranian Foreign Exchange Policy and the Black Market for Dollars," *International Journal of Middle East Studies* 24, no. 1 (1992): 101–121.

Price, Massoume. *Iran's Diverse Peoples: A Reference Sourcebook*. Santa Barbara, CA: ABC-Clio, 2005.

Rahimi, Babak. "The Politics of the Internet in Iran." In *Media, Culture and Society in Iran: Living with Globalization and the Islamic State*, edited by Mehdi Semati, 37–56. London and New York: Routledge, 2008.

Ram, Haggai. *Iranophobia: The Logic of an Israeli Obsession*. Stanford, CA: Stanford University Press, 2009.

Richard, Yann. "Intégrisme islamique en Iran," *Social Compass* 32, no. 4 (1985): 421–428.

Roy, Olivier. *L'échec de l'islam politique*. Paris: Seuil, 1992.

Sadeghi, Fatemeh. "The Foot Soldiers of the Islamic Republic's Culture of Modesty," *Middle East Report* 39, no. 250 (Spring 2009): 50–55.

———. "Lower Class Women and Tradition in Iran," *Goft-o-gu* no. 56 (Summer 2010): 127–146.

Salehi-Esfahani, Hadi and Farzad Taheripour. "Hidden Public Expenditures and the Economy in Iran," *International Journal of Middle East Studies* 34 (2002): 691–718.

Sanasarian, Eliz. *The Women's Rights Movement in Iran: Mutiny, Appeasement and Repression from 1900 to Khomeini*. New York: Praeger, 1982.

Sariolghalam, Mahmoud. *The Evolution of the State in Iran: A Political Culture Perspective*. Kuwait: Center for Strategic and Future Studies, 2010.

Schirazi, Asghar. "The Debate on Civil Society in Iran." In *Civil Society in the Middle East*, edited by Amr Hamzawy, 47–83. Berlin: Verlag Hans Schiler, 2002.

Shaery-Eisenlohr, Roschanack. "Imagining Shi`ite Iran: Transnationalism and Religious Authenticity in the Muslim World," *Iranian Studies* 40, no. 1 (2007): 17–35.

Shahrokni, Nazanin. "All the President's Women," *Middle East Report* 39, no. 4 (Winter 2009): 2–6.

Sherkat, Shahla. *Zanan: le journal de l'autre Iran*. Paris: CNRS Éditions, 2009.

Taheri, Amir. *Nest of Spies: America's Journey to Disaster in Iran*. New York: Pantheon, 1989.

Tezcür, Günes Murat. *Muslim Reformers in Iran and Turkey: The Paradox of Moderation*. Austin, TX: University of Texas Press, 2010.

Tilly, Charles. *La France conteste de 1600 à nos jours*. Paris: Fayard, 1986.

Tohidi, Nayereh. "Ethnicity and Religious Minority Politics in Iran." In *Contemporary Iran: Economy, Society, Politics*, edited by Ali Gheissari, 299–323. Oxford, UK: Oxford University Press, 2009.

———. "The Women's Movement and Feminism in Iran: A Glocal Perspective." In *Women's Movements in the Global Era: The Power of Local Feminisms*, edited by Amrita Basu, 375–414. Boulder, CO: Westview Press, 2010.

Touraine, Alain. *Le retour de l'acteur*. Paris: Fayard, 1984.

Vieille, Paul and Farhad Khosrokhavar. *Le Discours populaire de la révolution iranienne*. 2 vols. Paris: Éditions Contemporanéité, 1990.

Walbridge, Linda S., ed., *The Most Learned of the Shi`a: The Institution of the Marja` Taqlid*. Oxford, UK: Oxford University Press, 2001.

Wehrey, Frederic, Jerrold D. Green, Brian Nichiporuk, Alireza Nader, Lydia Hansell, Rasool Nafisi, and S. R. Bohandy. *The Rise of the Pasdaran: Assessing the Domestic Roles of Iran's Islamic Revolutionary Guards Corps*. Santa Monica, CA: RAND Corporation, 2009. http://www.rand.org/pubs/monographs/MG821.

Yount, Kathryn M. and Hoda Rashad, eds., *Family in the Middle East: Ideational Change in Egypt, Iran, and Tunisia*. London and New York: Routledge, 2008.

Zubaida, Sami. "Is Iran an Islamic State?" In *Political Islam: Essays from Middle East Report*, edited by Joel Beinin and Joe Stork, 103–119. Berkeley, CA: University of California Press, 1997.

Books and Articles in Persian

Abdi, Abbas. "Negahi jame`eh-shenakhti beh vaqe`eh-ye dovvom-e khordad: dar goft-o-gu ba Abbas Abdi" (A sociological look at the event of the Second of Khordad: in conversation with Abbas Abdi), *Rah-e naw*, no. 1, 5 Ordibehesht 1377/ April 25, 1998, 16–19.

———. "Seda-ye mokhalefan bayad saf shavad" (The voice of the dissidents must be made clear), *Rah-e naw*, no. 6, 9 Khordad 1377/ May 30, 1998, 3.

Ahmadi, Hamid. *Qawmiyyat va qawm-gara'i dar Iran* (Ethnicity and ethnic nationalism in Iran). Tehran: Nashr-e Ney, 1378/ 1999.

Al-Taie, Ali. *Bohran-e hoviyyat-e qawmi dar Iran* (The crisis of ethnic identity in Iran). Tehran: Shadegan, 1378/ 1999.

Armin, Mohsen, ed., *Eslahat va porseshha-ye asasi: majmu`eh maqalat* (Essential reforms and questions: collected essays). Tehran: Zekr, 1380/ 2001.

. *Nesbat-e din va jame`eh-ye madani* (The relationship between religion and civil society). Tehran: Zekr, 1378/ 1999.

Baba'i-Zarech, Ali-Mohammad. *Ommat va mellat dar andisheh-ye Emam Khomeini* (The *Umma* and nation in Imam Khomeini's thought). Tehran: Markaz-e asnad-e enqelab-e eslami, 1383/ 2004.

Baqi, Emadeddin. *Goft-o-gu ba Saeed Hajjarian: bara-ye tarikh.* (In conversation with Saeed Hajjarian: for the record). Tehran: Nashr-e Ney, 1379/ 2000.

———. *Hoquq-e mokhalefan: tamrin-e demokrasi bara-ye jame'eh-ye irani* (The Rights of dissidents: An exercise in democracy for the Iranian society). Tehran: Nashr-e Sara'i, 2000, 24.

———. *Jonbesh-e eslahat-e demokratik dar Iran: enqelab ya eslah* (The Democratic reform movement in Iran: revolution or reform). Tehran: Nashr-e Sara'i, 1383/ 2004.

———. "Mas'aleh-ye zanan: kodam mas'aleh?" (The woman question: what question?), *Zanan*, no. 57, Aban 1378/ October–November 1999, 23–25.

———. "Vezarat-e hoquq-e bashar ta'sis konid" (Establish a ministry for human rights), *E'temad-e melli: si sal, si khatereh*, Special Nawruz supplement, spring 2009, 109–110.

Fawzi-Toyserkani, Yahya. *Emam Khomeini va hoviyyat-e melli* (Imam Khomeini and national identity). Tehran: Markaz-e asnad-e enqelab-e eslami, 1385/ 2006.

Hajjarian, Saeed. *Az shahed-e qodsi ta shahed-e bazaari: 'urfi shodan-e din dar sepehr-e siyasat* (From the sacred witness to the profane witness: the secularization of religion in the sphere of politics). Tehran: Tarh-e Naw, 1380/ 2001.

———. "Dovvom-e Khordad: bimha va omidha, payamha va cheshmandazha, dar goft-o-gu ba Saeed Hajjarian" (The Second of Khordad: fears and hopes, messages and expectations, in conversation with Saeed Hajjarian), *Rah-e naw*, no. 5, 2 Khordad 1377/ May 23, 1998, 16–20.

———. "Hajjarian: eslahtalaban dar teori aqab mandehand" (Hajjarian: the reformists are lagging behind in theoretical thinking), *Sharq*, 29 Bahman 1383/ February 17, 2005.

———. *Jomhuriyyat: afsunzeda'i az qodrat* (Republicanism: the demystification of power). Tehran: Tarh-e Naw, 1379/ 2000.

Hosseini, Seyyedeh Zahra. *Da: Khaterat-e Seyyedeh Zahra Hosseini* (Da: Seyyedeh Zahra Hosseini's diarieis). Tehran: Soureh, 1388/ 2009.

Kar, Mehrangiz. "Aya hoquq-e zan yek maquleh-ye siyasi ast?" (Is women's rights a political topic?), *Zanan*, no. 23, Farvardin-Ordibehesht 1374/ March-May 1995, 22–26.

Khatami, Mohammad. "Jame'eh-ye madani az negah-e Eslam" (Civil society as seen by Islam), in *Nesbat-e din va Jame'eh-ye madani* (The relationship between religion and civil society), edited by Mohsen Armin. Tehran: Zekr, 1378/ 1999, 178–194.

Khomeini, Ruhollah. *Sahifeh-ye emam: majmu'eh-ye asar, bayanat, mosabehhehha, ahkam, ejazat-e shar'I va namehha.* (The Imam's book: the collection of works, speeches, interviews, decrees, legal certifications, and letters). Tehran: Mo'aseseh-ye Tanzim va Nashr-e asar-e Emam Khomeini, 2003, CD-ROM.

Malek Afzali, Hossein. "Jam'iyyat va tanzim-e khanevadeh dar jomhuri-ye eslami-ye iran" (Population and family planning in the Islamic Republic of Iran), *Nabze*, no. 2, 1371/ 1992, 3–7.

Mardiha, Seyyed Morteza. *Ba mas'uliyyat-e sardabir: moqadameh-i bar projeh-ye eslah* (With the responsibility of the editor: an introduction to the project of reform). Tehran: Jame'eh-ye Iraniyan, 1379/ 2000.

"Mohemtarin masa'el-e zanan-e Iran chist? Miz-e gerdi ba sherkat-e Shirin Ebadi, Alireza Alavitabar va Nahid Moti'" (What are the most important problems of Iranian women? A round-table with Shirin Ebadi, Alireza Alavitabar and Nahid Moti'), *Zanan*, no. 34, Ordibehesht 1376/ May 1997, 18.

Nazer, Behruz. "Dar nafy-e radikalism beh onvan-e ravesh" (In refuting radicalism as a method), *Rah-e naw*, no. 5, 2 Khordad 1377/ May 23, 1998, 7.

Quchani, Mohammad. *Bazi-ye bozorgan: Vaqaye`-negari-ye jonbesh-e eslahat-e demokratik dar Iran* (The Elite's game: Chronicling the democratic reform movement in Iran). Tehran: Jame`eh-ye Iraniyan, 1379/ 2000.

Sadr-ol-Ashrafi, Zia. *Kesrat-e qawmi va hoviyyat-e melli-ye iraniyan* (Ethnic diversity and national identity of Iranians). Tehran: Andisheh-ye Naw, 1377/ 1998.

Soroush, Abdolkarim. *Ideolozhi-ye sheytani* (Satanic Ideology). Tehran: Sarat, 1373/ 1994.

Selected Websites and Weblogs Cited

http://ayande.ir
http://www.emadbaghi.com
http://www.entekhabnews.com
http://www.esteghamat.ir
http://www.farsnews.com
http://www.iran-emrooz.net
http://www.iranian.com
http://www.iranonline.com
http://www.jahannews.com
http://www.kadivar.com
http://www.khabaronline.ir
http://www.ksabz.net
http://www.montazeri.com
http://www.president.ir
http://www.roozonline.com
http://www.shahabnews.com
http://www.shafaf.ir
http://www.tabnak.ir
http://www.webneveshteha.com

Contributors

Fariba Adelkhah is senior research fellow at the Institut d'Études Politiques (Sciences Po) in Paris and the author of numerous publications, among them *Être Moderne en Iran* (Being Modern in Iran) (Paris: Karthala, 2006); and *Les Mosquées: Espaces, Institutions et Pratiques* (Mosques: Spaces, Institutions and Practices) (coedited with Abdarahmane Moussaoui) (Paris, 2009.)

Rasmus Christian Elling is currently postdoctoral research fellow at the School of Oriental and African Studies (SOAS), University of London. He obtained his PhD in Iranian Studies at the University of Copenhagen with a dissertation on the politics of ethnic and national identity in postrevolutionary Iran. His forthcoming book is entitled *Minorities in Iran: Ethnicity and Nationalism after Khomeini*.

Farideh Farhi is an independent scholar and Iran analyst, and affiliate of the Graduate Faculty of Political Science at the University of Hawaii at Manoa.

Marie Ladier-Fouladi is a social demographer and researcher at the French National Center for Scientific Research (CNRS), and the Centre on Population and Development (CEPED), University of Paris Descartes. She is the author of several books and articles on demographic changes and sociopolitical transformation in Iran. Her most recent publication is entitled *Iran: un monde de Paradoxes* (Nantes: l'Atalante, 2009).

Negin Nabavi is associate professor of history at Montclair State University. She has taught at Princeton University, NYU and University of Maryland. She has authored a number of articles as well as books, among them, *Intellectuals and the State in Iran: Politics, Discourse and the Dilemma of Authenticity* (University Press of Florida, 2003).

Babak Rahimi is assistant professor of Iranian and Islamic Studies at University of California, San Diego. He has written many articles on the culture, religion, and politics of Iran as well as contemporary Iraq. His forthcoming book is entitled *Between Mourning and Carnival: the Emergence of the Early Modern Iranian Public Sphere in the Safavid Period, 1592–1618.*

Fatemeh Sadeghi is an independent scholar and Tehran-based researcher of political thought and women's studies. She was born in 1971 and has a PhD in Political Philosophy from Tarbiyat Modarres University in Tehran. Her book *Gender, Nationalism, and Modernity in Iran during the first Pahlavi Ruler* was published in Persian in 2005.

Kjetil Selvik is assistant professor at the University of Oslo and researcher at the Fafo Institute of Applied International Studies. He earned his PhD in Political Science from l'Institut d'Études Politiques (Sciences Po) in Paris in 2004 with a thesis on "Private Industrial Entrepreneurs in the Islamic Republic of Iran." He has also published on the social and political roles of the private sector in Syria, and is most recently (with Stig Stenslie), the author of *Stability and Change in the Modern Middle East* (I. B. Tauris, 2011).

Index